Dynamic Learning:
Photoshop CS3

with Digital Classroom Video Tutorials

Dynamic Learning:
Photoshop CS3

with Digital Classroom Video Tutorials

Jennifer Smith & AGI Creative Team

AGI

O'REILLY®

BEIJING · CAMBRIDGE · FARNHAM · KÖLN · PARIS · SEBASTOPOL · TAIPEI · TOKYO

Dynamic Learning: Photoshop CS3   By Jennifer Smith & AGI Creative Team

Additional writing: **Larry Happy, Jeremy Osborn, Christopher Smith, Jerron Smith, Robert Underwood**

Series Editor: **Christopher Smith**

Technical Editors: **Caitlin Smith, Cathy Auclair, Jeff Ausura, Linda Forsvall**

Additional Editing: **Edie Freedman**

Video Project Manager: **Jeremy Osborn**

Recording Technician: **Robert Beinhocker**

Cover Design: **Edie Freedman, O'Reilly Media**

Interior Design: **Ron Bilodeau, O'Reilly Media**

Graphic Production: **Lauren Mickol**

Additional Production: **Aquent Studios**

Indexing: **Joda Alian**

Video Editor: **Trevor Chamberlin**

Proofreading: **Jay Donahue**

Published by O'Reilly Media, Inc., 1005 Gravenstein Highway North, Sebastopol, CA 95472.

O'Reilly books may be purchased for educational, business, or sales promotional use. Online editions are also available for most titles (*safari.oreilly.com*). For more information, contact our corporate/institutional sales department: 800.998.9938 or *corporate@oreilly.com*.

The O'Reilly logo is a registered trademark of O'Reilly Media, Inc. *Learning Photoshop CS3*, the cover images, and related trade dress are trademarks of O'Reilly Media, Inc.

Many of the designations used by manufacturers and sellers to distinguish their products are claimed as trademarks. Where those designations appear in this book, and O'Reilly Media, Inc. was aware of a trademark claim, the designations have been printed in caps or initial caps. Adobe Photoshop™ is a registered trademark of Adobe Systems, Inc. in the United States and other countries. O'Reilly Media, Inc. is independent of Adobe Systems, Inc.

While every precaution has been taken in the preparation of this book, the publisher and author assume no responsibility for errors or omissions, or for damages resulting from the use of the information contained herein.

Please report any errors by sending a message to errata@aquent.com.

Print History: June 2007, First Edition.
ISBN 10: 0-596-51061-9
ISBN 13: 978-0-596-51061-9
[F]

Printed in Canada.

Contents

Starting Up

Lesson 1: What's New in Adobe Photoshop CS3?

Lesson 2: Exploring Adobe Photoshop CS3

Lesson 3: Getting to Know the Workspace

Lesson 4: Using Adobe Bridge

Lesson 5: The Basics of Photoshop CS3

Lesson 6: Creating a Good Image

Lesson 7: Making the Best Selections

Lesson 8: Painting and Retouching

Lesson 9: Getting to Know Layers

Lesson 10: Taking Layers to the Max

Lesson 11: Using Smart Objects

Lesson 12: Using Adobe Photoshop Filters

Lesson 13: Creating Images for Web and Video

DVD Contents

Resources on the DVD

The *Dynamic Learning: Photoshop CS3 Digital Classroom* DVD that is included with this book is loaded with useful information, video tutorials that accompany each lesson, and the lesson files that you'll need to complete the exercises contained in this book.

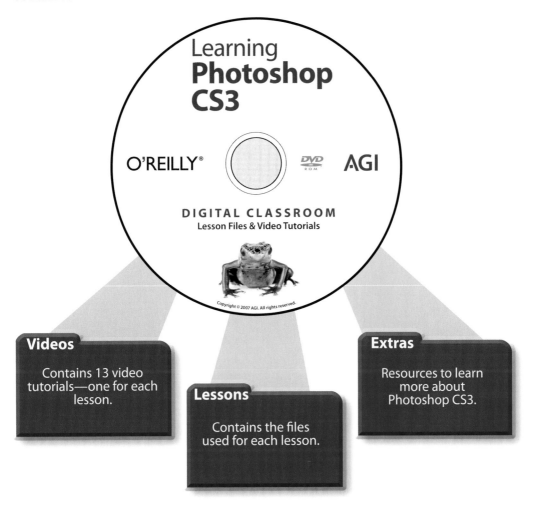

 The included video tutorials play on both Windows and Mac OS computers, using the free Adobe® Flash® player available at adobe.com/products/flashplayer.

Starting up

About Dynamic Learning

Adobe® Photoshop® CS3 is the leading digital image editing software. It is the perfect creative tool for designing and manipulating images for print layouts, Web publishing, multimedia, video, photography, and for visually expressing your creative ideas.

Dynamic Learning: Adobe Photoshop CS3 is like having your own personal instructor guiding you through each lesson, while you work at your own pace. This book includes 13 self-paced lessons that let you discover essential skills and explore new features and capabilities of Adobe Photoshop CS3. Each lesson includes step-by-step instructions, lesson files, along with video tutorials that complement the topics covered in each lesson. These accompanying files are provided on the included *Dynamic Learning: Photoshop CS3* DVD and are developed by the same team of Adobe Certified Instructors and Photoshop experts who have created many of the official training titles for Adobe Systems.

Prerequisites

Before you start the lessons in *Dynamic Learning: Photoshop CS3*, you should have a working knowledge of your computer and its operating system. You should know how to use the directory system of your computer so that you can navigate through folders. You need to understand how to locate, save, and open files. You should also know how to use your mouse to access menus and commands.

Before starting the lessons files in *Dynamic Learning: Photoshop CS3*, make sure that you have installed Adobe Photoshop CS3, or Adobe Photoshop CS3 Extended. The software is sold separately, and not included with this book. You may use the 30-day trial version of Adobe Photoshop CS3 available at the *adobe.com* web site, subject to the terms of its license agreement.

Adobe Photoshop CS3 versions

Photoshop CS3 comes in two versions: Adobe Photoshop CS3 and Adobe Photoshop CS3 Extended. The Extended version offers everything you find in Photoshop CS3, along with additional tools for editing video, motion-graphics, 3-D content, and performing image analysis. This book covers both versions of Photoshop CS3. Where appropriate, we have noted any features that are available only in the Extended version. Adobe Photoshop CS3 is used to refer to both versions of the software throughout the book.

System requirements

Before starting the lessons in *Dynamic Learning: Photoshop CS3*, make sure that your computer is equipped for running Adobe Photoshop CS3 or Adobe Photoshop CS3 Extended, which you must purchase separately. The minimum system requirements for your computer to effectively use the software are listed on the following page.

System requirements for Adobe Photoshop CS3, and CS3 Extended

Windows

- Intel® Pentium® 4, Intel Centrino®, Intel Xeon®, or Intel Core™ Duo (or compatible) processor
- Microsoft® Windows® XP with Service Pack 2 or Windows Vista™ Home Premium, Business, Ultimate, or Enterprise (certified for 32-bit editions)
- 512MB of RAM
- 64MB of video RAM
- 1GB of available hard-disk space, with additional free space required during the installation process
- 1,024x768 monitor resolution with 16-bit video card
- DVD-ROM drive
- QuickTime 7 software required for multimedia features
- Internet or phone connection required for product activation

Mac OS

- PowerPC® G4 or G5 or multicore Intel processor
- Mac OS X v.10.4.8
- 512MB of RAM
- 64MB of video RAM
- 2GB of available hard-disk space, with additional free space required during installation
- 1,024x768 monitor resolution with 16-bit video card
- DVD-ROM drive
- QuickTime 7 software required for multimedia features
- Internet or phone connection required for product activation

Starting Adobe Photoshop CS3

As with most software, Adobe Photoshop CS3 is launched by locating the application in your Programs folder (Windows) or Applications folder (Mac OS). If necessary, follow these steps to start the Adobe Photoshop CS3 application:

Windows

1   Choose Start > All Programs > Adobe Photoshop CS3.

2   When the Welcome Screen appears, click Close. You are now ready to use Adobe Photoshop CS3.

Mac OS

1   Open the Applications folder, and then open the Adobe Photoshop CS3 folder.

2   Double-click on the Adobe Photoshop CS3 application icon.

3   When the Welcome Screen appears, click Close. You are now ready to use Adobe Photoshop CS3.

Menus and commands are identified throughout the book by using the greater than symbol (>). For example, the command to print a document would be identified as File > Print.

Fonts used in this book

Dynamic Learning: Photoshop CS3 includes lessons that refer to fonts that were installed with your copy of Adobe Photoshop CS3. If you did not install the fonts, or have removed them from your computer, you may substitute different fonts for the exercises or re-install the software to access the fonts.

Loading lesson files

The *Dynamic Learning: Photoshop CS3* DVD includes files that accompany the exercises for each of the lessons. You may copy the entire lessons folder from the supplied DVD to your hard drive, or copy only the lesson folders for the individual lessons you wish to complete.

For each lesson in the book, the files are referenced by the file name of each file. The exact location of each file on your computer is not used, as you may have placed the files in a unique location on your hard drive. We suggest placing the lesson files in the My Documents folder (Windows) or at the top level of your hard drive (Mac OS).

Follow these instructions to copy the lesson files to your hard drive:

1   Insert the *Dynamic Learning: Photoshop CS3* DVD that is supplied with this book.

2   Using your directory system, open the DVD and navigate to the folder named pslessons.

3   You can install all of the files, or just specific lesson files. Do one of the following:

   •   Install all lesson files by dragging the pslessons folder to your hard drive.

   •   Install only some of the files by creating a new folder on your hard drive, named pslessons. Open the pslessons folder on the supplied DVD, select the lesson you wish to complete, and drag the folder(s) to the pslessons folder you created on your hard drive.

Resetting Adobe Photoshop CS3 preferences

When you start Adobe Photoshop, it remembers certain settings along with the configuration of the workspace from the last time you used the application. It is important that you start each lesson using the default settings so that you do not see unexpected results when working with the lessons in this book.

As you reset your preferences to the default settings, you may wish to keep your color settings. This is important if you have created specific color settings, or work in a color calibrated environment.

Use the following steps to reset your Adobe Photoshop CS3 preferences and save your color settings. If you are confident that you do not need to save your color settings, you can skip to the section, "Resetting Adobe Photoshop CS3 preferences."

Saving Adobe Photoshop CS3 color settings

1   Launch Adobe Photoshop.

2   Choose Edit > Color Settings, and then press the Save button. The Save dialog box opens. Enter an appropriate name for your color settings, such as the date. Leave the destination and format unchanged, then press the Save button. The Color Settings Comment dialog box opens.

3   In the Color Settings Comment dialog box, enter a description for the color settings you are saving, then press OK. Press OK again in the Color Settings dialog box to close it. You have saved your color settings so they can be accessed again in the future.

4   Choose File > Quit, to exit Adobe Photoshop CS3.

Resetting Adobe Photoshop CS3 preferences

Press and hold the Ctrl+Alt+Shift keys (Windows) or Command+Option+Shift keys (Mac OS) simultaneously and start Adobe Photoshop CS3. You can double-click on the Adobe Photoshop CS3 application icon (Mac OS or Windows), or start the application by choosing Start > Adobe Photoshop CS3 (Windows). A dialog box appears verifying that you want to delete the Adobe Photoshop settings. Release the keys, then press OK.

Resetting your Photoshop CS3 preferences.

To reset your Photoshop CS3 preferences, you must have the three modifier keys pressed before starting Photoshop.

Restoring previous Adobe Photoshop CS3 color settings

1   Start Adobe Photoshop CS3. Choose Edit > Color Settings. The Color Settings dialog box appears.

2   From the Settings drop-down menu, choose your saved color settings file. Press OK. Your color settings are restored.

A note about color warnings

Depending upon how your Color Settings are configured, there may be times when you will receive a Missing Profile or Embedded Profile Mismatch warning. Understand that if you reset your preferences before each lesson (without restoring your color settings) you should not see these color warnings. This is because the default color setting of North America General Purpose 2 has all warning check boxes unchecked.

If you do receive Missing Profile and Embedded Profile Mismatch warnings, choose the Assign working option, or Convert document's colors to the working space. What is determined to be your working space is what you have assigned in the Color Settings dialog box. Color Settings are discussed in more detail in Lesson 6, "Creating a Good Image," and in Lesson 8, "Painting and Retouching."

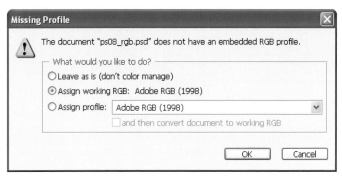

Missing color profile.

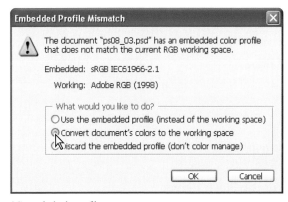

Mismatched color profile.

Working with the video tutorials

Your *Dynamic Learning: Photoshop CS3* DVD comes with video tutorials developed by the authors to help you understand the concepts explored in each lesson. Each tutorial is approximately 5 minutes long and demonstrates and explains the concepts and features covered in part of the lesson.

The videos are designed to supplement your understanding of the material in the chapter. We have selected exercises and examples that we feel will be most useful to you. You may want to view each lesson's entire video tutorial before you begin that lesson. Additionally, at certain points in a lesson, you will encounter the DVD icon. The icon, with the appropriate lesson number, indicates that an overview of the exercise being described can be found in the accompanying video.

DVD video icon.

Setting up for viewing the video tutorials

The DVD included with this book includes video tutorials for each lesson. Although you can view the lessons on your computer directly from the DVD, we recommend copying the folder labeled Videos from the *Dynamic Learning: Photoshop CS3* DVD to your hard drive.

Copying the video tutorials to your heard drive

1 Insert the *Dynamic Learning: Photoshop CS3* DVD that is supplied with this book.

2 Using your directory system on your computer, navigate to the DVD and locate the folder named Videos.

3 Drag the Videos folder to a location on your computer's hard drive.

Viewing the video tutorials with the Adobe Flash Player

To view the video tutorials, you need the Adobe Flash Player 8 or later, including Adobe Flash Player 9. Earlier versions of the Flash Player will not play the videos correctly. If you're not sure you have the latest version of the Flash Player you can download it for free from the Adobe web site: *http://www.adobe.com/support/flashplayer/downloads.html*

The accompanying video files use the Adobe Flash Video format to make universal viewing possible for users on both Mac OS and Windows computers. The most recent versions of the free Adobe Flash Player software generally improve playback performance of these video files.

Playing the video tutorials on your computer

1 Make sure you have at least version 8 of the Adobe Flash Player.

2 Using your directory system, navigate to the Videos folder on your hard drive or DVD.

3 Open the Video folder and right-click (Windows) or Ctrl+click (Mac OS) on the video tutorial you wish to view.

4 Choose Open > Open With> Flash Player. If there is no Flash Player option available, you may need to install the latest version of Flash Player.

Macintosh users on the new Intel-based Mac OS computers may need to download the stand-alone Flash Player from Adobe.com to see this option. You may also double-click the video tutorial file you wish to view.

5 The video tutorial opens using the Flash Player and begins to play. The Flash Player has a simple user interface that allows you to control the viewing experience, including stopping, pausing, playing, and restarting the video. You can also rewind or fast-forward, and adjust the playback volume.

A. Go to beginning. B. Play/Pause. C. Fast-forward/rewind. D. Stop. E. Volume Off/On. F. Volume control.

Playback volume is also affected by the settings in your operating system. Be certain to adjust your sound volume for your computer, in addition to the sound controls in the player window.

Additional resources

The Dynamic Learning series goes beyond this book and DVD. You can continue your learning online, with training videos, and at seminars and conferences.

Video training series

Expand your knowledge of the Adobe Creative Suite 3 applications with the Dynamic Learning video training series that complements the skills you'll learn in this book. Learn more at *agitraining.com* or *oreilly.com*.

Seminars and conferences

The authors of this book frequently conduct in-person seminars, and speak at conferences, including the annual CRE8 Conference. Learn more at *agitraining.com* or *oreilly.com*.

Resources for educators

Visit *oreilly.com* to access resources for educators, including teachers' guides for incorporating the Dynamic Learning series into your curriculum.

Images used in this book

The images provided on the DVD are to be used only in connection with the tutorials in this book. They are copyrighted, and may not be reproduced, copied, or used by you for any other work without first obtaining permission from the copyright owner. Licenses for many of the images used in this book are available from *istockphoto.com*, a great resource for stock images.

You can use Adobe Bridge to learn more details about the images, including information about the photographers, copyright information, and, where applicable, *istockphoto.com* image numbers. This information is listed under the IPTC Core metadata for each image.

Copyright information and other details are listed under the metadata for each image.

What you'll learn in this lesson:

- Merging images
- Using Smart Filters
- Using the new selection tools
- Working with text
- Using unsharp masking
- Using Camera Raw

What's New in Adobe Photoshop CS3?

Welcome to Photoshop CS3! In this lesson, you'll get a look at many of the new features, such as easier-to-use selection tools, improved Vanishing Point, and Live Filter. You will also explore these features in more detail in the lessons that follow.

This lesson provides an overview of new features in Photoshop CS3. If you'd prefer to get familiar with all that Photoshop CS3 has to offer, including some of the new features, you can jump ahead to Lesson 2, "Exploring Adobe Photoshop CS3."

A different Photoshop for different users

In this release of Photoshop, there are two versions: Photoshop CS3 and Photoshop CS3 Extended. Don't worry about one being better than the other; that is not necessarily true. Photoshop CS3 in any flavor is a full, digital editing application. Photoshop CS3 Extended includes additional features geared toward industries such as multimedia, animation, film, architecture, engineering construction (AEC), manufacturing, and medical professions. In this lesson, the features mentioned are included in both Photoshop CS3 and Photoshop CS3 Extended.

Starting up

Before starting, make sure that your tools and palettes are consistent by resetting your preferences. See "Resetting Adobe Photoshop CS3 preferences" on page 4.

You will work with several files from the ps01lessons folder in this lesson. Make sure that you have loaded your pslessons folder onto your hard drive from the supplied DVD. See "Loading lesson files" on page 3. Now, let's take a look at what's new in Photoshop CS3.

See Lesson 1 in action!

Use the accompanying video to gain a better understanding of how to use some of the features shown in this lesson. Open the file PS01.swf located in the Videos folder to view the video training file for this lesson.

Easy-to-manage workspace

The interface has been standardized across all of the CS3 applications, making them easier to use. The added bonus is that the interface now takes up less of your screen real estate. In the next section, you'll get your feet wet so you'll see the benefits of the interface. You will more fully explore the interface in Lesson 3, "Getting to Know the Workspace."

Using the new interface

This new interface is consistent with the interface you will find in the other Creative Suite 3 applications, allowing you to focus on your job, and not spend time searching for tools and menus. You will open a file using Adobe Bridge, which is the preferred workflow for the Creative Suite 3 applications.

Docking palettes

You can take advantage of new docking features that allow you to neatly store your palettes and tools until you need them. In fact, palettes can be collapsed to icons organized in a space-saving dock.

1   Choose File > Browse to open Adobe Bridge. Adobe Bridge provides you with image previews, as well as features to manage and organize your images. You'll find out more about Bridge in Lesson 4, "Using Adobe Bridge."

2   Click on the Folders panel that is in the upper left of the Adobe Bridge window to bring it forward, then click on Desktop. The items that are on your Desktop appear in the content panel on the right, including the pslessons folder that you have copied from the pslessons DVD supplied with this book.

    If your content from the Desktop does not appear in the Content pane in Adobe Bridge, choose Desktop from the Favorites panel instead.

Open the pslessons folder and then open the ps01lessons folder contained within it. Locate the file ps0101.psd and double-click on it to open the file. If a color profile warning dialog box appears, press OK.

You are not creating a project at this time, but, you will explore the interface using this image. Note the single column Tools palette on the left of the display and the collapsible palette icons in the dock on the right side of the display.

The new streamlined interface saves space and is easier to navigate.

3   Notice that the Tools palette is in a space-saving, one-column format. Click on the gray bar or the left-facing double arrows at the top of the Tools palette to change it to two columns. Click on it again to switch back to one column.

4   Reposition, or undock, the Tools palette from the left side by clicking on the gray bar directly above the Ps logo and dragging it to another location.

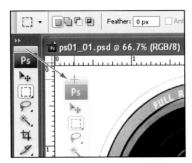

Click and drag to undock the Tools palette.

5   To re-dock the Tools palette, click on the gray bar again and drag it to the left side of the workspace. When you see a ghosted gray bar, release the mouse; the Tools palette is re-docked.

6   Leave ps0101.psd open for the next section.

Unified user interface panels

You are likely to find Photoshop's new palette docking system very intuitive.

1   Before starting, make sure that you are back to the standard Photoshop workspace by choosing Window > Workspace > Default Workspace. This returns you to the original Photoshop workspace. In Photoshop CS3, there are many workspaces that you can choose. You'll find out how to use them and create your own in Lesson 3, "Getting to Know the Workspace."

2   Click once on the left-facing double arrows in the gray area above the icons. The icons are expanded into full palettes, which is especially helpful for new users, as it can be difficult to decipher which palettes the icons represent.

Expand and collapse palettes to customize your workspace.

3   Click on the right-facing double arrows to collapse the palettes back to icons.

You'll notice that the expanded palettes on the right also have these arrows, so you can expand and collapse them as well.

4   Choose File > Close and close the ps0101.psd image. If you are asked to save changes, select No.

Now you will discover some of the other new features in Adobe Photoshop CS3.

Understanding the Smart Filter feature

With the Smart Filter feature, you have the ability to turn filters on or off and blend or mask filters without editing the original image content.

By choosing Filter > Convert for Smart Filters, you can save an original image that will not be affected when you apply filters. You can then add, adjust, and remove filters from the image without having to re-save the image or start all over again.

You'll now open a file with a Smart Filter already applied to it. You'll find out how to create and work with these filters more in Lesson 12, "Using Adobe Photoshop Filters."

1   Choose File > Browse. Adobe Bridge appears. If the ps01lessons folder is not visible, click on the Folders tab in the upper left side of the Adobe Bridge workspace, then click on Desktop and locate the ps01lessons folder inside the pslessons folder on your desktop.

2   Double-click on ps0102.psd to open the file. An image with an exaggerated radial blur appears. You'll tone this down a bit using the Smart Filter mask located in the Layers palette.

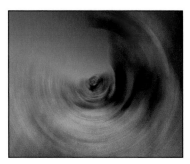

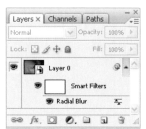

An image with a radial blur applied.   *The Smart Filter is visible on the layers palette.*

3   You'll now save this as a work file. Choose File > Save As. In the Save As dialog box, navigate to the ps01lessons folder. In the File name text field, type **ps0102_work**. Leave the format set to Photoshop and press Save.

4   If the Layers palette is not visible, choose Window > Layers. Note the Filters effects mask that is under the image layer.

5   Click on the eye icon (👁) to the left of Smart Filters. The unfiltered image appears. To turn the filter effect back on, click on the area where the eye icon was located.

    Now you will make an adjustment to the radial blur filter.

6   Double-click on the words Radial Blur underneath Smart Filters in the Layers palette. The Radial Blur dialog box appears.

7   Click and drag the Amount slider to approximately 15, or type **15** into the Amount text field.

8   Select Zoom for the Blur method, then press OK. Notice that much of the detail is returned to the image, as it retained the original image data as a Smart Object.

9   Choose File > Save, and then choose File > Close.

    You may use Smart Filters for simple processes, like clicking on the eye icon to turn filters that you applied off and on. You may want to take it further with creative masking techniques like painting on the Filter effects. Learn more about the Smart Filter feature, as well as the Smart Object feature, in Chapter 11, "Using Smart Objects."

See the Quick Selection tool in action!

Use the video that accompanies this lesson to gain a better understanding of how to take advantage of using the Quick Selection tool. Open the file PS01.swf located in the Videos folder to view the video training file for this lesson.

Select like a pro with the Quick Selection tool

Accurate selections in Photoshop are essential. If you do a good job using the selection tools, editing and retouching looks natural. Do it badly, and the image could look contrived. In Photoshop CS3, you can take advantage of new tools to make accurate selections more easily.

The new Quick Selection tool (✎) allows you to paint a selection on an image. Photoshop automatically completes the selection for you with very accurate results. Of course, this won't work for every selection, but it will do the trick for many types of selections.

Once Photoshop has completed the selection, you can then refine it—or any selection, for that matter—with the new Refine Edge feature.

In this next exercise, you'll make the background transparent and change the color of the little girl's shirt using this new selection tool.

1   Choose File > Browse, or click on the Go to Bridge button (📷) in the upper right of the options bar.

2   Locate the ps01lessons folder, and double-click on the image named ps0103.psd. An image of a young girl appears.

3   Choose File > Save As. In the Save As dialog box, navigate to the ps01lessons folder and type **ps0103_work** in the File name text field. Leave the format set to Photoshop and press Save.

4   In the Tools palette, click and hold on the Eraser tool (⌫) to reveal the Magic Eraser tool (⌫). Using the Magic Eraser tool, click on the white background behind the little girl.

    You just eliminated the background, essentially turning it from white to transparent, using the Magic Eraser tool. This is not a new tool, but many users have yet to discover its possibilities.

5   Now, select the Quick Selection tool (⟍) from the Tools palette and paint over the little girl's shirt. Watch as the selection is created with your cursor movement. If you accidently select the area beyond the shirt, choose the Subtract from selection button (⟍) in the options bar and paint over the area that should not be selected. You can make the brush size smaller by pressing the [(left bracket key) or larger by pressing the] (right bracket key).

Brushing a selection with the Quick Selection tool.

6.   Choose File > Save. Keep this image open for the next part of this lesson.

Making selections with the new Refine Edge feature

After making a selection, you can click on the Refine Edge button in the options bar. This opens a Refine Edge dialog box full of options to improve your selection. In this section, you will use these options.

1   With your ps0103_work.psd file still open, click on the Refine Edge button in the options bar. The Refine Edge dialog box appears. You can click on the Preview buttons at the bottom of the dialog box to choose the preview method that works best for the image. In this example, the preview was left at On White.

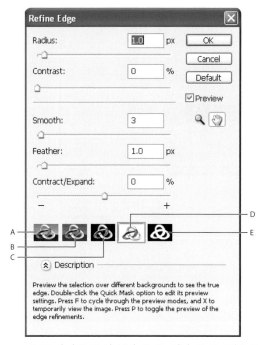

A. *Standard*. *B*. *Quick Mask*. *C*. *On Black*. *D*. *On White*. *E*. *Mask*.

You can experiment with these new selection features and learn some tried-and-true methods for using them in Lesson 7, "Making the Best Selections."

2 Click and drag the Contrast slider to approximately 40, or type **40** into the Contrast text field. Press OK.

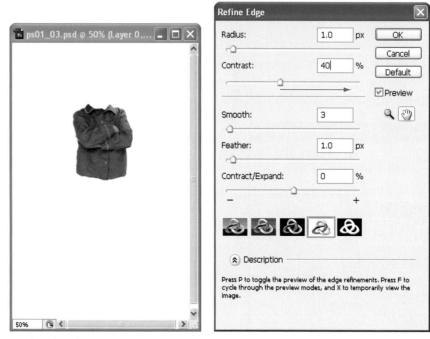

Use the Refine Edge feature to add contrast to the selection.

3 With the selection still active, locate the Layers palette. If it is not visible, choose Window > Layers, then click and hold on the Create new fill or adjustment layer button (⊘) and select to Hue/Saturation. The Hue/Saturation dialog box appears.

Choose the Hue/Saturation Adjustment layer.

4   You can drag the Hue slider to the left or right to change the color of the shirt. Don't worry if your selection is not perfect, as you will learn how to better create selections in Lesson 7, "Making the Best Selections." In this example, drag the slider to approximately +113 to change the color of the shirt to green, then press OK.

5   Choose File > Save, then choose File > Close.

Creating better composites

With the new Auto-Align feature in Photoshop CS3, you can align multiple layers quickly and accurately.

The Auto-Align Layers command quickly analyzes details and then moves, rotates, or warps layers to align them perfectly. This is a big boost for photographers who regularly shoot photos of groups, and for anyone else who wants to combine images more accurately.

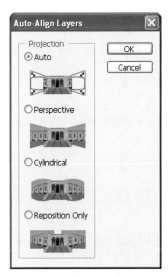

The new Auto-Align Layers feature.

This new feature includes the Auto-Blend Layer option, which blends color and shading seamlessly into the final image. You could achieve the same high-quality results in earlier versions of Photoshop, but it was very time consuming. The new automatic layer alignment and blending features get you there faster, and with less work. You'll have the opportunity to use the Auto-Align feature in the Lesson 2, "Exploring Adobe Photoshop CS3."

Camera Raw improvements

Camera Raw is a file format option for many digital cameras. Camera Raw file formats can vary depending on the camera manufacturer and model, but Photoshop CS3 can handle most Camera Raw files. The Raw format is gaining popularity, especially among serious photographers, because it stores the largest amount of original digital image data—almost no processing occurs in the camera. This means that you have a lot more information to work with when you make adjustments, such as lighting, sharpening, and color changes.

Photoshop's improved Camera Raw processing

Photoshop has supported Camera Raw files in the past, but Photoshop CS3 is faster and supports more than 150 different versions of the Raw file format.

Photoshop CS3 now supports opening Raw, JPEG, and TIFF images in the Camera Raw Plug-in. By simply selecting a file from Adobe Bridge (see Lesson 4, "Using Adobe Bridge") or choosing File > Open, you can open most Raw files. The Camera Raw interface in Photoshop CS3 allows you to make incredibly precise adjustments to an image. It includes new Fill Light controls, which are used to reduce the contrast of a scene and provide illumination in the shadows, and Vibrance controls, which are used to enhance or diminish the intensity of the colors in less-saturated areas of an image.

In this exercise, you'll open a Camera Raw file so you can investigate the capabilities of working with these files using Photoshop CS3.

1   Choose File > Browse, or select the Go to Bridge button (📷) in the options bar.

2   Double-click on the image named ps0104.CR2, a Camera Raw image from a Canon EOS Digital Rebel camera. The Camera Raw window opens.

The Camera Raw window.

3   Click and drag the Recovery slider to the right to a value of approximately 50. Notice that the detail is recovered in the sky. You will learn more about working with Camera Raw files in Lesson 6, "Creating a Good Image."

4   When you are finished experimenting, click Open Image to open the Camera Raw file in Adobe Photoshop.

5   While you could continue to edit this file using Photoshop, you will not be performing additional edits at this time. Choose File > Close. If you are asked to save the changes, choose No.

Understand the improved Vanishing Point filter

You can now edit images in perspective with more creative options using the enhanced Vanishing Point feature. You can create multiple planes in an image—areas that are built in perspective—connect them at any angle, and then wrap graphics, text, and images around them. This is especially useful for package designers.

Artwork pasted into multiple perspective planes, such as the fence on the left which was added to the image.

The painting tools also work in perspective, allowing you to clone and to take advantage of retouching tools for healing. You can learn all about using the Vanishing Point filter in Lesson 12, "Using Adobe Photoshop Filters."

Photoshop CS3 vs. Photoshop CS3 Extended

If you purchased the Creative Suite 3 Design Premium Suite, Web Premium, or Master Collection Suite, you have Photoshop CS3 Extended. If you purchased the Design Standard Suite, you have Photoshop CS3. You can find out easily which version of Photoshop you have by choosing Help > About Photoshop (Windows) or Photoshop > About Photoshop (Mac OS). The version of Photoshop is listed in the welcome screen. Photoshop CS3 Extended is for multimedia and video professionals, as well as other users who have a need for extended capabilities to analyze data and build 2-D images from 3-D files. The features discussed below are available only in the Extended version.

Create animation with the Animation palette

With Photoshop CS3 Extended, you can use the new Advanced Timeline palette to create animation from a series of images, such as time-series data. The animation can then be exported to QuickTime, MPEG-4, and Adobe Flash Video (FLV) formats.

If you are working with video, you can now open video files in Photoshop, where it is opened as a Movie layer. Using the Timeline controls, you can select footage and retouch video frame-by-frame using Photoshop's painting and editing tools. Find out more about the timeline in Lesson 13, "Creating for Web and Video."

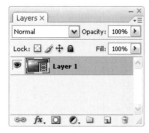

Movie layer.

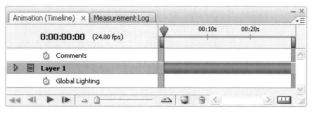

Advanced Timeline palette.

3-D compositing and texture editing

Using Photoshop CS3 Extended, you can also render and incorporate rich 3-D content into 2-D composites—and can even edit textures on 3-D models directly within Photoshop, and immediately see the results. Photoshop Extended supports common 3-D interchange formats including 3DS, OBJ, U3D, KMZ, and COLLADA, so you can import, view, and interact with most 3-D models.

2-D and 3-D measurement tools

If you work in the architecture, construction, engineering, manufacturing, or health care industries, you can use the new measurement tools in Photoshop CS3 Extended to extract quantitative information from images.

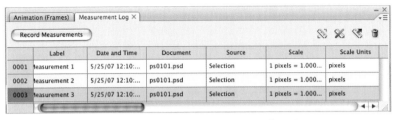

New measurement tools in Photoshop help you to extract quantitative information.

With the new measurement tools, you can easily calibrate or set the scale of an image, and then use any of the Photoshop selection tools to define and calculate distance, perimeter, area, and other measurements. You can also record data points in a measurement log and export data, including histogram data, to a spreadsheet for further analysis.

These advanced features are not covered in this book, but look for the *Photoshop CS3 Expert Answers* book and the Dynamic Learning training videos for more information.

Lesson 2

What you'll learn in this lesson:

- Creating panoramic images
- Using Smart Filters
- Making more accurate selections
- Creating vector shapes and text

Exploring Adobe Photoshop CS3

In this lesson, you'll dive right into Photoshop CS3 and create a composition using the new selection tools, layers, masks, and text. All these features and tools are also covered in detail in later lessons, but, in this lesson, you'll get up and running quickly, and discover the possibilities of Photoshop CS3.

Starting up

Relax and have fun with this lesson. You will complete a fast-paced exercise that incorporates many of the new features in Photoshop CS3. Use this lesson to discover the many possibilities Photoshop CS3 has to offer. Don't worry about absorbing all the information about these features right away, as they are covered in more detail in the following lessons. You don't have to be an expert to complete this lesson, but you won't be bored if you are.

Before starting, make sure that your tools and palettes are consistent by resetting your preferences. See "Resetting Adobe Photoshop CS3 preferences" on page 4.

You will work with several files from the ps02lessons folder in this lesson. Make sure that you have loaded your pslessons files onto your hard drive from the supplied DVD. See "Loading lesson files" on page 3.

See Lesson 2 in action!

Use the accompanying video to gain a better understanding of how to use some of the features shown in this lesson. Open the file PS02.swf located in the Videos folder to view the video training file for this lesson.

Viewing the completed lesson file

You will now have an opportunity to examine the finished lesson file.

1 If you don't have Photoshop CS3 open, launch it now. Note that Photoshop CS3 Extended is used throughout this book, but, unless noted, all lessons can be completed in both Photoshop CS3 and Photoshop CS3 Extended.

2 Choose File > Browse. This launches Adobe Bridge, a stand-alone application that can be accessed using the File menu in any of the Creative Suite 3 applications, or via the Go to Bridge button (⬛) that is found on the options bar or control panels of most of the Creative Suite 3 applications. Navigate to the ps02lessons folder inside the pslessons folder you have copied on to your desktop.

3 Locate the file named ps0201_done.psd and double-click to open it in Photoshop. A composite image appears.

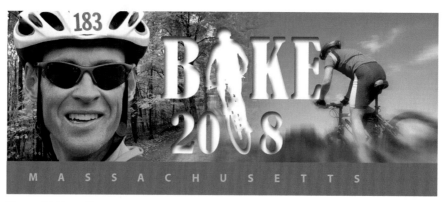

The completed lesson file.

4 The ps0201_done.psd file is the complete file that you will make in this lesson. You can close it now by choosing File > Close, or keep it open for reference.

Creating a panorama

In the first part of the lesson, you'll use tools available in Adobe Bridge to take three images and merge them into one. These images were created by taking several shots while moving at a constant pace along a path. Most people have had grand ideas of shooting images like these and then piecing them back together, but not everyone gets that far. Now is your chance to take advantage of the newly enhanced Photomerge feature. Using Photomerge not only saves you hours of time blending images together; it is also likely to do a better job than you can do by hand.

Take several images and combine them, using the Photomerge feature.

1   To access the images for the final panoramic image, choose File > Browse or select the Go to Bridge button (▣) in the options bar. Navigate to the ps02lessons folder inside the pslessons folder you have copied onto your desktop.

2   Hold down the Ctrl key (Windows) or Command (Mac OS), and select the images named ps0201.psd, ps0202.psd, and ps0203.psd. By holding down the Ctrl or Command key while selecting, you are able to select multiple files.

Note that there are tools for several applications built into Adobe Bridge; you will work only with the Photoshop tools in this lesson.

3 Choose Tools > Photoshop > Photomerge. The Photomerge dialog box appears, with the three images you selected as the source files.

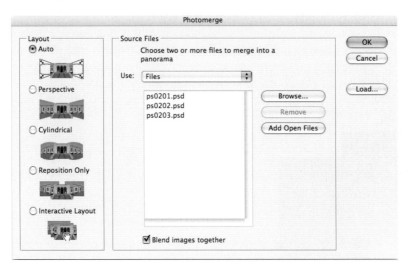

The Photomerge feature offers many possibilities when combining images.

Photomerge options

When merging files or layers together, you have multiple layout options from which to choose. Here is what each option can do:

Auto: Analyzes the source images and applies either a perspective or cylindrical layout, depending on which produces a better final Photomerge result.

Perspective: Creates a consistent composition by designating one of the source images (by default, the middle image) as the reference image. The other images are then transformed so that overlapping content across layers is matched.

Cylindrical: Reduces the distortion that can occur with the perspective layout by displaying individual images as if they appeared on the surface of an unfolded cylinder. Overlapping content across layers is still matched. The reference image is placed at the center.

Reposition Only: Aligns the layers and matches overlapping content, but does not transform (stretch or skew) any of the selected layers.

Interactive Layout: Allows you to open the source images in a dialog box and position them manually.

4 Leave the Photomerge settings at their default and press OK. The Photomerge process takes some time as it goes through its calculations, but in the end it produces a merged file created from the original three images.

Notice that your images are now on three separate layers. This is helpful if you need to make any minor tweaks, but in this instance, you will choose to combine, or merge, them into one layer. Before you merge these layers together, take a look at the layers that Photomerge has just created.

5 Click on the visibility eye icons (👁) to the left of the layer names, one at a time, to see the edges of the images and how they were created to provide you with the best merged image possible. Click where the eye icon was on each layer to turn the visibility back on. All layers should now be visible.

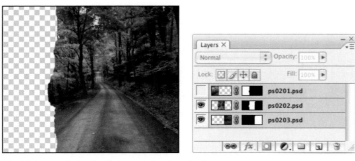

The Photomerge feature builds layer masks automatically.

6 Select the layer named ps0201.psd, and then Shift+click to select ps0202.psd and ps0203. psd. All three layers are now selected.

7 From the Layers palette menu, choose Merge layers, or you can use the keyboard shortcut Ctrl+E (Windows) or Command+E (Mac OS). The three layers become one layer.

8 Double-click on the text ps0201.psd to activate the layer name text field. When the layer name becomes highlighted, type **forest**.

9 When you used the Photomerge feature, a new file was automatically created, named Untitled _Panorama1. Choose File > Save; the Save As dialog box appears. In the File name text field, type **ps0201_work**, then navigate to the ps02lessons folder and choose Photoshop in the Format drop-down menu and press Save.

10 Leave this image open for the next part of this lesson.

Placing another image into the file

In the next part of the exercise, you'll add another image to this document and apply some filter effects to the image, using the new Smart Filter feature.

1 Choose File > Browse, or press the Go to Bridge button (📷) in the upper right of the options bar.

2 Navigate to the ps02lessons folder, and double-click on the image named ps0204.psd to open it in Photoshop. The image of a bicycle rider appears. Position the image so that you can see both the panoramic image and the bicycle rider image at the same time.

3 Select the Move tool (✛), then click and drag the bicycler image over and on top of the panoramic image. Do not release the mouse until you see an outline, or border, appear around the ps0201_work.psd document.

If a Paste Profile Mismatch box appears, leave it set to convert (preserve color appearance) and press OK. The image of the bicycler is now added as a second layer (Layer 1) in your file.

Drag and drop one image to another.

4   Using the Move tool (⊹), click and drag to position Layer 1 so that it is on the right side of the image. The exact location of this layer is not important.

Use the Move tool to reposition the bicycler image.

5   Double-click on the layer name, Layer 1, to activate the name text field, and type **bicycler**.

6   Choose File > Save. Keep this file open for the next part of this exercise.

7   Choose Window > ps204.psd to bring that image to the front, then choose File > Close to close the file. If asked to save changes choose No.

Using Smart Filters

By using filters in Photoshop, you can dramatically change the content of an image. You can change a photograph to make it appear as though it was hand-drawn with a pencil, or even painted with watercolors. You can add depth of focus, blurring parts of an image to attract the viewer to a main focal point, and apply a neon glow, if that is the type of effect you want. Up until this version, filters have changed the original image data; with Photoshop CS3, you can convert a layer to a Smart Object before applying a filter. The Smart Object is actually a copy of the original image that becomes embedded in the file. This allows you the freedom to experiment, without worrying about destroying the original image data. Read more about Smart Objects in Lesson 11, "Using Smart Objects." This new feature is referred to as "Smart Filters." In this next section, you will discover the benefits of using Smart Filters, and how you can take advantage of the filter masks for more creative effects.

1   Select the bicycler layer to make sure that it is the active layer.

2   Choose Filter > Convert for Smart Filters. A warning message appears, informing you that this layer will now be converted to a Smart Object. Press OK.

    A Smart Object icon (⬚) appears in the layer thumbnail, indicating that it is now a Smart Object.

3   Select Filter > Blur > Radial Blur. A rather long warning message may appear, informing you that the newly added filter will not preview. Press OK. The Radial Blur dialog box appears.

    You will now use the Radial Blur filter to create motion and excitement in the image.

4   In the Radial Blur dialog box, type **30** into the Amount text field. Blur Method should be Zoom and Quality should be Best.

5   To have the blur center generate from the area where the bicycler is, click slightly towards the right in the Blur Center pane. Press OK to apply the Radial Blur to the bicycler layer.

6   Choose File > Save. Keep the file open for the next part of this lesson.

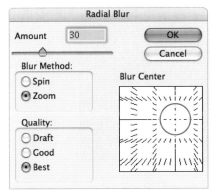

Click in the Blur Center pane to determine where the canter of the radial blur will occur.

Result.

Applying a second filter

You can have multiple filters applied to one layer. In this part of the lesson, you will add the Mosaic filter to give the image a digital look.

1   Select the bicycler layer to make sure that it is the active layer.

2   Choose Filter > Pixelate > Mosaic. The Mosaic dialog box appears.

3   Type **25** in the Cell Size text field, and press OK. The Mosaic filter creates square blocks of color, producing a pixelated effect.

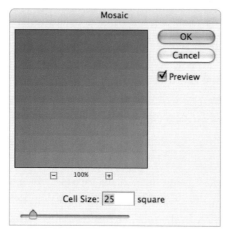

Applying the Mosaic filter.   *Result.*

You can change the results of a Smart Filter by changing the stacking order in the Layers palette.

4   Select the Mosaic Filter (under Smart Filters) and drag and drop it under Radial Blur. Don't release the Mosaic filter until you see a dark line appear under Radial Blur. Notice that by changing the order of your Smart Filters, you can change the affect they have on your image.

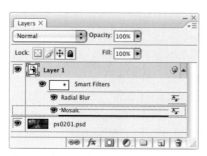

Changing the order of the filters.   *Result.*

Masking a Smart Filter

Now that you have applied the Radial Blur and Mosaic filters to the bicycler layer, you'll adjust the visibility of the effect.

1 First of all, notice that you can easily return to your original image at any time. Click on the eye icon (👁) to the left of Smart Filters; this turns the filter effect off. Click the location of the eye icon again to turn the visibility of the filter effect back on.

2 Second, notice that there is a Filter effects mask thumbnail to the right of the eye icon. Click to activate the mask. You will know the mask is selected when you see corner marks appear on the edges.

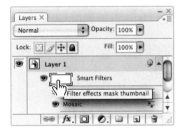

Click on the Filter effects mask thumbnail to activate it.

3 Choose the Gradient tool (▣) from the Tools palette.

4 In the options bar, select the Radial Gradient button (▣), and press **D**. By pressing D, you revert back to the default foreground and background colors of black and white. Make sure that the Mode drop-down menu is set to Normal and that the Opacity is set at 100%. Check the Reverse checkbox. This reverses the order in which the black and white appear in the gradient.

Setting up the Radial Gradient tool.

5   With the Gradient tool still selected, click and drag from the center of the bicycler to about halfway to the edge of the bicycler image, then release. The filters are now masked, using the gradient you just created. Notice that where there is black on the mask, the filter is masked, or blocked, from view. Where there is white, the filter is visible.

Click and drag with the Radial Gradient.

Result.

6   You are finished with the Smart Filter section of this lesson. Find out more about Smart Filters in Lesson 12, "Using Adobe Photoshop Filters." Choose File > Save. Keep this file open for the next part of this lesson.

Applying a layer mask

In this next section, you'll create a gradient mask for the entire layer you just created.

1   Click on the bicycler layer in the Layers palette to activate the layer.

2   Click on the Add layer mask button (◙) at the bottom of the Layers palette. A Layer mask thumbnail appears to the right of the bicycler layer.

3   Select the Gradient tool (■), then, in the options bar, select the Linear Gradient button (■). Press **D** to make sure you are back at the default foreground and background colors of black and white. Make sure that the Mode drop-down menu is set to Normal, the Opacity is set at 100%, and the Reverse checkbox is checked.

4   With the Gradient tool selected, click and drag from the left of the bicycler image to the right, stopping at about the middle of the bicycler image. Hold down the Shift key to constrain the gradient you are creating to a straight line. Release the mouse. A gradient mask has been created, and the bicycler layer is now transitioning smoothly into the forest image. You can repeatedly click and drag new gradients until you find one that works best for the image.

Click and drag a gradient over the image.

If you decide that you do not want to use the layer mask, you can delete it by selecting it and clicking on the Delete button (🗑) at the bottom of the Layers palette, or you can temporarily turn the effects of the layer mask off and on by Shift+clicking on the layer mask thumbnail. Shift+click again on the layer mask thumbnail to turn it back on.

5   Choose File > Save, and leave this file open for the next part of this lesson. Find out more about layers in Lesson 9, "Getting to Know Layers," and Lesson 10, "Taking Layers to the Max."

See new selection techniques in action!

Use the video that accompanies this lesson to gain a better understanding of how to take advantage of using new selection techniques. Open the file PS02.swf located in the Videos folder to view the video training file for this lesson.

Using new selection techniques

There are several new and improved selection techniques that you can take advantage of in Photoshop CS3.

Using the Quick Selection tool

In Photoshop CS3, you can select regions of your image quickly and accurately using the new Quick Selection tool (✎). You can then refine the edge using the new Refine Edge feature.

1   If you do not still have the ps0201_work.psd file open, choose File > Open Recent, and choose ps0201_work.psd from the list of recently opened documents.

2   Choose File > Browse to open Adobe Bridge. Navigate to the ps02lessons folder and double-click on the image named ps0205.psd to open it. A portrait of a bicycler appears. You will create a layer mask on this image from a selection you will make using the Quick Selection tool.

3   Select the Quick Selection tool (✎) and start painting the section of the man's helmet, head and shirt. The areas that you paint become part of a selection. As you paint additional regions, they are added to the selection.

4   If you inadvertently paint an area that should not be included, hold down the Alt key (Windows) or Option key (Mac OS) and paint over that region again. No modifier key is needed to add to the selection, as that is the default. Continue painting the selection, making sure that you get in the holes of the helmet and don't leave the ears behind.

5 Make sure that you have removed the area between the helmet strap and the biker's shirt from the selection. Holding down the Alt/Option key while painting with the Quick Selection tool will deselect that section.

Use Alt/Option to subtract from the selection.

Saving your selection

It is wise to save a selection, especially if you put a lot of effort into creating it. In this next section, you will save your selection.

1 With the selection of the man's face still active, choose Select > Save Selection. The Save Selection dialog box appears.

2 Type **portrait** into the Name text field and press OK. If you accidently deselect your selection, you can now retrieve it by choosing Select > Load Selection and choosing portrait from the Channels drop-down menu.

3 Leave this file open, with the selection active, for the next part of this lesson.

Refining the edge of the selection

Once you have created a selection, you can modify it using the Refine Edge feature. The Refine Edge feature is available in the options bar when you have any selection tool active.

The Refine Edge feature gives you more control over selections after they have been created. Using the Refine Edge dialog box, you can better define a selection's edges with controls that change the radius, contrast, smoothness, and feather, or contract or expand the selection.

1 You should still have ps0205.psd open with the active selection. If not, please review the previous section.

2 Make sure you have a selection tool selected, such as the Marquee, Lasso, or Quick Selection tool, then press the Refine Edge button in the options bar. The Refine Edge dialog box appears.

3   You can choose from several viewing options across the bottom of the Refine Edge dialog box. Starting with the first one (Standard), click on each preview option to see how your image and its selection are displayed. Depending upon the image and the selection, you may have to change the preview to get the best view of your selection.

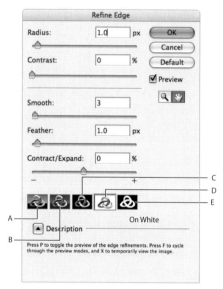

*A. Standard. **B**. Quick Mask. **C**. On Black. **D**. On White. **E**. Mask.*

As you are investigating your selection, use the Hand (☝) and Zoom tools (🔍) that appear in the Refine Edge dialog box. If you prefer, you can use the standard zoom keyboard shortcuts, such as Ctrl++(plus sign) (Windows) and Command++ (plus sign) (Mac OS). Once zoomed in, you can hold down the spacebar and click and drag to pan (or push) around your image. Ctrl+0 (zero) (Windows) or Command+0 (zero) (Mac OS) fits the image back into the window.

4   Select the On White preview option.

What the Refine Edge options mean

Here are some brief descriptions of how each option affects your selection.

Radius: Determines the size of the region around the selection where you want the Refine Edge to be applied. You can increase the radius to create a better selection in areas with soft transitions, like hair.

Contrast: Sharpens selection edges and removes fuzzy artifacts.

Smooth: Reduces irregular areas ("hills and valleys") in the selection.

Feather: Creates a soft-edged transition between the selection and its surrounding pixels.

Contract/Expand: Shrinks or enlarges the selection boundary. This setting is useful for making subtle adjustments to soft-edged selections.

5   Experiment with different settings, previewing the result in the preview pane. When you are finished experimenting, hold down the Alt (Windows) or Option (Mac OS) key. The Cancel button turns into a Reset button. Press the Reset button to return to the original Refine Edge dialog settings.

6   For this image, slide the Radius slider to about the 5 mark, or type **5** in the Radius text field. This setting controls the size of the area that Refine Edge affects.

7   Slide the Contrast slider to the right to about the 30 mark, or type **30** into the Contrast text field. This removes the fuzzy artifacts in the selection.

8 Click and drag the Smooth slider to about the 40 mark, or type **40** into the Smooth text field. This setting smooths out any bumpy selection areas that you may have inadvertently created. Leave all the other settings at their defaults and press OK. The entire image appears with the selection region still active.

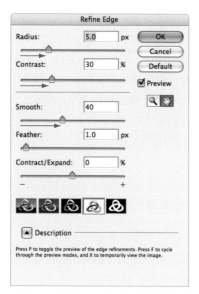

Adjust your selection.

9 Choose File > Save. Keep this file open, with the selection region active, for the next part of this lesson.

Creating a layer mask

If the Layers palette is not visible, choose Window > Layers. Notice that this document has a Background layer, as is the case with most images that are opened in Photoshop. To create a layer mask, you must convert this Background layer to a regular layer. In this part of the exercise, you will turn the Background layer into a regular layer, and then create a layer mask from your selection.

1 With the ps0205.psd file open and the Layers palette visible, hold down the Alt (Windows) or Option (Mac OS) key and double-click on the text Background (to the right of the layer thumbnail) in the Layers palette. The Background layer is now Layer 0.

2 With your selection still active, press the Add layer mask button (▣), at the bottom of the Layers palette. The background is transparent (as represented by the checked background). You are viewing only the selected area.

Creating a layer mask from your selection.

3 Make sure that you still have your ps0201_work.psd image open. If not, choose File > Open Recent and choose ps0201_work from the list of recent files.

4 Position your images so that you can see both the ps0201_work.psd image and the ps0205.psd image on your screen. Make sure that ps0205.psd is in front by clicking on its titlebar.

5 Switch to the Move tool (▸₊), or press **V**, the keyboard shortcut for the Move tool, and click and drag the portrait of the bicycler over to the ps0201_work.psd image, making sure that you do not release the image until you see a border appear around the ps0201_work.psd image. The layer and the layer mask are moved to the ps0201_work.psd document.

6 With the Move tool still selected, click and drag the bicycler portrait image to the left side of the document window.

The new image is combined with the original work file.

7 Double-click on the layer name (Layer 1), to the right of the newly placed layer thumbnail. This activates the text so that you can change the name. Type **portrait** and press the Return or Enter key.

8 Choose File > Save to save this file. Keep it open for the next part of this lesson.

9 Choose Window > ps0205.psd to bring the portrait of the bicycler forward again, then choose File > Close. Choose No when asked if you want to save changes to the file.

Creating a vector shape

In this section, you'll discover how to use a basic vector shape with the vector tools available in Adobe Photoshop. Use the vector tools for creating artwork that can be resized and output at any resolution. Since the vector tools create graphics with paths, not pixels, the shapes you create will be scalable without any loss of image quality.

1   Have the ps0201_work.psd file open. If you do not see gray area (pasteboard) showing around the outside of the image, click on the lower right corner of the document window and drag it to the lower right of your screen. It is helpful to have some of the pasteboard showing when creating shapes or selections that are positioned at the edges of an image.

Click and drag open the image area.

2   Select the Rectangular tool (□), or press **U**, the keyboard shortcut for the Rectangle Vector tool. Make sure that you do not select the Rectangular Marquee tool, as you are creating a shape, not a selection.

3 In the options bar, make sure that the Shape layers (⊡) option is selected, then click and drag across the lower eighth of the image to the lower right corner. You might cross over part of the bicycler's chin, which is fine; he can be repositioned later. The exact size of the rectangle is not critical, and can be adjusted later. When you release, a vector shape layer is created. The color of the shape is based upon the last selection you made for the foreground color. You will change that color now.

Click and drag to create a rectangular vector shape layer.

4 If the Layers palette is not visible, choose Window > Layers. You see a newly added Shape 1 layer. In the Shape 1 layer is a Layer thumbnail (on the left) that includes the color of your vector shape. Double-click on that thumbnail to open the Color Picker. A dialog box appears, asking you to pick a solid color. You will sample a color from the image.

5 When you position the cursor over the image, it changes into the Eyedropper tool (⌁), so that you can sample colors directly from your image. Position the cursor over a green area of the trees and click. The color is selected in the Color Picker. If you don't like your first choice, continue selecting various areas in the image until you find a color you like. In our example, we used these color values: Red 101, Green 110, and Blue 57. Press OK.

You will now reposition the portrait layer. First, ensure that the Shape 1 layer is the active layer.

6 Select the Move tool (⊹). You can easily switch from one active layer to another by selecting the layer in the Layers palette, or you can use this helpful keyboard shortcut: hold down the Ctrl (Windows) or Command (Mac OS) key and click on the image content that you want to activate. In this example, click on the portrait of the bicyclist in the image file. The portrait layer becomes active.

By holding down the Ctrl or Command key, you have activated an auto-select feature available in Photoshop. If you have Auto-Select checked in the options bar, this keyboard shortcut will not work.

7   With the portrait layer selected, click and drag to reposition the portrait layer so that the bicycler's chin is not being covered by the vector box.

8   Choose File > Save. Leave this file open for the next part of this lesson.

Adding artwork from Adobe Illustrator

You can import, or place, graphics from many different applications into Photoshop files, including native Adobe Illustrator files. In this section, you will place Adobe Illustrator artwork as a Smart Object, then you will edit the Smart Object, resizing and applying effects to it.

For this part of the lesson, you need to have Adobe Illustrator installed. If you do not have Adobe Illustrator installed, you can follow the steps up to the Editing a Smart Object section, and then just read the steps that explain the process.

Placing artwork

1   Choose File > Place; the Place dialog box appears. Navigate to the ps02lessons folder that you dragged onto your hard drive from the pslessons DVD. Select the file named bikelogo.ai. Choose Place.

2   When the Place PDF dialog box appears, leave it at the defaults and press OK. The image is placed into the document. Note that there is an active bounding box surrounding the image. Photoshop offers the opportunity to scale the logo before approving its placement. For this example, you'll leave the size of the logo as is. Confirm the placement by pressing the Return or Enter key, or by selecting the Commit transform button (✔) in the options bar.

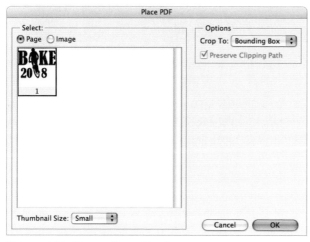

Placing an Adobe Illustrator file into Photoshop.

The image has been placed, but it is not at the final size. Though you could have adjusted the size upon placement, you were instructed not to. Not to worry; Photoshop automatically turned the logo into a Smart Object. This Smart Object maintains its original image data, and, as long as it is a Smart Object it can be scaled, edited, and even have effects applied to it without destroying the original artwork.

3   Make sure the bikelogo is still the active layer. Then, press Ctrl+T (Windows) or Command+T (Mac OS), the keyboard shortcut for the Free Transform feature. The bounding box reappears.

4   Hold down the Shift key and click and drag the lower right corner to the right and down. This not only scales the logo to make it larger, but also constrains the scale so that it is proportional. The exact size to which you scale the logo is not important right now. If you want to follow the example in this lesson, drag until you see a value close to 225% in the options bar, then press the Return or Enter key.

Hold down the Shift key when scaling the logo to constrain the proportions.

5   Choose File > Save. Keep the file open for the next part of this lesson.

Editing the Smart Object

Keep in mind that Photoshop has embedded a copy of the original artwork into your image file. The artwork is not linked to the original bikelogo that you have just placed. This is helpful when you need to make adaptations to artwork multiple times to make it work on various images. For instance, if you have a company logo that is blue, and you are placing it on a blue sky, you might want to change the color for just that one instance. Give this workflow a try by following the next part of the lesson. You must have Adobe Illustrator installed for this part of the lesson, but if you do not have Adobe Illustrator, skip to the next part of this lesson, Apply layer effect to the artwork.

1   Double-click on the bikelogo layer in the Layers palette (make sure you double-click on the thumbnail of the bike logo). An Adobe Photoshop warning dialog box appears; press OK. The artwork opens in Adobe Illustrator CS3.

2   In Adobe Illustrator, choose Select > All or press Ctrl+A (Windows) or Command+A (Mac OS).

3   Click on the Fill drop-down menu in the options bar across the top and select white. The bikelogo is now not visible, as it is the same color of the paper.

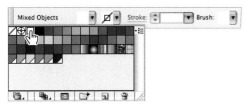

Select the white from the Swatches panel.

4   Choose File > Save, and then File > Close to close the file. Note that this Illustrator file is embedded in your Photoshop image file.

5   Return to Adobe Photoshop, where you see that the logo has been automatically updated.

6   Choose File > Save. Keep the file open for the next part of the lesson.

If you do not have Adobe Illustrator installed, you can continue the exercise from this point forward.

Applying layer effects to the artwork

Even though the artwork is a Smart Object, you can still add Photoshop layer styles such as drop shadows, inner shadows, and outer glows. In the next part of the lesson, you'll apply an inner shadow to the logo to add some depth to it.

1   Make sure the bikelogo layer is active, then click and hold on the Add a layer style button (*fx*) at the bottom of the Layers palette. Scroll up to select Inner Shadow; the Layer Style dialog box opens.

In the Layer Style dialog box, you see a list of all available layer styles on the left. Inner Shadow is checked, as that is the style you originally selected. You can add multiple styles, but for this lesson you will only add one.

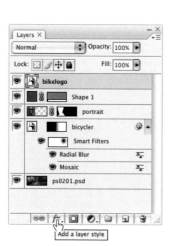
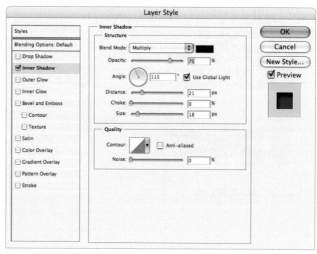

Click on the Add a layer style button.   *The Layer Style dialog box.*

If you want to re-use a Layer Style, you can click on New Style and name the style. The style then appears in the Styles palette. Simply activate a layer and then click on the saved style in the Styles palette to apply it to another layer.

2   Experiment with the settings pane on the right side of the Layer Style dialog box, and watch as you change the attributes of the inner shadow. When you are finished experimenting, hold down the Alt (Windows) or Option (Mac OS) key and press the Reset button.

3   Position your mouse over the image and click and drag; note that you can change the distance, direction, and angle of the drop shadow visually. You can also enter exact values in the structure section on the right. Position the shadow where you feel it works well; no exact settings are necessary for this lesson.

4   Soften the shadow by dragging the Size slider to the right to about 18 px, or type **18** into the Size text field. Press OK.

The logo with the inner shadow applied.

5   Choose File > Save and leave this file open for the next part of the lesson.

Adding a text layer

In Photoshop, you have all the features that you need to create text, including spellcheck and paragraph formatting controls. In the next section, you'll add the word "Massachusetts" to the bottom of your image, completing the final composition.

1   Select the Type tool (T) and click in the area of the vector rectangle you created. A cursor appears.

2   Before typing, select the Center text button (≡) in the options bar.

3   Type **MASSACHUSETTS**. If you need to reposition the text, DO NOT SELECT THE MOVE TOOL. To reposition the text, keep the Type tool selected, hold down the Ctrl (Windows) or Command (Mac OS) key, and then click and drag the type to fit in the approximate center of your vector shape.

You'll learn more about type in Lesson 9, "Getting to Know Layers," but you can pick up some helpful tips in the next few steps.

4   With the Text tool still selected, choose Select > All, or Ctrl+A (Windows) or Command+A (Mac OS) to select all the letters in the word Massachusetts.

5   Hold down Ctrl+Shift (Windows) or Command+Shift (Mac OS) and press the > (greater than) or < (less than) keys until the text is a size that you like. In this example, the text size is 22 points. Using this keyboard shortcut, you can visually resize text without having to type numbers into the Size text field in the options bar.

6   Hold down Alt (Windows) or Option (Mac OS) and press the right arrow key repeatedly to apply tracking to the word, essentially spreading out the space between the letters. If you go too far and want to decrease the space, press Alt/Opt and the left arrow.

7   With your text still selected, click on the Set the text color box in the options bar. The Color Picker appears.

8   With the Color Picker open, position your cursor over a region of the image that contains yellow, such as the leaves, and click. Yellow is applied to the text. Press OK.

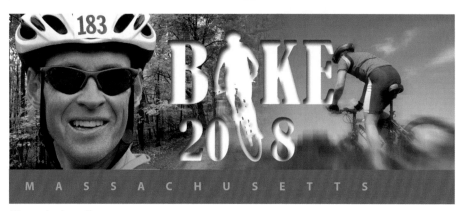

The complete image file.

9   Choose File > Save. Keep your file open for the last part of this exercise, saving the file for use on the Web.

Using the new Zoomify feature

Perhaps you want to send someone this image, or post it on the Web. You have created many layers; the image is relatively large. In fact, if you look in the lower left corner of the document window, you might notice that your layered image is close to 23 MB. The number on the left of the forward slash is the size your file would be if it were flattened. Now you will use the new Zoomify feature to export an .swf file, decreasing the size of the file and offering your viewer the ability to pan and zoom into your final image.

1   Choose File > Export > Zoomify. The Zoomify Export dialog box appears.

2 Press the Folder button in the Output Location section and choose the ps02lessons folder. For this example, leave the other settings at their defaults. Press OK.

The completed Zoomify image.

Your image is instantly saved as a Zoomify image and opened in the browser. Note that you can scale and pan, using the navigation tools at the bottom of the .swf image. If you want to use the image in this form, you must keep all the elements together in ps0201_work_img folder that was created in your ps02lessons folder.

Congratulations! You have finished the Exploring section for Adobe Photoshop CS3. Now you can dive into the rest of the lessons in this book to learn more about some of the features and tools you used in this lesson.

What you'll learn in this lesson:

- Opening a file using Adobe Bridge
- Using Photoshop tools
- Moving around in your image
- Using palettes

Getting to Know the Workspace

In this lesson, you'll learn how to best use the Adobe Photoshop work area. You will also discover how to open a document using Adobe Bridge, how to use the Tools palette, ways to easily navigate around images as you work with them, and also how to manage the many tools and palettes.

Starting up

Adobe Photoshop is an image editing program that can open an image captured by a scanner or digital camera or downloaded from the Web. It can also open captured video images and vector illustrations. In addition, you can create new documents in Photoshop, including vector graphics, which are scalable image files, i.e., the images can be enlarged or reduced in size with no loss of clarity.

Before starting, make sure that your tools and palettes are consistent by resetting your preferences. See "Resetting Adobe Photoshop CS3 preferences" on page 4.

You will work with several files from the ps03lessons folder in this lesson. Make sure that you have loaded the pslessons folder onto your hard drive from the supplied DVD. See "Loading lesson files" on page 3.

See Lesson 3 in action!

Use the accompanying video to gain a better understanding of how to use some of the features shown in this lesson. Open the file PS03.swf located in the Videos folder to view the video training file for this lesson.

Opening an existing document in Adobe Bridge

As mentioned previously, Adobe Bridge is a standalone application that can be accessed using the File menu in any of the Creative Suite 3 applications or via the Go to Bridge button ( ) that is found on the options bar or control palettes of most of the Creative Suite 3 applications.

1   Launch Adobe Photoshop CS3. If the Welcome menu appears, choose Close.

2   Choose File > Browse to open Adobe Bridge. If the Folders panel is not in the foreground, click on it now to bring it forward, then click on Desktop, the first list item in the Folders panel.

3   Open the pslessons folder that you have already copied onto your desktop and then open the ps03lessons folder.

4   Locate and then double-click on the image named ps0301.psd to open it in Photoshop. An image of a girl with a dandelion appears.

As you practice with the files throughout this book, you will find that you are instructed to save a work file immediately after opening the original file. This way you can be assured that you have an original to return to if you want to run through the lesson again.

5   Choose File > Save As to save a copy of this document to your ps03lessons folder.

6   Navigate to the ps03lessons folder. In the File name text field, type **ps0301_work**, and choose Photoshop from the Format drop-down menu. Press Save.

The Save As dialog box.

Discovering the Tools palette

When you start Photoshop, the Tools palette appears docked on the left of the screen—it is not a floating Tools palette, as it was in earlier versions of Photoshop. There are five main groups of tools, separated by functionality on the Tools palette: selection, cropping and slicing, retouching and painting, drawing and type, and annotation, measuring, and navigation tools.

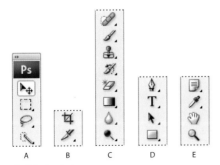

A. Selection tools.
B. Crop and Slice tools.
C. Retouching and Painting tools.
D. Drawing and Type tools.
E. Annotation, Measuring, and Navigation tools.

Selection Tools

ICON	TOOL NAME	USE	WHERE IT'S COVERED
	Move (V)	Moves selections or layers.	Lesson 3
	Marquee (M)	Makes rectangular, elliptical, single row, and single column selections.	Lesson 7
	Lasso (L)	Makes freehand, polygonal (straight-edged), and magnetic selections.	Lesson 7
	Quick Selection (W)	Paints selections.	Lessons 2, 7

Crop and Slice Tools

ICON	TOOL NAME	USE	WHERE IT'S COVERED
	Crop (C)	Crops an image.	Lesson 3
	Slice (K)	Creates HTML slices. Also contains the Slice Selection tool.	Lesson 13

Retouching and Painting Tools

ICON	TOOL NAME	USE	WHERE IT'S COVERED
	Spot Healing (J)	Removes imperfections.	Lesson 8
	Brush (B)	Paints the foreground color.	Lesson 8
	Clone Stamp (S)	Paints with a sample of the image.	Lesson 8
	History (Y)	Paints a duplicate of the selected state or snapshot.	Lesson 8
	Eraser (E)	Erases pixels—or reverts to saved history state.	Lesson 8
	Gradient (G)	Creates a gradient.	Lessons 2, 8
	Blur (R)	Blurs pixels.	Lesson 12
	Dodge (O)	Lightens pixels in an image.	Lesson 7

Drawing and Type Tools

ICON	TOOL NAME	USE	WHERE IT'S COVERED
✎	Pen (P)	Draws a vector path.	Lesson 10
T	Type (T)	Creates a type layer.	Lesson
▸	Path Selection (A)	Allows you to manipulate a path.	Lesson 7
☐	Shape (U)	Draws vector shapes.	Lessons 2, 10

Annotation, Measuring, and Navigation Tools

ICON	TOOL NAME	USE	WHERE IT'S COVERED
▤	Annotation (N)	Makes notes and audio comments.	Not referenced in this book
⚲	Eyedropper (I)	Samples pixels.	Lesson 8
✋	Hand (H)	Navigates the page.	Lesson 3
⚲	Zoom (Z)	Increases and decreases the relative size of the view.	Lesson 3

Can't tell the tools apart? You can view tooltips that reveal a tool's name and keyboard shortcut by positioning your cursor over the tool.

If you have used previous versions of Photoshop, you'll see that the Tools palette is now in a space-saving, one-column format. Click on the gray title bar area above the Tools palette to bring the Tools palette into the two-column view. Click on the title bar again to bring the Tools palette back to the default, single-column view. Keep the Tools palette set to whichever format works best for you.

See the tools and workspace in action!

Use the accompanying video to gain a better understanding of how to navigate the tools and work with palettes. Open the file PS03.swf located in the Videos folder to view the video training file for this lesson.

Hidden tools

Some of the tools in the toolbox display a small triangle at the bottom right corner; this means there are additional tools hidden under the tool.

1 Click and hold the Blur tool to see the hidden Sharpen and Smudge tools.

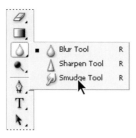

Selecting a hidden tool.

2 Drag to the Smudge tool (👄) and release. The Smudge tool is now the visible tool.

Most tools have options that you can adjust, using the options bar that runs across the top of your document window. In this case, you will change an option for the Smudge tool before using it on your image.

3 Click on the arrow to the right of Brush in the options bar to open up the Brush options drop-down menu. Using the Master Diameter slider, slide to the right until you reach approximately the 100 mark, or type **100** into the Master Diameter text field.

Now you can try painting with the tool you just customized.

4 Click and drag over the seeds flying away in the image. Use freeform brush strokes, as you want the smudging to look like part of the image is being stirred up by the wind. Have fun with this part of the lesson and smudge any part of the image you like. Don't worry; your next step is to revert the file back to its last saved version.

Smudging the seeds.

5 Choose File > Revert. The image is returned to its last saved version.

As noted above, you will spend much more time working with many of these tools in future lessons.

Getting around your image

To work most efficiently in Photoshop, you'll want to know how to zoom (magnify) in and out of your image. Changing the zoom level allows you to select and paint accurately and helps you see details that you might otherwise have overlooked. The zoom function has a range from down to a single pixel up to a 3200% enlargement, which gives you a lot of flexibility in terms of viewing your images.

You'll start out using the View menu to reduce and enlarge the document view, ending with fitting the entire document on your screen.

1 Choose View > Zoom In to enlarge the display of ps0301_work.psd.

2 Press Control+plus sign (Windows) or Command+plus sign (Mac OS) to zoom in again. This is the keyboard shortcut for the Zoom In command that you accessed previously from the View menu.

3 Press Control+minus sign (Windows) or Command+minus sign (Mac OS) to zoom out. This is the keyboard shortcut for View > Zoom Out.

Now you will fit the entire image on the screen.

4 Choose View > Fit on Screen, or use the keyboard shortcut Ctrl+0 (zero) (Windows) or Command+0 (zero) (Mac OS), to fit the document to the screen.

5 You can also display artwork at the size it will print by choosing View > Print Size.

Using the Zoom tool

When you use the Zoom tool (Q), each click increases the view size to the next preset percentage, and centers the display of the image around the location in the image that you clicked on. By holding the Alt (Windows) or Option (Mac OS) key down (with the Zoom tool selected), you can zoom out of an image, decreasing the percentage and making the image view smaller. The magnifying glass cursor is empty when the image has reached either its maximum magnification level of 3200% or the minimum size of one pixel.

1 Choose View > Fit on Screen.

Fitting the image on the screen.

2 Select the Zoom tool (🔍), and click four times on the dandelion to zoom in.

You can also use key modifiers to change the behavior of the Zoom tool.

3 Press Alt (Windows) or Option (Mac OS) while clicking with the Zoom tool to zoom out.

You can accurately zoom into the exact region of an image by clicking and dragging a marquee around that area in your image.

4 With the Zoom tool still selected, hold down the mouse and click and drag from the top left of the dandelion to the bottom right of the dandelion. You'll see that you are creating a rectangular marquee selection over the dandelion. Once you release the mouse, the area that was included in the marquee is now enlarged to fill the document window.

Dragging a marquee over the dandelion.

5 Double-click the Zoom tool in the Tools palette to return to a 100% view.

Because the Zoom tool is used so often, it would be tiresome to continually have to change from the Zoom tool back to the tool you were using. The good news is that you can activate the Zoom tool at any time without deselecting your current tool.

6 Select the Move tool (➤₊) at the very top of the Tools palette.

7 Hold down Ctrl+spacebar (Windows) or Command+spacebar (Mac OS) and the Move tool is temporarily converted into the Zoom In tool. While still holding down the Ctrl/Command+spacebar, click and drag over the dandelion again, then release. Note that although you have changed the zoom level, the Move tool is still active.

You can zoom out by holding down Ctrl+Alt+spacebar (Windows) or Command+Option+spacebar (Mac OS).

8 Choose View > Fit on Screen.

Using the Hand tool

The Hand tool allows you to move or pan the document. It is a lot like pushing a piece of paper around on your desk.

1 Select the Zoom tool (⊕), and click and drag on an area surrounding the dandelion.

2 Select the Hand tool (✋), and click and drag to the right to push the picture to the right.

Now try accessing the Hand tool without deselecting your current tool.

3 Select the Zoom tool and hold the spacebar. Notice that the cursor turns into the Hand tool. Click and drag left to view the dandelion again.

4 Double-click the Hand tool in the Tools palette to fit the entire image on your screen. This is the same as using Ctrl+0 (zero) (Windows) or Command+0 (zero) (Mac OS).

Navigation Shortcuts	Windows	MAC OS
Zoom In	Ctrl + (plus sign) Ctrl+spacebar	Command + (plus sign) Command+spacebar
Zoom Out	Ctrl – (minus sign) Ctrl+Alt+spacebar	Command – (minus sign) Command+Option+spacebar
Turn Zoom tool into Zoom Out tool	Alt	Option
Fit on Screen	Ctrl+0 (zero) or double-click the Hand tool	Command+0 (zero) or double-click the Hand tool
View at 100%	Double-click the Zoom tool	Double-click the Zoom tool
Hand tool (except when Type tool is selected)	Press spacebar	Press spacebar

Maximizing productivity with Screen Modes

Now that you can zoom in and out of your document as well as reposition it in your image window, it's time to learn how to take advantage of screen modes. You have a choice of four screen modes in which to work. Most users start and stay in the default—standard screen mode—until they accidentally end up in another. Screen modes control how much space your current image occupies on your screen, and whether you can see other Photoshop documents as well.

By changing the screen modes, you can locate over-extended anchor points and select more accurately up to the edge of your image. Changing modes can also help you to present your image to clients in a clean workspace.

1 Press **F**, and the screen mode is changed from the Standard mode to the Maximized Screen Mode. Maximized Screen Mode displays a maximized document window that fills all available space between the palette docking areas. (You'll find out more about the palette docking area later in this lesson.)

You can also change your screen mode by clicking and holding on the Change Screen Mode button at the bottom of the Tools palette.

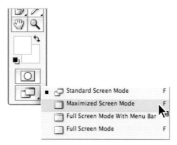

The Change Screen Mode button.

Notice that the gray background area (pasteboard) appears. One of the benefits of working in this mode is that you can click outside the image area without worrying about selecting another image or exiting Photoshop, which happens frequently to Macintosh users. You can also color-correct images without color interference from your desktop pattern.

The Maximized Screen Mode.

2 Position your cursor on the vertical line that runs down the left side of the palette docking area. Click on the line and drag to the left. Notice that this not only expands the palette docking area, it also dynamically changes the image window when you release the mouse. The document window is resized when dock widths change.

The image area dynamically changes as the palette docking area is resized.

3 Press **F** to cycle to the next screen mode, which is Full Screen Mode with Menu Bar. This view surrounds the image out to the edge of the work area with a neutral gray (even behind the docking area). This mode prevents you from accidentally clicking out of an image and exiting Photoshop, but it also eliminates the Close, Minimize, and Restore functions of the image window.

Full Screen Mode with Menu.

4 Press the Tab key; the Tools palette and other palettes disappear, creating much more workspace. Press the Tab key again to bring the Tools palette and other palettes back.

5 Press Shift+Tab to hide the other palettes while keeping the Tools palette visible. Press Shift+Tab to bring the other palettes back. Both the Tools palette and other palette docking area should now be visible.

As you position your cursor over various tools, you see a letter to the right of the tool name in the Tooltip. This letter is the keyboard shortcut that you can use to access that tool. You could, in fact, work with the Tools palette closed and still have access to all the tools.

You are going to hide the palettes once more so you can take advantage of a new, hidden feature in Photoshop CS3.

Press the Tab key to hide the palettes. Then, position your cursor over the area where the Tools palette had been, and, when a gray bar appears, pause. The Tools palette reappears. Note that the Tools palette appears only while your cursor is in the Tools palette area, and they disappear if you move your cursor out of that area. Try this with the palette docking area to the right of the screen and watch as that also appears and disappears as your cursor moves over it.

6 Press **F** on the keyboard again to see the last screen mode, Full Screen Mode.

The Full Screen Mode with no Menu.

7   Press Tab to hide the Tools palette and other palettes.

This is Full Screen Mode, no Menu. This view is a favorite with multimedia folks. It allows you to show others your document full-screen with no distracting screen elements.

8   Press Tab again to reveal all the palettes.

9   Press the **F** key twice to cycle back into Maximized Screen Mode, or click and hold on the Change Screen Mode button at the bottom of the Tools palette and select Maximized Screen Mode. Stay in this mode throughout this lesson.

Using palettes

Much of the functionality in Photoshop resides in the palettes, so you will want to know how to navigate them and find the ones you need quickly and easily. In Photoshop CS3, the palette docking area has become streamlined and is very much like the panel docking areas in the other CS3 applications. In this lesson, you will learn how to resize, expand, and convert palettes to icons and then back to palettes again. You will then find out how to save your favorite workspaces so that you don't have to set them up every time you work on a new project.

The default palette locations.

Putting the new palette system to use

If you want to maximize your workspace, convert your palettes to icons. You can get an idea of what the complete icon view for palettes looks like by switching to the Basic workspace.

1 Click and hold down on the Workspace button in the options bar and select Basic. A warning message appears, verifying that you want to change your menu and keyboard shortcut sets. Select Yes. Notice that all the palettes are now converted to small icons. Move your cursor over the icons to see tooltips indicating the names of the palettes associated with each icon.

2 Click on the Navigator palette icon (*); the Navigator palette opens.

The Navigator palette shows the entire image. A red box (called the proxy view) in the image area of the Navigator palette identifies the area currently being viewed in the active window. You can change the proxy view by clicking and dragging the red box to other locations in the Navigator palette. The view percentage—how much of the whole image you're currently able to see—is shown in the lower left corner of the Navigator palette. To zoom in or out, you can either type in a new percentage or use the sliders at the bottom of the palette.

Move the proxy view (red box) to navigate your image.

3 In the Navigator palette, drag the bottom slider to the right to approximately 200% to zoom into the image. The image on-screen updates once you release the mouse.

Use the slider to adjust the zoom level.

Notice the box to the left of the slider automatically updates and indicates the percentage of the image you are able to see as you drag the slider left or right.

4 Move your cursor over the image in the Navigator palette. The cursor becomes a pointer ( ). Click anywhere over the preview image in the Navigator palette to move the area that is being previewed.

5 Now, move the cursor over the proxy view. Your pointer turns into the Hand tool ( ). Drag the proxy view to the top left. This allows you to quickly scroll to that part of the image.

Next, you will control your zoom with a key modifier.

Reposition the proxy view.

6 Hold Ctrl (Windows) or Command (Mac OS) while hovering with your cursor over the Navigator palette; your cursor becomes the Zoom tool (🔍). Click and drag over the part of the image that contains the dandelion. When you release, the exact location of the region you created is enlarged to the maximum level. Leave this image open for the next part of this lesson.

Use Ctrl (Windows) or Command (Mac OS) to zoom.

Choosing other palettes

Now you will focus on a different palette, the Actions palette. To move from the Navigator palette to the Actions palette, select the Actions palette icon (▶). The Navigator palette changes back to an icon as the Actions palette appears. Actions are very useful tools; Photoshop comes with many predefined actions installed that can help you perform common tasks. You can use these actions as is, customize them to meet your needs, or create new actions. Actions are stored in sets to help you stay organized.

1 Select the arrow to the left of Default Actions to expand the folder, then use the Scroll bar to locate the action named Sepia Toning (layer).

2 Select the Sepia Toning (layer) action by clicking on it, and then press the Play selection button (▶) at the bottom of the Actions palette. The image is immediately converted to a sepia-toned image.

3 Now, select the History palette icon (🔁). The Actions palette disappears and the History palette appears. Select the first state in the History palette, called Open. The image file is reverted back to the original image data. You can read more about the History palette in Lesson 8, "Painting and Retouching."

Expanding your palettes

If you do not like deciphering what the palette icons represent, you can expand your palettes. You can do this automatically with a preconfigured workspace, or you can choose to expand only the palettes you wish to see.

1   Click and hold on the Workspace button on the options bar and select Legacy. The Legacy workspace provides a workspace with most of the palettes expanded. Only the Brushes, Tool Presets, and Layer Comps remain in icon view.

2   Collapse palettes by clicking on the gray bar (titlebar) at the top of each palette. Click on the gray area again to expand them.

Collapse a palette by clicking on the titlebar.

Customizing your palettes

A palette group is made up of two or more palettes that are stacked on top of each other. To view the other palettes in a group, select the name on the tab of the palette. You will now learn how to organize your palettes the way that you want.

1   Select the tab that reads Actions; the Actions tab is brought forward.

2   Now, select the History tab to return the History palette to the front of the palette group.

3 Click on the tab of the History palette and drag it away from the palette group and into the image area. The palette looks slightly transparent as you drag it away from the group. Release it—you have just removed a palette from a palette group and the docking area. Rearranging palettes can help you keep palettes that you frequently use together in one area.

The History palette appears to be transparent as it is dragged away from a palette group.

Now that the History palette is away from the Actions palette, you will resize it.

4 Position your cursor over the bottom-right corner of the History palette. Note that the cursor is now displayed as a double arrow.

Click and drag the History palette to enlarge the palette.

5 Click and drag diagonally to the lower right to enlarge the palette, click and drag diagonally to the upper left to reduce the size of the palette.

6   Click the title bar area at the top of the Actions palette and drag it over the History palette. It appears slightly transparent as you drag. As soon as you see an outline around the History palette, release the mouse. You have now made a palette group.

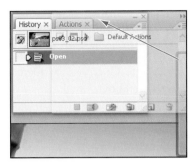

The Actions palette dragged over the History palette.

You'll now save a custom workspace. Saving a workspace is a good idea if you have production processes that often use the same palettes. Saving workspaces is also helpful if you are in a situation where multiple users are sharing Photoshop on one computer.

7   Choose Window > Workspace > Save Workspace.

8   In the Save Workspace dialog box, type **1st Workspace**, and press Save.

The Save Workspace dialog box.

9   You have completed the "Getting to Know the Workspace" lesson. You can choose File > Save and then File > Close to close this file, or keep it open while you continue through the Self study and Review sections.

Self study

Choose File > Browse to access a practice file in your ps03lessons folder. You can double-click on ps0302.psd to explore workspaces further.

1   Using the Zoom tool (Q), zoom into different parts of the picture. Then practice using the keyboard shortcuts referenced in this lesson to increase or decrease the zoom level.

2   Using the Navigator palette, zoom into the image. Try holding down the Ctrl or Command key for the Zoom tool shortcut available in the Navigator palette. Once you are zoomed in, navigate to different parts of the image using the proxy view (red box).

3   Click on the tabs of various palettes and practice clicking and dragging palettes from one group to another. You can put your palettes back in order when you are finished experimenting by selecting Window >Workspace > Default Workspace.

4   Use the Window menu to open the Info, Navigator, Histogram, and Layers palettes, then save a new workspace called color correction.

5   Take a look at some of the pre-built workspaces Photoshop has already made for you. They won't change the palette locations, but they will highlight things in the menu that are relevant to workspace. For instance, try selecting What's New in CS3 to see all the new features become highlighted in the menus.

Review

Questions

1   What is the Maximized screen mode?

2   Name two ways to fit your image to the screen.

3   What happens in the default workspace when you exit one palette and select another?

4   How do you save a workspace?

5   Can you delete a workspace?

Answers

1   The Maximized screen mode displays a maximized document window that fills all the available space between docks. In this mode, the document window resizes when dock widths change.

2   You can fit your image to the screen by using the View menu, or by double-clicking the Hand tool (✋), right-clicking while you have the Zoom (Q) or Hand tool selected, or by pressing Ctrl+0 (zero) (Windows) or Command+0 (zero) (Mac OS).

3   When you leave one palette to select another, the initial palette returns to its original location in the docking area.

4   You can save your own workspace by selecting Window > Workspace > Save Workspace.

5   Yes, you can delete a workspace by selecting Window > Workspace > Delete Workspace.

Lesson 4

What you'll learn in this lesson:

- Navigating Adobe Bridge
- Using folders in Bridge
- Making a favorite
- Creating metadata
- Using keywords
- Opening a file
- Using automated tools for Photoshop

Using Adobe Bridge

Adobe Bridge is the command center of the Creative Suite. In Adobe Bridge, you can manage and organize your files, utilize and modify XMP metadata for faster searches, and quickly preview files before opening them.

Starting up

Before starting, make sure that your tools and palettes are consistent by resetting your preferences. See "Resetting Adobe Photoshop CS3 preferences" on page 4.

You will work with several files from the ps04lessons folder in this lesson. Make sure that you have loaded the pslessons folder onto your hard drive from the supplied DVD. See "Loading lesson files" on page 3. For this lesson, it may be easier to follow if the ps04lessons folder is on your desktop.

See Lesson 4 in action!

Use the accompanying video to gain a better understanding of how to use some of the features shown in this lesson. Open the file PS04.swf located in the Videos folder to view the video training file for this lesson.

What is Adobe Bridge?

Adobe Bridge is an application included with Adobe Photoshop and the other Adobe Creative Suite 3 components. Adobe Bridge helps you locate, organize, and browse the documents you need to create print, Web, video, and audio content. If you have Photoshop or any one of the Creative Suite applications, you can start Adobe Bridge from any one of them using the File menu, or you can select the Go to Bridge button (📷).

You can use Bridge to access documents such as images, text files, and even non-Adobe documents, such as MS Word or Excel files. Using Adobe Bridge, you can also organize and manage images, videos, and audio files, as well as preview, search, and sort your files without opening them in their native applications.

Once you discover the capabilities of Adobe Bridge, you'll want to make it the control center for your Photoshop projects. With Bridge, you can easily locate files using the Filters panel and import images from your digital camera right into a viewing area that allows you to quickly rename and preview your files. This is why the recommended workflow throughout this book includes opening and saving files in Adobe Bridge. Reading through this lesson will help you to feel more comfortable with Adobe Bridge, and will also build some awareness of some of the more advanced features that are available to you for your own projects.

Adobe Bridge contains more features when installed as part of one of the Creative Suites. The tools and features demonstrated in this lesson are available in both the single product install or the Suite install, unless otherwise noted.

Navigating through Bridge

In order to utilize Adobe Bridge effectively, you'll want to know the available tools and how to access them. Let's start navigating!

1   Even though Adobe Bridge is accessible directly from the File menu in the Creative Suite applications, you'll launch it separately for this part of the lesson. To launch Adobe Bridge on Windows, go to the Start button, choose All Programs, and select Adobe Bridge CS3. On the Mac, navigate to the Applications folder, open the Adobe Bridge CS3 folder, and double-click on Adobe Bridge CS3 to launch the application.

2 Once Adobe Bridge appears, you will see two panels in the upper left corner. Click on the Favorites tab to make sure it is in front. The list of names or locations you see there includes some of the places you will visit frequently while using Adobe Bridge. You'll create a Favorite later in this lesson.

The Favorites panel.

3 Click on the Folders panel to bring it forward. Navigate to the ps04lessons folder inside the pslessons folder that you have copied to your hard drive. You will notice that as you open each folder in the Folders panel, the contents of that folder is displayed in the Content panel in the center of the Adobe Bridge window. You can also navigate by double-clicking on the folders in the Content pane, or by clicking on the Folder drop-down menu in the upper left corner of the Bridge window.

The contents of the Desktop.

4 You can also navigate through your navigation history by clicking on the Go back and Go forward arrows in the upper left corner of the window. Double-click on the ps04lessons in the center pane of Adobe Bridge to open it.

5 Click on the Go back arrow to return to the desktop view.

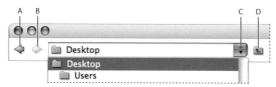

A. Go back. B. Go forward. C. Drop-down list. D. Go up button.

6 Click on the Go forward arrow to return to the last view, which is the ps04lessons.

7 Now, click the Go up folder (▣) to return to the Desktop. This method follows the folder hierarchy of nested folders.

Using folders in Adobe Bridge

Adobe Bridge is used for more than just navigating your file system. Bridge is also used to manage and organize folders and files.

1 Click on the tab of the Folders panel in the upper left corner of the Bridge window. Then, click on the arrow to the left of Desktop so that it turns downward and reveals its contents.

2 Double-click on My Computer (Windows) or Computer (Mac OS) to reveal its contents in the center pane of Bridge. Continue to double-click on items to reveal their contents. This is basically a view of everything on your computer, through the eyes of Adobe Bridge.

Managing folders

Adobe Bridge is a great tool for organizing folders and files. It is a simple task of drag and drop to reorder items on your computer. You can create folders, move folders, move files from one folder to another, copy files and folders to other locations; basically any organizing task that can be performed on the computer can also be performed in Adobe Bridge. This is a great way to help keep volumes of images organized for easy accessibility, as well as easy searching. The advantage of using Adobe Bridge for these tasks is that you have bigger and better previews of images, PDF files, and movies, with much more information about those files at your fingertips.

3 Click on the Desktop to reveal its contents.

4   Click on ps04lessons to view its contents. You'll now add a new folder into that lessons folder.

Reveal Desktop.   *Then click on the ps04lessons folder.*

5   Click on the Create a new folder icon (🗂) in the upper right corner of Adobe Bridge to create a new folder inside of the ps04lessons folder. Type the name **Music extras**.

Creating a new folder in Bridge.

6   Click once on the image named IMG_1381.JPG, then hold down the Ctrl (Windows) or Command (Mac OS) key and select image IMG_1426.JPG. By holding down the Ctrl/ Command key you can select non-consecutive items in Adobe Bridge. The two images appear simultaneously in the Preview panel, located in the upper right corner of Adobe Bridge.

Multiple images selected in Adobe Bridge.

You can use Adobe Bridge to organize images. Because you can see a preview of each file, you can more easily rename them, as well as relocate them to more appropriate locations in your directory system. In the next step, you will move files from one folder to the new Music extras folder you have just created.

7   Click and drag the selected images to the Music extras folder. When the folder becomes highlighted, release the mouse. The files have now been moved into that folder.

8   Double-click on the Music extras folder to view its contents. You see the two images that you moved.

9   Click the Go up folder (🗁) to return to the ps04lessons.

Making a Favorite

As you are working in Photoshop, you will find that you are frequently accessing the same folders. One of the many great features in Bridge is that you can designate a frequently used folder as a Favorite, allowing you to quickly and easily access it from the Favorites panel. This is extremely helpful, especially if the folders that you are frequently accessing are stored deep into your file hierarchy. To put it simply, Favorites are a great way to gain quick access without clicking through folder hierarchies.

1   Select the Favorites panel in the upper left corner of Adobe Bridge to bring it to the front. In the listing of Favorites, click on Desktop. Since the ps04lessons is going to be frequently accessed in this lesson, you'll make it a Favorite.

2   Place your cursor over the ps04lessons in the center pane (Content), and click and drag the pslesson04 folder until you see a horizontal line appear in the Favorites panel. When a cursor with a plus sign (🔾) appears, release the mouse. The folder is now listed as a Favorite.

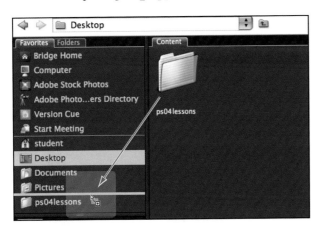

Adding a Favorite.

3   Click on the ps04lessons folder shown in the Favorites panel to view its contents. Note that creating a Favorite simply creates a shortcut for quick access to a folder; it does not copy the folder and its contents.

Creating and locating metadata

Metadata is information that can be stored with images. This information travels with the file, and makes it easy for identification and searching. In this section, you are going to find out how to locate and create metadata.

1   Make sure that you are viewing the contents of the ps04lessons in the center pane of Adobe Bridge. If not, navigate to that folder now, or click on the ps04lessons folder in the Favorites panel.

2   Choose Window > Workspace > Reset to Default Workspace. This ensures that all of the default panels for Adobe Bridge are visible.

3   Click once on IMG_1374.JPG, and look for the Metadata and Keywords panels in the lower right area of the Adobe Bridge workspace.

4   If Metadata is not in front, click on the Metadata panel now. In this panel, you see the image data that is stored with the file. Take a few moments to scroll through the data and view the information that was imported from the digital camera that was used to take the photo.

5   Select the arrow to the left of IPTC Core (IPTC Core is the schema for XMP that provides a smooth and explicit transfer of metadata) to reveal its contents.

6   Here you see a series of pencils. The pencils indicate that you can enter information in these fields.

7 Scroll down until you can see Description Writer, and click on the pencil next to it. All editable fields are highlighted; a cursor appears in the Description Writer field.

8 Type your name, or **student**.

Reveal the IPTC contents.   *Enter metadata information.*

9 Click on City, type the name of your city, then press the Tab key. The cursor is now in the State text field. Enter your state information. You have now edited metadata that is attached to the image, information that will appear whenever someone opens your image in Bridge or views the image information in Adobe Photoshop, using File > File Info.

Using keywords

Keywords can reduce the amount of time it takes to find an image on a computer, by using logical words to help users locate images more quickly.

1 In the Metadata panel, under the IPTC Core section, select Keywords.

2 Type **guitar**, press the Return/Enter key and type **Gibson**.

3   Select the Apply checkbox at the bottom of the Metadata panel, or press the Enter key on the numeric keypad to apply the metadata. Notice that a semicolon is placed between the entries.

Adding information in the Metadata panel.

4   Click on the Keywords panel next to Metadata. Notice that the keywords you added in metadata appear at the top, under Assigned Keywords. Also notice that there is a category entitled Other Keywords.

5   Click on the New Keyword button (◻) at the bottom of the Keywords panel; a blank text field appears. Type **Austin** and check the box next to the new entry to make it active.

   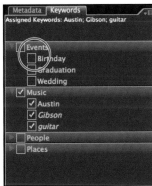

Add a new keyword.   *Rename the keyword set.*

You can add as many keywords as you like to an image. Adding new sets, by clicking on the folder icon at the bottom of the Keywords panel, helps organize keyword categories.

6   Right-click (Windows) or Control+click (Mac OS) on the Other Keywords category, and choose the option Rename. When the text field becomes highlighted, type **Music**.

You can also enter information directly in the image by opening the image in Adobe Photoshop, then choosing File > File Info. The categories that appear on the left include Description, Camera Data, IPTC Contact, and IPTC Content, among others. Once it is entered in the File Info dialog box, the information is visible in Adobe Bridge.

Opening a file from Adobe Bridge

Opening files from Adobe Bridge is a great way to begin the work process in Adobe Photoshop. Not only is it very visual, but important data stored with the files makes it easier to locate the correct file.

1   Make sure you are viewing the contents of the ps04lessons, and then double-click on image IMG_1402.JPG to open the file in Adobe Photoshop.

 Sometimes you will find that double-clicking on a file opens it in a different application than expected. This can happen if you are working in generic file formats such as JPEG and GIF. To avoid this problem, you can Right-click (Windows) or Ctrl+click (Mac OS) on the image and choose Open With to select the appropriate application.

2   Choose File > Close to close the file in Photoshop and return to Adobe Bridge.

3   You can also click once to select an image and then choose File > Open, or use the keyboard shortcut Ctrl+O (Windows) or Command+O (Mac OS).

Automation tools in Adobe Bridge

Adobe Bridge provides many tools to help you automate tasks. In this section, you will learn how to access and take advantage of some of these features.

Automated tools for Photoshop: Contact Sheet

Many of the automated features available in Photoshop are also available in Adobe Bridge. Performing these tasks in Adobe Bridge can make them easier to execute, due to Bridge's visual interface. By creating a contact sheet, you can assemble a series of images into one file for such purposes as client approval and summaries of folders, among others.

1   Make sure you are viewing the contents of the ps04lessons, then click once on image IMG_1374.JPG.

2   Hold down Shift key and click on the last image, IMG_1443.JPG. By holding down the Shift key, you have selected the two files that you clicked on, and all the files in between.

3 Select Tools > Photoshop > Contact Sheet II. The Contact Sheet II dialog box appears.

The Contact Sheet II option in Adobe Bridge.

Since you have selected images in Adobe Bridge, you see "Selected Images from Bridge" in the Use drop-down menu.

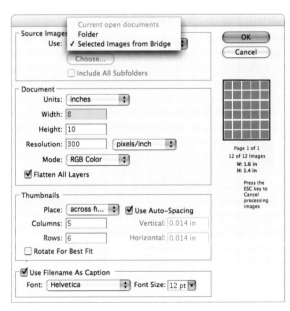

Settings for Contact Sheet II.

4 If the values in the Document section of the dialog box are not already set, select inches from the Units drop-down menu.

5   Type **8** into the Width text field and **10** in the Height text field. In the Resolution text field, type **150**, and choose pixels/inch. In the Mode drop-down menu, choose RGB Color, and check the Flatten All Layers checkbox.

6   In the Thumbnails section of the dialog box, choose across first in the Place drop-down menu, and check the Use Auto-Spacing checkbox. Type **2** in the Columns text field and **5** in the Rows text field. Leave all other settings at their defaults.

7   Select OK. The contact sheet feature processes for a moment as it creates an image file containing thumbnails of your images, along with the file names. If the number of images exceeds the amount that can fit on one page, additional pages are automatically created.

Contact Sheet result.

8   Choose File > Save; in the Save As dialog box, navigate to the ps04lessons folder and type **lesson4images** in the File name text field. Choose Photoshop PDF from the Format drop-down menu, and click Save. An Adobe Photoshop dialog box may appear, stating that your settings in the Save As dialog box can be overridden. Press OK.

9   Select OK to the Adobe Photoshop dialog box informing you that the PDF settings will override the Save As settings.

10 Choose a preset from the Adobe PDF Preset drop-down menu. If you are e-mailing these pages, or choose to post them on the Web, choose Smallest File Size and click Save PDF. You have now saved a PDF file that you can post on the Web or send via e-mail.

Create a smaller version of a contact sheet to make a CD cover by entering 4.724 x 4.724 in the Width and Height text fields (in the Contact Sheet II dialog box) and unchecking Use filename.

See the Web Photo Gallery in action!

Use the video that accompanies this lesson to gain a better understanding of how to take advantage of the Web Photo Gallery. Open the file PS04.swf located in the Videos folder to view the video training file for this lesson.

Automated tools for Photoshop: Web Photo Gallery

If you want to share images online you can use Web Photo Gallery, which creates a web site that features a home page with thumbnail images and gallery pages with full-size images. You select the images you want to include in the site and Adobe Bridge does the rest, from automatically creating navigation images, like arrows, links, and buttons, to creating Flash files. This is a fun feature that you can take advantage of quickly, even if you have no coding experience. For those with coding experience, or if you want to edit the pages further, you can open the pages in Adobe Dreamweaver or GoLive to customize them.

Before you start this part of the lesson, make sure that you are in Adobe Bridge and are viewing the contents of the ps04lessons folder.

1 Click once on image IMG_1374.JPG then press the Shift key and click on the last image, IMG_1443.JPG. As previously mentioned, this selects both images and all the images in between.

2 Choose Tools > Photoshop > Web Photo Gallery.

3 Click on the Styles drop-down menu and choose Horizontal Slideshow.

4   Type your e-mail address in the E-mail text field (this is not necessary for this test run, but is helpful when you post a real gallery).

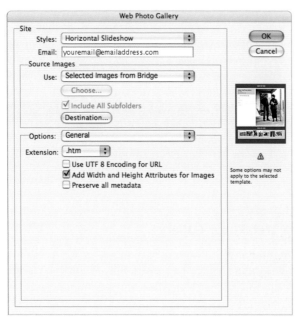

Settings in Web Photo Gallery.

5   In the Source Images section, leave Selected Images from Bridge selected in the Source Images section. Note that you could also choose an entire folder from this drop-down menu.

6   Next, you'll instruct Adobe Bridge where to put all the files that are going to be created. The Web Photo Gallery feature creates an index page, individual gallery pages, and images, so you need to find a location to store them. Click the Destination button, then browse to the ps04lessons folder, where there is an empty folder that was created for this use. Double-click to open the folder. If you are a Macintosh user, press Choose to select this folder.

7   Click on the Options drop-down menu to investigate other Web page options that you can customize. Here are some of those options:

General: These are general options for encoding, image attributes and metadata.

Banner: This is the information that is visible in the banner of the Web Photo Gallery. Set up the site name and put in contact information, such as your name and contact information.

Large Images: The Web Photo Gallery produces small thumbnail images and large gallery images. You can change the resolution of the images in this section. To maintain image quality, do not increase the resolution any higher than the original image's current resolution.

Thumbnails: Use this section to adjust the size of the thumbnails that appear in the initial gallery pages.

Custom Colors: Adjust the default web colors for text and links in this section. It is best to adjust background color in a web editing program, as some styles that you might select here do not give you access to these color options.

Security: This option provides you with additional options for copyright, credit, and title information, to name a few.

If you like, you can enter information in these sections, but it is not necessary for this exercise. Press OK.

8   Once the automated task is complete, your Web Photo Gallery opens in your default web browser, and the slide show begins. The page is complete with thumbnails and navigational arrows.

Web Photo Gallery result.

Changing the view

Work the way you like by adjusting the look and feel of Adobe Bridge. Click on the view icons in the lower right corner to change your Bridge image previews. As a default, they are set to Default, Horizontal Filmstrip, and Metadata Focus, but you can click and hold on each numbered preview to select a different view for that option.

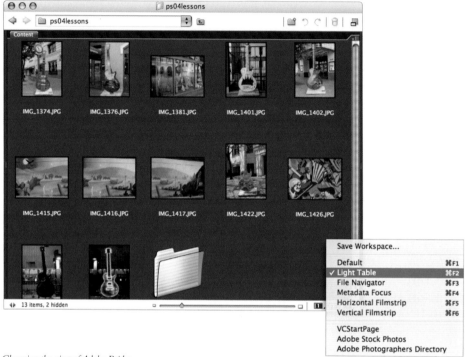

Changing the view of Adobe Bridge.

If you want to adjust the size of the image previews, simply click and drag on the slider to the left of the view buttons.

Other Bridge features worth investigating

You have discovered how to use Adobe Bridge for file management, organization, and automated tools, but there is even more to Bridge. Bridge can also be used to find tips and tricks, using Bridge Home. You can start collaboration meetings on documents using Adobe Connect, and locate the perfect stock photo, using Adobe Stock Photos.

Adobe Bridge Home: Adobe Bridge Home delivers up-to-date learning resources for all your Adobe Creative Suite 3 components in one convenient location. Watch in-depth video tutorials, listen to podcasts by leading designers, learn about training events, and more. Discover tips to help you work smarter and faster, and make the most of your Adobe products.

Start Meeting: From Bridge, you can start a real-time web conference to share your desktop and review documents. Others can join your meeting by logging in to a web-based meeting space from their computers. You must have an account to start and attend meetings. You can subscribe or set up a trial account by clicking the Start Meeting button in Bridge. If you are not familiar with Acrobat Connect, find out more at adobe.com.

Adobe Stock Photos: Select Adobe Stock Photos in the Favorites panel to start searching for that perfect image. You can locate, download, compare, and, when you are ready, buy your image right through Adobe Bridge.

Adobe Photographers Directory: Not looking for stock images, but want to locate a photographer? Select Adobe Photographers Directory in the Favorites panel and enter the information requested. You'll be provided with contact information for photographers meeting your specifications.

Locate photographers using Adobe Bridge.

Self study

As you work with Bridge, create some new Favorites of folders that you frequently use. You might also want to practice removing Favorites: highlight the Favorite and choose File > Remove from Favorites. Also, explore creating a Slideshow from the View menu. This will give you a full-screen presentation of the images in the Content panel of Adobe Bridge. For more control over the slideshow, choose View > Slideshow Options.

Review

Questions

1 How do you access Photoshop automation features from within Adobe Bridge?

2 Where do you find the metadata for an image and how do you know if the metadata is editable?

3 Which panel in Adobe Bridge enables you to organize your files on your computer?

Answers

1 You can access automated tools for Adobe Photoshop, as well as other Creative Suite applications if you purchased the suite, by choosing Tools > Photoshop.

2 You find metadata information in the Metadata and Keywords panels in the lower right of the Bridge workspace. Metadata is editable if it has the pencil icon next to it.

3 You can use the Folders panel to organize your files.

What you'll learn in this lesson:

- Combining images
- Understanding document settings
- Removing backgrounds
- Saving files

The Basics of Photoshop CS3

In this lesson, you'll learn how to combine images while gaining an understanding of image resolution and file size. You'll also learn about file formats and options for saving your files for use on the Web or in print.

Starting up

Before starting, make sure that your tools and palettes are consistent by resetting your preferences. See "Resetting Adobe Photoshop CS3 preferences" on page 4.

You will work with several files from the ps05lessons folder in this lesson. Make sure that you have loaded the pslessons folder onto your hard drive from the supplied DVD. See "Loading lesson files" on page 3.

In this lesson, you'll use multiple images to create a composite image that will then be saved for both print and online use. While this lesson covers some basic information about working with files for online distribution, you can learn even more about saving files for the Web in Lesson 13, "Creating for Web and Video."

See Photoshop Basics in action!

Use the accompanying video to gain a better understanding of some of the concepts and features shown in this lesson. The video uses some different examples to expand your understanding of the concepts covered in this lesson. The files used in the video can be found in the ps05video_lessons folder. Open the file PS05.swf located in the Videos folder to view the video training file for this lesson.

A look at the finished project

In this lesson, you will develop a composite using several images, while addressing issues such as resolution, resizing, and choosing the right file format.

To see the finished document:

1 Choose File > Browse to open Adobe Bridge, or select the Go to Bridge icon (⬚) in the options bar. Using Adobe Bridge, navigate to the pslessons folder on your hard drive and open the ps05lessons folder.

2 Double-click on the ps05_done.psd file, and the completed image is displayed in Photoshop.

The completed lesson file.

3 You can keep this file open for reference, or choose File > Close to close the file now.

Opening an existing document

Now you will assemble all the images that are a part of the final combined image.

1 Choose File > Browse to open Adobe Bridge, or select the Go to Bridge icon (⬚) in the options bar.

2 Navigate to the pslessons folder you copied onto your system and open the ps05lessons folder.

3 From the ps05lessons folder, select the file named ps0501.psd. Hold down the Ctrl key (Windows) or Command key (Mac OS), and also select the ps0502.psd and ps0503.psd images. Choose File > Open or double-click any one of the selected files. All the selected images open in Adobe Photoshop.

If you receive an Embedded Profile Mismatch warning when opening the images, you may have forgotten to reset your preferences using the instructions on page 4. If you receive the warning, choose the Use Embedded Profile option, then click OK.

Understanding document settings

In this section, you will move images from one file to another to create your mock-up. Before you combine the images, you need to be familiar with each document's unique attributes, such as size, resolution, and color mode. Moving layers between documents that have different resolutions may create unexpected results, such as causing the images to appear out of proportion.

Viewing an image's size and resolution

1 Click on the title bar of the image of the barn, ps0501.psd, to make it active. Press the Alt key (Windows) or Option key (Mac OS) and click the file information area in the status bar, located in the lower left corner of the document window. The resolution of the barn image is displayed as 885 pixels wide by 542 pixels tall.

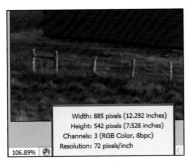

Width: 885 pixels (12.292 inches)
Height: 542 pixels (7.528 inches)
Channels: 3 (RGB Color, 8bpc)
Resolution: 72 pixels/inch

106.89%

Image size and resolution information.

2 If the picture of the rooster, ps0502.psd, is not visible, choose Window > ps0502.psd to make it the active window. After confirming that this is the active document, select Image > Image Size to open the Image Size window.

The Image Size window appears.

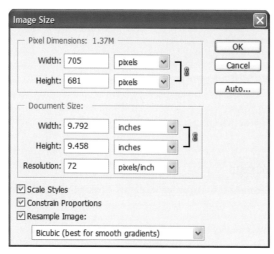

Image size plays an important role when combining images.

The Image Size window is divided into two main areas: Pixel Dimensions and Document Size. Pixel Dimensions shows the number of pixels that make up the image. For Web graphics, the pixel dimensions are more relevant than the document's actual printing size. Document Size shows the resolution information, as well as the actual physical size of the image.

The most important factors for size and resolution of Web images are the pixel dimensions and the pixels/inch (ppi). If you are designing content for the Web you should reference the top (Pixel Dimensions) section of the Image Size dialog box. As a print designer, you should reference the bottom (Document Size) section of the Image Size dialog box.

3 The image size of the rooster is 705 pixels x 681 pixels. At this size, the rooster is taller than the barn, which would be apparent when we combine the two files. While this might work for an Attack of the Roosters horror movie, we're interested in making the rooster smaller.

Make sure that the Resample Image and Constrain Proportions checkboxes are both selected. In the Image Size window, type **200** pixels for height in the Pixel Dimensions portion at the top half of the window. Press OK to apply the transformation and close the Image Size window.

The rooster is now an appropriate size to combine with the barn image.

Combining the images

For this project, you'll use several methods to combine the images.

Using Copy and Paste

1   If necessary, click the title bar of the rooster image, ps0502.psd, to make it active.

You can have many documents open at once in Photoshop, but only one of them is active at any given time.

2   Choose Select > All to select the entire image. This creates a selection marquee around the outside edge of the image. You can learn more about selections in Lesson 7, "Making the Best Selections."

3   Choose Edit > Copy to copy the selected image area. The image is now in your computer's clipboard, ready to be pasted into another document.

4   Select the title bar of barn picture, ps0501.psd, to make it the active document. Choose Edit > Paste to place the image of the rooster into the picture of the barn.

    The rooster appears on top of the barn, and the background surrounding the rooster blocks part of the image. Both these items will be addressed in future steps in this lesson.

The image of the rooster is now in the middle of the barn.

5   Select the titlebar of the rooster image, ps0502.psd and choose File > Close to close the file. Do not save any changes.

Dragging and dropping to copy an image

In this section, you'll drag and drop one image into another.

1   Choose Window > Arrange > Tile Vertically to view both the cow (ps0503.psd) and
the barn (ps0501.psd) pictures at the same time. The Arrange commands allow you to
determine how windows are displayed on your monitor; the Tile command allows you to
see all the open images.

2   Select the Move tool (✥), and then select the picture of the cow, which is the
ps0503.psd image. Click and drag the cow image over to the barn image. When your cursor
is positioned over the picture of the barn, release your mouse. The cow picture is placed
into the barn picture on a new layer.

Like using the Copy and Paste command, you can use the Move tool to copy images from
one document to another.

Click and drag the cow image, ps0502.psd, into the picture of the barn, ps0501.psd.

3 Select the title bar of ps0503.psd and choose File > Close to close the file containing the picture of the cow. Do not save any changes to the file.

4 With the composite image of the barn, rooster, and cow active, choose View > Fit on Screen, or use the keyboard shortcut Ctrl+0 (zero) (Windows) or Command+0 (zero) (Mac OS). This fits the entire image into your document window.

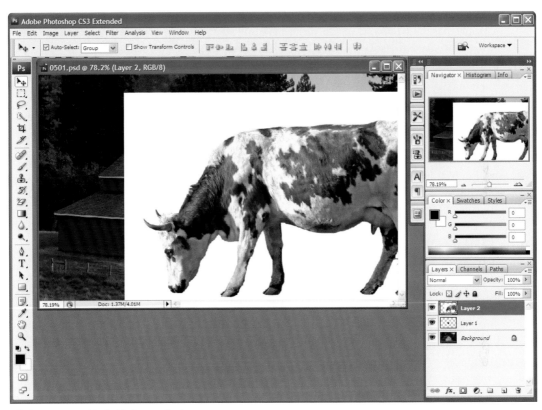

The barn picture combined with the two other images.

Transforming and editing combined images

While you have combined three images together, they still require some work. The background remains in the two imported images, and the picture of the cow is out of proportion when compared with the barn.

In order to use the transform options, the affected area must reside on a layer. Layers act as clear overlays on your image and can be used in many ways. Find out more about layers in Lesson 9, "Getting to Know Layers" and Lesson 10, "Taking Layers to the Max."

In this section, you will do the following:

- View the stacking order of the layers that were automatically created when you combined the images;
- Remove the background from the copied images;
- Refine the edges of the combined images;
- Name the layers to organize them.

Changing the size of a placed image

While you could have adjusted the image size prior to dragging and dropping it into the barn picture, you can also make adjustments to layers and the objects that reside on the layers. Here you will adjust the size and position of the placed images.

1 Make sure the Layers palette is visible. If you do not see the Layers palette, choose Window > Layers.

The Layers palette, with the layers that are part of the combined file.

2 Double-click on the words Layer 1, to the right of the image thumbnail of the rooster in the Layers palette. When the text field becomes highlighted, type **rooster**, then press the return key to accept the change. Repeat this process to rename layer 2, naming it **cow**.

The layers renamed.

3 With the cow layer selected in the Layers palette, choose Edit > Free Transform. Handles appear around the edges of the cow. Keep the cow selected.

4 Press and hold the Alt+Shift keys (Windows) or Option+Shift keys (Mac OS), then click and drag any one of the handles on the outside corner edges of the cow toward the center. The image size is reduced.

Notice that the scale percentages in the options bar change as you scale the image. Reduce the size to approximately 30% of its original size. Holding the Shift key maintains the proportions as you scale, while the Alt or Option key scales the image toward its center.

5 In the options bar, click the Commit Transform button or press the Return key to accept the changes.

6 In the Layers palette, click to activate the rooster layer, then choose Edit > Free Transform.

7   Press and hold the Alt (Windows) or Option (Mac OS) key and reduce the size of the rooster to approximately 60%, using the options bar as a guide to the scaling you are performing. Click the Commit Transform button or press the Return key to accept the changes.

The cow layer being reduced in size, using the Free Transform command.

Removing a background

Photoshop CS3 makes it easy to remove the background of an image. Here you'll use a method that works well with solid backgrounds, such as the white behind the cow and rooster.

1   If necessary, click in the Layers palette to select the cow layer.

2   In the Tools palette, click to select the Magic Eraser tool (⌦). You may need to click and hold on the Eraser tool to access the Magic Eraser tool.

3   Position the Magic Eraser tool over the white area behind the cow and click once to remove the white background.

Using the Magic Eraser tool to remove the background behind the cow.

4   In the Layers palette, click to activate the rooster layer.

5   Position the cursor over the white area adjacent to the rooster, and click once to remove the white background.

Understanding the stacking order of layers

Layers are much like pieces of clear film that you could place on a table. The layers themselves are clear, but anything placed on one of the layers will be positioned on top of the layers that are located beneath it.

1 Confirm that the rooster layer remains selected. Click to select the Move tool (⊹) from the Tools palette.

2 Position the Move tool over the rooster image in the document window, and drag the rooster so your cursor is positioned over the head of the cow. Notice that the rooster is positioned under the cow. This is because the cow layer is on top of the rooster layer in the Layers palette.

3 In the Layers palette, click and hold the rooster layer. Drag the layer up so it is positioned on top of the cow layer. Notice in the document window how the stacking order of the layers affects the stacking order of the objects in the image.

Click and drag the rooster layer up to place it on top of the cow layer.

4 Using the Move tool, click and drag the rooster to position it in the lower left corner of the image, in front of the fence and along the side of the barn.

5 Click to activate the cow layer, then, continuing to use the Move tool, click and drag the cow to position it in the lower right corner of the image. Position the cow so it appears to be grazing on the grass.

Refining the edges of copied images

When the images were copied, they maintained very hard edges, making it very clear where the picture of the cow or rooster stops and the original image starts. This hard edge makes the images look contrived. You will blend the images so they look more natural together.

1 Click to select the cow layer in the Layers palette. Choose the Zoom tool (⊕) from the Tools palette, then click and drag to create a zoom area around the entire cow. The cow is magnified to fill the entire display area.

2   Press **H** on the keyboard to choose the Hand tool (✍), then choose Layer > Matting > Defringe. The Defringe window opens.

3   In the Defringe window, maintain the default setting of 1 pixel, then press OK. The Defringe command blends the edges of the layer into the background, making it appear more natural.

The cow after it is defringed.

4   Use the Hand tool to click and drag in the image window to view the rooster. Click and drag the window to the right to reveal the content positioned on the left side of the image. Stop dragging when the rooster is visible.

5   In the Layers palette, click to activate the rooster layer, then choose Layer > Matting > Defringe. The Defringe window opens.

6   In the Defringe window, once again maintain the default setting of 1 pixel, then click OK. The Defringe command affects only the selected layer.

Notice that both the rooster and the cow now look more naturally blended into the background.

7   Press Ctrl+Z (Windows) or Command+Z (Mac OS) to undo the application of the Defringe command. Notice the hard edge around the perimeter of the rooster. Press Ctrl+Z or Command+Z again to re-apply the Defringe command.

The rooster before and after it is defringed.

8 Double-click the Hand tool in the Tools palette to fit the entire image in the document window. This can be easier than choosing View > Fit on Screen, yet it achieves the same result.

9 Choose File > Save As. In the File name field, type **farm done**, keep the format as Photoshop (PSD), then click Save. If the Photoshop Format Options window appears, click OK without changing any settings.

Adding text

You will now add text to the image.

1 With the farm done file still open, click to select the cow layer in the Layers palette.

2 In the Tools palette, click to select the Type tool (T) and click in the upper left corner of the image, just above the roof of the barn. Notice that a layer appears on top of the cow layer in the Layers palette.

3 In the options bar, select the following:

- From the font family drop-down menu, choose Myriad Pro. If you do not have this font, you can choose another.

- From the font style drop-down menu, choose Bold Italic.

- From the font size drop-down menu, choose 72.

4 Click once on the Set text color box (■) in the options bar. The text Color Picker appears. Click on white or any light color that appear in the upper left corner of the color pane, then press OK to close the Color Picker window.

5 Type **Big Red Barn**; the text appears above the roof of the barn. When you are finished typing, press the check mark (✔) in the options bar to confirm the text.

6 With the text layer still active, select the Add a layer style button (*fx*) at the bottom of the Layers palette, and choose Stroke. The Layer Style dialog box opens, with the Stroke options visible. Press OK to accept the default settings. A stroke is added to the border of the text.

7 Choose File > Save. Keep the file open for the next part of this lesson.

Saving files

Adobe Photoshop allows you to save your files in a variety of file formats, which makes it possible to use your images in many different ways. You can save images to allow for additional editing of things such as layers and effects you have applied in Photoshop, or save images for sharing with users who need only the finished file for use on the Web or for printing. In all, Photoshop allows you to save your file in more than a dozen unique file formats.

As you work on images, it is best to save them using the default Photoshop format, which uses the PSD extension at the end of the file name. This is the native Photoshop file format, and retains the most usable data without a loss in image quality. Because the Photoshop format is developed by Adobe, many non-Adobe software applications do not recognize the PSD format. Additionally, the PSD format may contain more information than you may need, and may be a larger file size than is appropriate for sharing via e-mail or posting on a web site. While you may create copies of images for sharing, it is a good idea to keep an original version in the PSD format as a master file that you can access if necessary. This is especially important because some file formats are considered to be *lossy* formats; they remove image data in order to reduce the size of the file.

Understanding file formats

While Photoshop can be used to create files for all sorts of media, the three most common uses for image files are in print, on the Web, and for use in video production. The following is a list of the most common formats and how they are used.

Print Production Formats	
PSD (Photoshop document)	The Photoshop format (PSD) is the default file format and the only format, besides the Large Document Format (PSB), that supports most Photoshop features. Files saved as PSD can be used in other Adobe applications, such as Adobe Illustrator, Adobe InDesign, Adobe Premiere, Adobe After Effects, Adobe Dreamweaver, and Adobe Flash. The programs can directly import PSD files and access many Photoshop features, such as layers saved within files that use the PSD format.
TIFF or TIF (Tagged Image File Format)	TIFF is a common bitmap image format. Most image-editing software and page-layout applications support TIFF images up to 2 GB in file size. TIFF supports most color modes and can save images with alpha channels. While Photoshop can also include layers in a TIFF file, most other applications cannot use these extended features and see only the combined (flattened) image. Similarly, capabilities such as annotations and transparency saved in a Photoshop TIFF file may not be accessible in other software applications.

Print Production Formats

EPS (Encapsulated PostScript)	EPS files may contain both vector and bitmap data. As a common file format used in print production, most graphics software programs support the EPS format for importing or placing images. EPS is a subset of the PostScript format. Some software applications cannot preview the high resolution information contained within an EPS file, so Photoshop allows you to save a special preview file for use with these programs, using either the EPS TIFF or EPS PICT options. EPS supports most color modes, and also supports clipping paths, which are commonly used to silhouette images and remove backgrounds.
Photoshop PDF	Photoshop PDF files are extremely versatile, as they may contain bitmap and vector data. Images saved in the Photoshop PDF format can maintain the editing capabilities of most Photoshop features, such as vector objects, text, and layers, and most color spaces are supported. Photoshop PDF files can also be shared with other graphics applications, as most of the current versions of graphics software are able to import or manipulate PDF files. Photoshop PDF files can even be opened by users with the free Adobe Reader software.

Web Production Formats

JPEG (Joint Photographic Experts Group)	A common format for digital camera photographs and the primary format for full-color images shared on the Web. JPEG images may use lossy compression, which degrades the quality of images and discards color and pixel data. Once the image data is lost, it cannot be recovered.
GIF (Graphic Interchange Format)	GIF files are used to display limited (indexed) color graphics on the Web. It is a compressed format that reduces the file size of images saved in this format, but it only supports a limited number of colors and is thus more appropriate for logos and artwork rather than photographs. GIF files support transparency.
PNG (Portable Network Graphics)	PNG was developed as an alternative to GIF for display of images on the Web. It uses lossless compression, and supports transparency. Some web browsers do not support PNG images, which has limited its widespread use.

Video Production Formats

TIFF or TIF	*See Print Production Formats, above.*
TARGA (Truevision Advanced Raster Graphics Adapter)	The legacy file format is used for video production. The TARGA format supports millions of colors, along with alpha channels.

Choosing a file format

In this section, you will save your file to share online and for printing. You will use two common formats, JPEG and Photoshop PDF.

Saving a JPEG file

To save a copy of your image for sharing online, whether on a web site or to send via e-mail, you will save it using the JPEG file format. In this lesson, you will use the Save menu, but in Lesson 13, "Creating for Web and Video," you will discover additional features when saving files for use online, including how to use the Save for Web & Devices capability, which is enhanced with this release of Photoshop.

1   Choose File > Save As.

2   In the Save As window, type **farm** in the File name text field. From the Format drop-down menu, choose JPEG. If necessary, navigate to the ps05lessons folder so the file is saved in this location, then press the Save button. The JPEG Options window appears.

3   In the JPEG Options window, confirm the quality is set to maximum, and leave the format options and matte set to their default options. Press OK. This completes the Save process for your file.

4   Choose File > Close to close the file.

Because JPEG is supported by web browsers, you can check your file by opening it using any web browser such as Firefox, Internet Explorer, or Safari. Open the browser and choose File > Open, which may appear as Open File or Open Location, depending upon the application. Navigate to the ps05lessons folder and double-click to open the file you saved.

Saving for print

In this part of the lesson, you will change the color settings to choose a color profile more suitable for print to help you preview and prepare your file for printing. You will change the resolution of the image before saving it.

Changing the color settings

You will now change the color settings to get a more accurate view of how the file will print.

1 Choose File > Open Recent > farm done.psd. You can use the Open Recent command to easily locate the most recently opened files. The file opens.

2 Choose Edit > Color Settings. The Color Settings window appears.

3 From the Settings drop-down menu, choose North America Prepress 2. This provides you with a color profile based upon typical printing environments in North America. Press OK to close the Color Settings window.

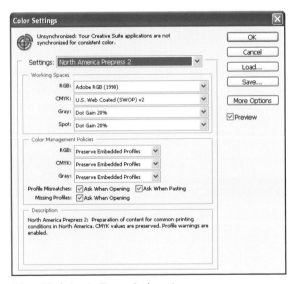

Select a North America Prepress 2 color setting.

4 Choose the Zoom tool (🔍) from the Tools palette, then click and drag to create a zoom area around the entire rooster. The rooster is magnified to fill the entire display area.

5   Choose View > Proof Colors. Notice a slight change in the color of the rooster's feathers, as they appear more subdued. The Proof Colors command allows you to work in the RGB format while approximating how your image will look when converted to CMYK, the color space used for printing. While you will work on images in the RGB mode, they generally must be converted to CMYK before they are printed.

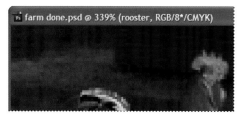

The title bar reflects that you are previewing the image in CMYK.

Adjusting image size

Next you will adjust the image size for printing. When printing an image, you generally want a resolution of at least 150 pixels per inch. For higher quality images, you will want a resolution of at least 300 pixels per inch. While this image was saved at 72 pixels per inch, it is larger than we need. By reducing the physical dimensions of the image, the resolution (number of pixels per inch) can be increased.

1   Choose Image > Image Size; the Image Size window appears. The image currently has a resolution of 72 pixels per inch.

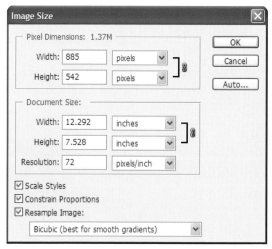

The image is at a low resolution of 72 pixels per inch.

This low resolution affects the image quality, and should be increased to print the best image possible. For this to occur, the dimensions of the image will need to be reduced so the image will be of a higher quality, but will be smaller in size. This process in known as resampling.

Resampling changes the amount of image data. When you resample up, you increase the number of pixels. New pixels are added, based upon the interpolation method you select. While resampling adds pixels, it can reduce image quality if it is not used carefully.

2   In the Image Size dialog box, uncheck Resample Image. By unchecking the Resample checkbox, you can increase the resolution without decreasing image quality.

You can use this method when resizing large image files, like those from digital cameras that tend to have large dimensions but are low resolution.

3   Type **300** in the Resolution field. The size is reduced in the Width and Height textbox to accommodate the new increased resolution. For quality printing at the highest resolution, this image should be printed no larger than approximately 2.9 x 1.8 inches. Press OK.

In this image, you are not adding pixels, you are simply reducing the dimensions of the image to create a higher resolution.

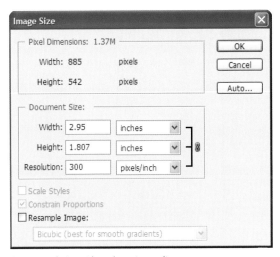

Increase resolution without decreasing quality.

4   Choose File > Save. Keep this file open for the next part of this lesson.

Saving a Photoshop PDF file

Images containing text or a vector shapes may appear fine in low resolution when viewed on a computer display, even if the vector information is rasterized. When the same images are used for print projects, they should retain the resolution-independent vector elements. This keeps the text and other vector graphics looking sharp, so you do not need to worry about the jagged edges that occur when text and shapes are rasterized. To keep the vector information, you need to save the file using a format that retains both vector and bitmap data.

1   With the farm done.psd image still open, choose File > Save As. The Save As dialog box appears.

2   In the Save In menu, navigate to the ps05lessons folder. In the File name field, type **farm print version**. From the Format drop-down menu, choose Photoshop PDF, then press Save. Click OK to close any warning windows that may appear. The Save Adobe PDF window appears.

3   In the Save Adobe PDF window, choose Press Quality from the Adobe PDF Preset drop-down menu, then click Save PDF. If a warning appears indicating that older versions of Photoshop may not be able to edit the PDF file, click Yes to continue.

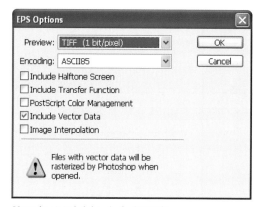

Vector data is included in the final EPS file.

Your file has been saved in the Adobe PDF format, ready to be used in other applications such as Adobe InDesign, or it can be shared for proofing with a reviewer who may have Adobe Acrobat or the Adobe Reader.

Congratulations! You have finished the lesson.

Self study

1 Adjust the stacking order of the layers in the composite image.

2 Scale and move the layers to place the cow and rooster in different positions.

3 Add your own images to the composition, adjusting their position and scaling.

4 Save the images as PDF and JPEG using the different compression options and presets to determine the impact these have on quality and file size.

5 Use the files in the ps05_video_lessons folder, inside the ps05lessons folder to create a composite similar to the one demonstrated in the PS05video.

Review

Questions

1 Explain two ways to combine one image with another.

2 What is created in the destination image when you cut and paste or drag and drop another image file into it?

3 What are the best formats (for print) in which to save a file that contains text or other vector objects?

Answers

1 **Copy and Paste**: Select the content from your source document and choose Edit > Copy. Then select your destination document and Edit>Paste the artwork into it.

   Drag and Drop: Make sure both your source and destination documents are visible. With the Move tool selected, click and drag the image from one file to the destination file.

2 When you cut and paste or drag and drop one image into another, a new layer containing the image data is created.

3 If your file contains text of vector objects, it is best to save the file in one of these three formats: Photoshop (PSD), Photoshop (EPS), or Photoshop (PDF).

What you'll learn in this lesson:

- Choosing color settings
- Using the histogram
- Discovering a neutral
- Using curves
- Unsharp Masking
- Using Camera Raw

Creating a Good Image

You can create interesting imagery in Photoshop, including compositions, filter effects, and even animation and video when using Photoshop CS3 Extended. But it is important to have a great-looking image to serve as the foundation of your work.

Starting up

There are simple steps that you can take to create a brighter, cleaner, more accurate image. In this lesson, you'll learn how to use the new improved Curves controls and how to sharpen your images. You'll learn what a neutral is and how to use it to color correct your images. You'll also have the opportunity to work with a Camera Raw image, using the improved Camera Raw plug-in.

Although the steps may at first seem time-consuming, they go quickly when not accompanied by the "whys and hows" included in this lesson. In fact, the process works almost like magic; a few steps and your image looks great!

Before starting, make sure that your tools and palettes are consistent by resetting your preferences. See "Resetting Adobe Photoshop CS3 preferences" on page 4.

You will work with several files from the ps06lessons folder in this lesson. Make sure that you have loaded the pslessons files onto your hard drive from the supplied DVD. See "Loading lesson files" on page 3.

See Lesson 6 in action!

Use the accompanying video to gain a better understanding of how to use some of the features shown in this lesson. Open the file PS06.swf located in the Videos folder to view the video training file for this lesson.

Choosing your color settings

What many Photoshop users do not understand is the importance of knowing where an image is going to be published; whether for print, the Web, or even a digital device like a cell phone. Photoshop has pre-defined settings that help adapt the colors and values of an image for these different uses. If not set properly, your images may appear very dark, especially in the shadow areas. For this lesson, you will use generic color settings that work well for a typical print image. You are also introduced to settings for other types of output, including the Web.

1 Choose Edit > Color Settings in Photoshop CS3. The Color Settings dialog box appears. In this example, the icon in the upper left corner indicates that Photoshop's Color Settings are not in synch with the other applications in the Creative Suite. Read Lesson 8, "Painting and Retouching," for more information about editing Color Settings in Adobe Bridge.

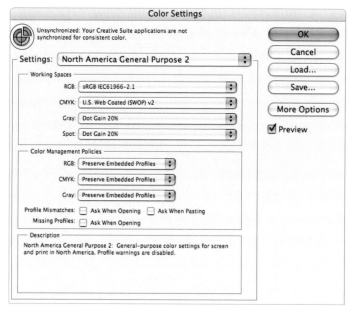

The Color Settings dialog box at its default settings.

2   As a default, North America General Purpose 2 is selected. This setting is good for images that are to be printed on coated paper stock. Coated paper has a coating that allows the paper to be printed without significant ink absorption. If you plan on printing on an uncoated stock, which, due to ink absorption, tends to produce a darker image, choose U.S. Sheetfed Uncoated v2 from the CMYK drop-down menu.

When you see U.S. Web Coated in the CMYK drop-down menu, it is not referring to the Web, as in Internet. A web press is used for printing books, catalogs, newspapers, and magazines. It is a high-run, high-speed, printing press that uses rolls of paper rather than individual sheets.

3   For this example, make sure that the default settings of North America General Purpose 2 are selected. Press OK to exit the Color Settings dialog box.

Opening the file

1   Choose File > Browse. When Adobe Bridge is forward, navigate to the ps06lessons folder that you copied onto your hard drive.

2   Locate the image named ps0601.psd and double-click on it to open it in Photoshop. You can also choose to Right-click (Windows) or Ctrl+click (Mac OS) and select Open with Adobe Photoshop CS3.

Note the comparison of images: the one on the left that is uncorrected, and the one on the right that is corrected. You'll correct the image on the left in the next few steps.

Image before color correction.

Image after color correction.

3   Choose File > Save As. The Save As dialog box appears. Navigate to the ps06lessons folder on your hard drive. In the File name text field, type **ps0601_work,** choose Photoshop from the Format drop-down menu, and press Save. Leave the image open.

Why you should work in RGB

In this lesson, you start and stay in the RGB (Red, Green, Blue) color mode. There are two reasons for this: you will find more tools are available in this mode and changes to color values in RGB degrade your image less than if you are working in CMYK. If you were sending this image to a commercial printer, you would convert it to CMYK at the end of process by choosing Image > Mode > CMYK Color.

Want to see the CMYK preview while working in RGB? By pressing Ctrl+Y (Windows) or Command+Y (Mac OS), you can work in the RGB mode while you see the CMYK preview on your screen. This is a toggle key command, meaning that if you press Ctrl+Y or Command+Y again, the preview is turned off.

Reading a histogram

Understanding image histograms is probably the single most important concept to become familiar with when working with images in Photoshop. A histogram can tell you whether your image has been properly exposed, the lighting correct, and what adjustments will work best to improve your image. You will reference the Histogram palette throughout this lesson.

1   If your Histogram palette is not visible, choose Window > Histogram. The Histogram palette appears.

A histogram shows the tonal values that range from the lightest to the darkest in an image. Histograms can vary in appearance, but typically you want to see a full, rich, mountainous area representing tonal values. See below for an example of a histogram with many values, and one with very few values, and the images relating to each.

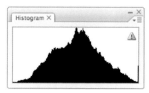

A good histogram and its related image.

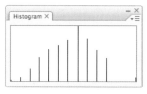

A poor histogram and its related image.

Keep an eye on your Histogram palette. Simply doing normal corrections to an image can break up a histogram, giving you an image that starts to look posterized. Avoid breaking up the histogram by learning to use multi-function tools, like the Curves palette, and making changes using adjustment layers, which don't change your original image data.

2   To make sure that the values you read in Photoshop are accurate, select the Eyedropper tool (🖊). Notice that the options bar (across the top of the document window) changes to offer options specific to the Eyedropper tool. Click and hold on the Sample Size drop-down menu and choose 3 by 3 Average. This ensures a representative sample of an area, rather than the value of a single screen pixel.

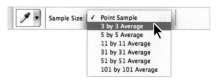

Set up the Eyedropper tool to provide a better reading.

3   If the Layers palette is not visible, choose Window > Layers. Click and hold on the Create new fill or adjustment layer button (⬤) at the bottom of the Layers palette, select Curves, and release. The Curves dialog box appears.

4   Click on the arrow to the left of Curve Display Options to show additional controls that you will need later in this lesson.

Select the Curves Adjustment.

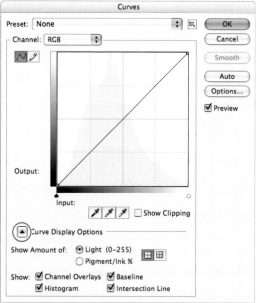

The Curves dialog box appears. This dialog box has additional options displayed.

By using an Adjustment layer, you can make curve adjustments without destroying the original image data. See Chapter 10, "Taking Layers to the Max," for more information about how to use Adjustment Layers.

5   Leave the Curves dialog box open for the next section.

Finding the highlight and shadow

Finding the lightest and darkest areas on an image is critical to getting the best output. Photoshop CS3 has made this easier by including a clipping checkbox right in the Curves palette.

1   Check Show Clipping and click the Highlight slider (△). The lightest parts of the image are highlighted.

Now you'll mark the light area with the Color Sampler tool (✸) so that you can find it later.

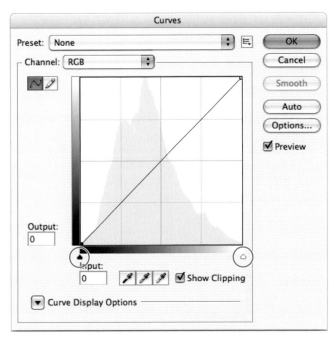

The Shadow and Highlight sliders.

2   Hold down the Shift key (shortcut to the Color Sampler tool), and click in the highlighted light area of the image. Depending upon the tonal values in the image, you may have a smaller or larger area to choose from. If it would help you to see the actual image, uncheck Preview. Once you Shift+click on the image, a Color Sampler marker is created.

If you need to move the position of the Color Sampler marker, hold down the Shift key while dragging the marker. If you accidently add more markers (you can have up to four), hold down Alt+Shift (Windows) or Option+Shift (Mac OS) and click on the marker to delete it.

3 Now, click on the Shadow slider (▲). On this image, you have to drag the Shadow slider slightly to the right to see the shadow areas.

4 Hold down the Shift key and click on the shadow area that appears in the area of the girl's eyes.

5 Uncheck Show Clipping, but leave the Curves dialog box open for the next section.

The image as it appears with Color Samplers on it.

If you accidentally press OK and close the Curves palette, you can re-open it by double-clicking on the Curves Adjustment Layer thumbnail in the Layers palette.

Defining the highlight and shadow

You located the highlights and shadows of the image, but still haven't made any changes to the image. In this section, you'll set the highlight and shadow to predetermined values using the Set White Point and Set Black Point tools. Before you do this, you'll determine what those values should be. This is a critical part of the process, as the default for the white point is 0, meaning no value will be printed, and any detail in this area is lost.

Some images can get away with not having tonal values in very bright areas. Typically, reflections off metal, fire, extremely sunlit areas, as well as reflections off other shiny objects like jewelry do not have value in those reflective areas.

These are referred to as specular highlights. By leaving them without any value, it helps the rest of the image look balanced, and allows the shine to "pop" out of the image. See below for an example.

This image has specular highlights, which should be left with a value of zero.

Defining the white and black point values

The process of defining values for the lightest and darkest points in your image is not difficult, but it helps if you know where the image is going to be used. If you have a good relationship with a printer, they can tell you what values work best for their presses, or you can just use the generic values suggested in this book. The values shown in this example are good for typical printing setups and for Web display.

1   Double-click on the Set White Point button (✐); the Select target highlight color dialog box appears. Even though you are in RGB, you can set values in any of the color environments displayed in this window. In this example, you'll use CMYK values.

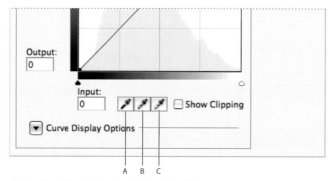

A. Set Black Point. B. Set Gray Point. C. Set White Point.

2 Type **5** in the C (Cyan) textbox, **3** in the M (Magenta) textbox, and **3** in the Y (Yellow) textbox. Leave K (Black) at 0. Then click OK.

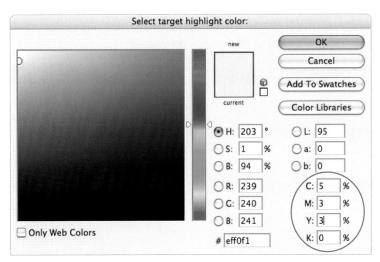

Set the values for your light point in the highlight color dialog box.

3 Now, double-click on the Set Black Point button (🖊). The Select target shadow color dialog box appears.

4 Type **65** in the C (Cyan) textbox, **53** in the M (Magenta) textbox, **51** in the Y (Yellow) textbox, and **95** in the K (Black) textbox. Press OK.

It is important to note that your printer may be able to achieve a richer black than the one offered here. If you have a relationship with a printer, ask for their maximum black value and enter it here. Otherwise, use these standard values.

5 Now, select the Set White Point button (✒), and then click on the #1 Color Sampler marker you created in the image.

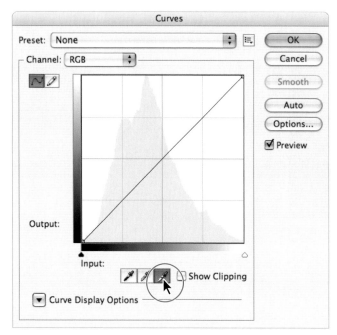

Select the Set White Point button.   Then click on the #1 marker.

The image highlight is adjusted to your new color values.

6 Select the Set Black Point button (✒), and then click on the #2 marker. The color values for the shadows are applied.

You should already see a difference in the image—a slight color cast has been removed and the colors look a little cleaner, but you are not done yet. The next step involves balancing the midtones (middle values) of the image.

7 Leave the Curves dialog box open for the next step.

Adjusting the midtones

In many cases, you need to lighten the midtones (middle values of an image) in order to make details more apparent in an image. In an RGB image, the default for the Curves dialog box is to display the curves based upon light values. It can sometimes be more logical to adjust color based upon actual pigment, or ink.

1 With the Curves palette still open, make sure that the Curves Display Options are visible (If they are not visible, click on arrow to the left of Curve Display Options). Then click on the Pigment/Ink % radio button in the Show Amount of: section.

2 Now, select the center (midtone area) of the black curve and drag downwards (don't worry about the colored curves, as Photoshop is making an overall change in this window). Move the curve downwards slightly to lighten the image in the midtones. This is the only visual correction that you will make to this image. You want to be careful that you do not adjust too much, as you can lose valuable information.

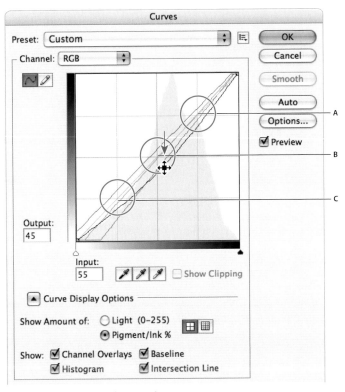

A. Three-quartertones. *B. Midtones.* *C. Quartertones.*

3   Add a little contrast to your image by clicking on the three-quarter tone area (the area between the middle of the curve and the top), then clicking and dragging up slightly. Again, this is a visual correction, so don't make too drastic a change.

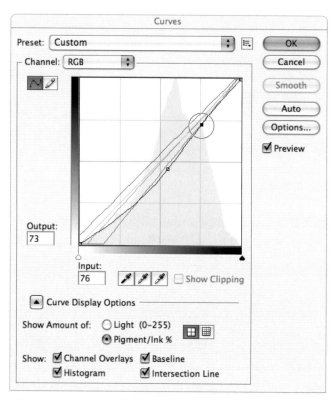

Add contrast to the image by adjusting the three-quarter tones.

4   Keep the Curves dialog box open for the next section of this lesson.

You can usually see a color cast by looking at the white and gray areas of an image, but, in some cases, you may not have any gray or white objects in your image. If these are art images, you may not want to neutralize them (e.g., orange sunsets on the beach, nice yellow candlelight images). Use the technique shown in this lesson at your discretion. It helps with a typical image, but it takes practice and experience to correct for every type of image.

Understanding neutral colors

A neutral is essentially anything in the image that is gray: a shade of gray, or even light to dark grays. A gray value is a perfect tool to help you measure color values, as it is composed of equal amounts of red, green, and blue. Knowing this allows you to pick up color inaccuracies by reading values in the Photoshop Info palette, rather than just guessing which colors need to be adjusted.

The first image you see below is definitely not correct, but exactly what is wrong? By looking at the Info palette, you can tell that the RGB values are not equal. In the second image, they are almost exactly equal. By looking at only the RGB values, you can tell that the image on the bottom is much more balanced than the image on the top.

The neutrals in this image are not balanced; as you can tell because the RGB values are not equal in value.

The neutrals in this image are balanced; as you can tell because the RGB values are close to equal.

Setting the neutral

In this section, you'll balance the neutrals in the image.

1   With the Curves palette still open, set another Color Sampler marker by Shift-clicking in the gray driveway in the lower right corner of the image. In this image, this is the neutral that you are using as a reference for this example. In your images, you might find a neutral in a shadow on a white shirt, a gray piece of equipment, or a countertop.

Some photographers like to include a gray card (available at photo supply stores) in their images to help them color-balance their images.

2   If the Info palette is not open, choose Window > Info. The Info palette appears.

In the Info palette, you'll see general information about RGB and CMYK values, as well as pinpoint information about the three Color Sampler markers you have created. You'll only focus on the #3 marker, as the first two were to indicate highlight and shadow.

Notice that to the right of the #3 marker in the Info palette there are two values separated by a forward slash. You'll focus only on the set of values to the right of the slash. Depending upon where you clicked in the driveway, you could have different values. The numbers to the left of the forward slash are the values before you started making adjustments in the Curves palette. The numbers to the right of the forward slash are the new values that you are creating with your curve adjustments.

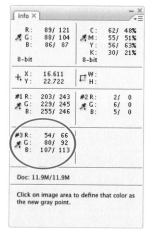

Focus on the values to the right of the forward slash.

3   Select the Set Gray Point button (🖋).

4 Click once on the #3 marker you created. The new color values may not be exactly the same, but they come closer to matching each other's values.

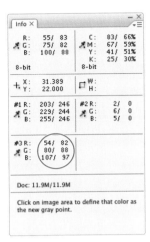

The Info palette after the #3 marker was selected as a gray point.

 If you want more advanced correction, you can enter each of the individual color curves and adjust them separately.

5 Press OK. An Adobe Photoshop window appears, asking if you want to save the new target values that you entered for your white and black points. Press Yes. This way you can keep the values for the next time you adjust curves.

Save yourself steps next time you adjust curves by saving the target colors.

The image has been adjusted, using the Curves adjustment layer.

6 Click on the visibility eye icon (👁) to the left of the Curves 1 adjustment layer to toggle off and on the curves adjustment you just made. Make sure that the Curves layer's visibility is turned back on before you move on to the next section.

Click on the eye icon to turn off and on the adjustment layer.

7 Choose File > Save. Keep this file open for the next part of this lesson.

Sharpening your image

Now that you have adjusted the tonal values of your image, you'll want to apply some sharpening to the image. In this section, you'll discover how to use unsharp masking. It is a confusing term, but is derived from the traditional (pre-computer) technique used to sharpen images.

To simplify this example, you'll flatten the adjustment layer into the background layer.

1 Choose Flatten image from the Layers palette menu, as shown in the figure below.

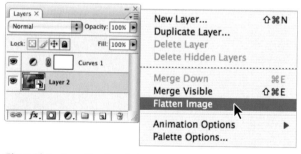

Choose Flatten image from the palette menu.

2 Choose View > Actual pixels. The image may appear very large; you can pan the image by holding down the spacebar and pushing the image around on the screen. Position the image so that you can see an area with detail, such as one of the eyes. Note that you should be in Actual Pixel view when using most filters, or you may not see accurate results on your screen.

Hold down the spacebar, and click and drag on the image area to adjust the position of the image in the window.

3 Choose Filter > Convert for Smart Filters. If an Adobe Photoshop dialog box appears informing you that the layer is being converted into a Smart Object, press OK.

This turns your image into a Smart Object, which allows you to edit filter applications after they are completed. Read more about Smart Objects in Lesson 11, "Using Smart Objects."

An icon (⊞) appears in the lower right corner of the layer thumbnail, indicating that this is now a Smart Object.

4 Choose Filter > Sharpen > Unsharp Mask. The Unsharp Mask dialog box appears.

You can click and drag inside the preview pane to change the part of the image that appears there.

Unsharp masking defined

Unsharp masking is a traditional film compositing technique used to sharpen edges in an image. The Unsharp Mask filter corrects blurring in the image, and it compensates for blurring that occurs during the resampling and printing process. Applying the Unsharp Mask filter is recommended whether your final destination is print or online.

The Unsharp Mask filter assesses the brightness levels of adjacent pixels and increases their relative contrast: it lightens the light pixels that are located next to darker pixels, as it darkens those darker pixels. You set the extent and range of lightening and darkening that occurs, using the sliders in the Unsharp Mask dialog box. When sharpening an image, it's important to understand that the effects of the Unsharp Mask filter are far more pronounced on-screen than they appear in high-resolution output, such as a printed piece.

In the Unsharp Mask dialog box, you have the following options:

Amount determines how much the contrast of pixels is increased. Typically an amount of 150% or more is applied, but this amount is very reliant on the subject matter. Overdoing Unsharp Mask on a person's face can be rather harsh, so that value can be set lower (150%) as compared to an image of a piece of equipment, where fine detail is important (300%+).

Radius determines the number of pixels surrounding the edge pixels that are affected by the sharpening. For high-resolution images, a radius between 1 and 2 is recommended. If you are creating oversized posters and billboards, you might try experimenting with larger values.

Threshold determines how different the brightness values between two pixels must be before they are considered edge pixels and thus are sharpened by the filter. To avoid introducing unwanted noise into your image, a minimum Threshold setting of 10 is recommended.

5 Type **200** into the Amount textbox. Since this is an image of a child, we can apply a higher amount of sharpening without bringing out unflattering detail.

 Click and hold on the Preview pane to turn the preview off and on as you make changes.

6 Type **1** in the Radius textbox and **10** in the Threshold textbox, and press OK.

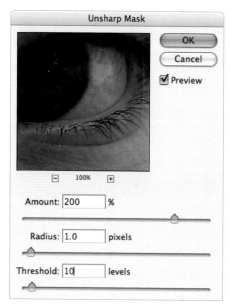

Using the Unsharp Mask dialog feature.

7 Choose File > Save. Keep the file open for the next part of this lesson.

Since you used the Smart Filter feature, you can turn the visibility of the filter off and on at any time by clicking on the eye icon to the left of Smart Filters in the Layers palette.

Comparing your image with the original

You can use the History palette in Adobe Photoshop for many functions. In this section, you'll use the History palette to compare the original image with your finished file.

1 If the History palette is not visible, choose Window > History.

2 Make sure that you have the final step you performed selected. In this case, it should be the Unsharp Mask filter. If you have some extra steps because you were experimenting with the Smart Filter thumbnail, just click on the Unsharp Mask state in the History palette.

3 Click on the Create new document from current state button (▣) at the bottom of the History palette. A new file is created.

4 Click back on your original image, ps0601_work.psd, and press Ctrl+0 (zero) (Windows) or Command+0 (zero) (Mac OS) to fit the image on your screen.

5 Click on the original snapshot located at the top of the History palette. This returns you to the original state. Drag to place the images side by side. You should see quite a difference between the images.

Comparing your corrected image with the original image.

6 Choose File > Close. Do NOT save the ps0601_work.psd.

7 Choose File > Close for the unsharp mask file created from your History palette. Do NOT save these changes.

Congratulations! You have finished the color-correction part of this lesson.

See Camera Raw in action!

Use the video that accompanies this lesson to gain a better understanding of how to take advantage of using the Camera Raw Plug-in. Open the file PS06.swf located in the Videos folder to view the video training file for this lesson.

Using the Camera Raw plug-in

In this section, you'll discover how to open and make changes to a Camera Raw file. Camera Raw really deserves more than can be covered in this lesson, but this will give you an introduction, and hopefully get you interested enough to investigate further on your own.

What is a Camera Raw file?

A Camera Raw image file contains the unprocessed data from the image sensor of a digital camera; essentially it is a digital negative of your image. By working with a Raw file, you have greater creative control and flexibility, while still maintaining the original image file.

The Raw format is proprietary and differs from one camera manufacturer to another, and sometimes even between cameras made by the same manufacturer. This differentiation can lead to many issues, mostly that you also need the camera's proprietary software to open the Raw file, unless of course, you are using Photoshop CS3's Camera Raw plug-in. The Camera Raw plug-in supports more than 150 camera manufacturers, and allows you to open other types of files into the Camera Raw plug-in, including TIFFs and JPEGs. If you are not sure whether your camera is supported by the Camera Raw plug-in, go to adobe.com and type **Support Camera Raw cameras** in the Search textbox.

1   Choose File > Browse to launch Adobe Bridge, if it is not already open. You can also select the Go to Bridge icon (🖼) in the options bar to launch Adobe Bridge.

2   Make sure that the folders panel is in front, and select Desktop.

3   Navigate to the ps06lessons folder, inside the pslessons folder on your hard drive. Select the image named ps0602.CR2. This is a Camera Raw file from a Canon Rebel digital camera. Note that each manufacturer has its own extensions; the CR2 extension is unique to Canon cameras.

4 Double-click on the ps0602.CR2 file to automatically launch and open the file in Photoshop's Camera Raw plug-in.

The Camera Raw plug-in automatically launches when a Raw file is opened.

If you attempt to open a Raw file that is not recognized by the Camera plug-in, you may need to update your plug-in. Go to adobe.com to download the latest version.

When the Camera Raw plug-in opens, you'll see a Control palette across the top, as well as additional tabbed palettes on the right. See the table below for definitions of each button in the Control palette.

ICON	TOOL NAME	USE
🔍	Zoom tool (Z)	Increases or decreases the magnification level of a Camera Raw preview.
✋	Hand tool (H)	Allows you to reposition a Raw image, when magnified, in the preview pane.
✐	White Balance tool (I)	Balances colors in a Raw image when you click on a neutral gray area in the image.
✐	Color Sampler tool (S)	Used to read image data and leave markers on the Raw image.
⊬	Crop tool (C)	Crops a Raw image right in the preview pane.
✎	Straighten tool (A)	Realigns an image.
✑	Retouch tool (B)	Heals or clones a Raw image in the preview pane.
👁	Red-Eye Removal (E)	Removes red eye from a Raw image.
☰	Open preferences dialog (Ctrl+K)	Used to change preferences, such as where xmp files are saved.
↺	Rotate image 90 degrees counterclockwise (L)	Rotates image 90 degrees counterclockwise.
↻	Rotate image 90 degrees clockwise (R)	Rotates image 90 degrees clockwise.

You'll have an opportunity to use several of these tools in the next lesson. Before starting, have a look at the palettes on the right, and learn a bit about how they are used.

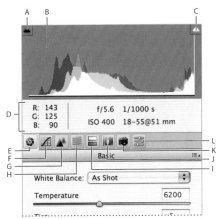

A. Shadow clipping warning button. B. Histogram. C. Highlight clipping warning button. D. Info.
E. Basic palette. F. Tone Curve palette. G. Detail. H. HSL/Grayscale. I. Split Toning. J. Lens Correction.
K. Camera Calibration. L. Presets.

A. Shadow clipping warning button

Indicates if an image is underexposed, with large areas of shadow being clipped. Clipped shadows appear as a solid dark area if not corrected using the exposure controls.

B. Histogram

Shows you where image data resides on the tone curve.

C. Highlight clipping warning button

Indicates if an image is overexposed, with large areas of highlight being clipped. A clipped highlight appears as a solid white area if not corrected using the exposure controls.

D. Info

Displays the RGB readings that enables you to check your colors and balance.

E. Basic palette

Contains the main controls, such as White Balance, Exposure, and Fill Light (new in CS3), among others.

F. Tone Curve palette

Adjusts the tone curve. The Point tab must be brought to the front (by clicking on it) to activate point-by-point controls.

G. Detail

Adjusts Sharpening and Noise Reduction.

H. HSL/Grayscale

Allows you to create grayscale images with total control over individual colors and brightness.

I. Split Toning
Introduces additional color tones into image highlights and shadows.

J. Lens Correction
Corrects for lens problems, including fringing and vignetting.

K. Camera Calibration
With the Camera Calibration tab, you can shoot a Macbeth color reference chart (available from camera suppliers). Then you can set Color Samplers on the reference chart, and use the sliders to balance the RGB values shown in the Info section. Settings can be saved by selecting the Presets tab and clicking on the New Preset button in the lower right, or by choosing Save Settings from the palette menu.

L. Presets
Stores settings for future use in the Presets tab.

Using Camera Raw controls

In this section, you'll use a few of the controls you just reviewed.

1   Make sure that the Camera image is back to its original settings by holding down the Alt key (Windows) or Option key (Mac OS) and clicking on Reset. The Cancel button becomes Reset when you hold down the Alt or Option key.

2   The first thing you are going to do with this image is balance the color. You can do this with the White Balance controls. In this instance, you'll keep it simple by selecting the White Balance tool (✐) from the Control palette.

A good neutral to balance from is the light gray section of the name tag. With the White Balance tool selected, click on the white part of the name tag. The image is balanced, using that section of the image as a reference.

With the White Balance tool selected,
click on the name tag.

You'll now adjust some of the other settings available in the Basic tab, to make the image more colorful while still maintaining good color balance.

The image looks a bit underexposed; the girl's face is somewhat dark. You'll bring out more detail in the girl's face with the Brightness slider. By using a combination of the Brightness and Recovery sliders, you can bring out additional detail without overexposing the highlights.

3 Click on the Exposure slider and drag to the left until you reach the –0.35 mark, or type **–.35** in the Exposure textbox.

4 Click on the Brightness slider in the Basic tab and drag to the right to about the +120 mark, or type **120** into the Brightness textbox.

5 Recover some of the lost highlights by clicking and dragging the Recovery slider right, to the 60 mark, or by typing **60** in the Recovery textbox.

Whenever the original image has a high luminance (brightness) range, a highlight recovery in Camera Raw can help extend the range of the processed image. By adjusting the Exposure down and the Brightness up, you can maintain highlight detail that would otherwise be lost.

6 Increase the contrast in the image by clicking and dragging the contrast slider right, to the 60 mark, or by typing **60** into the Contrast textbox.

Increase the richness of color by using the new Vibrance slider. Do not increase it too much if you plan on printing the image, as oversaturated, rich colors do not generally convert well to CMYK.

7 Drag the Vibrance slider right, over to the 25 mark, or type **25** into the Vibrance textbox.

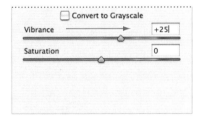

Drag Vibrance slider to the right.

8 Select the Crop tool (⌗) from the Control palette, and click and drag to select an image area that is a little closer to the girl's face.

Cropping an image in the Camera Raw Plug-in.

Now you'll save your settings.

9 Click on the Presets tab. Press the Save Preset button (⌐) in the lower right corner of the Presets palette. Type the name **Canon_outdoor** and press OK.

10 Keep the Camera Raw Plug-in window open for the next step.

Saving a DNG file

Next, you will save your image as a DNG file. A DNG file is essentially a digital negative file that maintains all the corrections you have made, in addition to the original unprocessed Raw image.

Adobe created the DNG format to provide a standard for Raw files. As mentioned previously, camera vendors have their own proprietary Raw formats and their own extensions and proprietary software to open and edit them. The DNG format was developed to provide a standard maximum-resolution format that all camera vendors would eventually support directly in their cameras. Right now, DNG provides you with the opportunity to save your original Camera Raw files in a format that you should be able to open for many years to come. Note that you can reopen the DNG over and over again, making additional changes without degrading the original image.

1 Press the Save Image button in the lower left corner of the Camera Raw window. The Save Options window appears.

2 Leave the Destination set to Save in Same Location, and click on the arrow to the right of the second drop-down menu in the File Naming section and choose 2 Digit Serial Number. This will automatically number your files, starting with the original document name followed by 01.

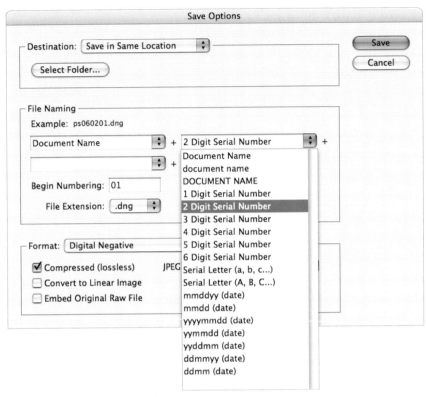

The Camera Raw Save Options dialog box.

3 Press Save. You are returned to the Camera Raw dialog box.

4 Click the Open Image button. The adjusted and cropped image is opened in Photoshop. You can continue working on this file. If you save the file now, you will see the standard Photoshop Save As dialog box. Note that whatever you save is a copy of the original Camera Raw file—your DNG file remains intact.

Reopening a DNG file

You'll now use Bridge to access your saved DNG file.

1 Access Bridge by choosing File > Browse, or by selecting the Go to Bridge (🔳) icon in the upper right corner of the Photoshop window.

2 If you are not still in the ps06lessons folder, navigate to it now. Double-click on the file you have created, ps060201.dng.

Note that the file reopens in the Camera Raw plug-in dialog box and that you can undo and redo settings, as the original has remained intact.

Congratulations! You have completed the lesson on Camera Raw images.

Self study

In this section, you can complete some exercises on your own.

Painting the Smart Filter

In this section, you'll learn how to take advantage of the Smart Objects and Smart Filters features using a technique that includes painting on the Filter effects mask thumbnail.

1   Choose File > Browse and locate the file named ps0603.psd, located in the ps06lessons folder.

2   Alt (Windows) or Option (Mac OS) double-click on the Background layer to turn it into a layer (Layer 0).

3   Select Filter > Convert for Smart Filters, and press OK if a Photoshop dialog box appears. Then choose Filter > Blur > Gaussian Blur. Again, press OK if an Adobe Photoshop dialog box appears. The Gaussian Blur dialog box appears. Use the slider at the bottom of the dialog box to apply a blur to the image. Move the slider until you can easily see the results; there's no exact number that you should set for this exercise, but make sure it is set at an amount high enough that you can see the results easily. Press OK when done. After you apply the Blur filter, a Smart Filter layer appears with a Filter effects mask thumbnail.

4   Select the Filter effects mask to activate it.

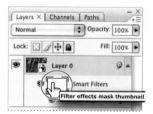

Click to activate the Filter effects mask.

5   Choose the Paintbrush tool (✐) from the Tools palette, and press **D** on your keyboard. This changes your foreground and background colors to the default colors of black and white.

6   If black is not set as your foreground color, press **X** to swap the foreground and background colors. Using the Paintbrush tool, paint over the image; note that where you paint with black, the blur disappears. Press **X** to swap the colors so that white is now the foreground color, then paint over areas where the blur is not visible, to restore it. While painting, try various values: for instance, if you press the **5** key, you are painting with a 50% opacity; if you enter **46**, you will paint with a 46% opacity. Press **0** to return to 100% opacity. This is a technique that is worth experimenting with—try other filters on your own to explore painting on Filter effect masks to hide or reveal the effect of each filter.

Review

Questions

1 Name an example of how a color sampler can be used.

2 What color mode is typically used for color-correcting an image?

3 What is a neutral? How can you use it to color-correct an image?

4 How can you tell if an image has been corrected in Adobe Photoshop?

5 What is a DNG file?

Answers

1 It is common for the Color Sampler tool to be used inside the Curves palette, where it can be used to mark white, black, or gray points on the image. Using a Color Sampler makes it much easier to read the data from one particular point of the image from the Info palette.

2 There are many theories as to which color mode is the best working environment for color correction. Unless you are in a color calibrated environment (using LAB), RGB should be the mode you choose to work in for color correction.

3 A neutral is a gray, or a shade of gray. You can often find a gray area in an image that can be used as a measuring tool to see if your colors are balanced. Some photographers like to introduce their own gray card in order to have a neutral against which to balance. They then crop the gray card out of the image when they are finished correcting the color balance.

4 By viewing the Histogram palette, you can tell if an image's tone curve has been adjusted. Even if you make just one simple curve adjustment, some degradation (splitting up) of the histogram occurs.

5 The DNG (Digital Negative) format is a non-proprietary publicly documented and widely supported format for storing raw camera data. The DNG format was developed to provide a standard format that all camera vendors would eventually support. You may also use DNG as an intermediate format for storing images that were originally captured using a proprietary camera raw format.

What you'll learn in this lesson:

- Using the selection tools
- Refining your selections
- Transforming selections
- Using the Pen tool
- Saving selections

Making the Best Selections

Creating a good selection in Photoshop is a critical skill. Selections allow you to isolate areas in an image for retouching, painting, copying, or pasting. If done correctly, selections are inconspicuous to the viewer; if not, images can look fake or over-manipulated. In this lesson, you will learn the fundamentals of making good selections.

Starting up

Before starting, make sure that your tools and palettes are consistent by resetting your preferences. See "Resetting Adobe Photoshop CS3 preferences" on page 4.

You will work with several files from the ps07lessons folder in this lesson. Make sure that you have loaded the pslessons folder onto your hard drive from the supplied DVD. See "Loading lesson files" on page 3.

See Lesson 7 in action!

Use the accompanying video to gain a better understanding of how to use some of the features shown in this lesson. Open the file PS07.swf located in the Videos folder to view the video training file for this lesson.

The importance of a good selection

"You have to select it to affect it" is an old saying in the image editing industry. To make changes to specific regions in your images, you must activate only those areas. To do this, you can use selection tools such as the Marquee, Lasso, and Quick Selection tools, or you can create a selection by painting a mask. For precise selections, you can use the Pen tool. In this lesson, you'll learn how to select pixels in an image with both pixel and pen (vector) selection techniques.

You'll start with some simple selection methods and then progress into more difficult selection techniques. Note that even if you are an experienced Photoshop user, you will want to follow the entire lesson; there are tips and tricks included that will help all levels of users achieve the best selections possible.

Using the Marquee tools

The first selection tools you'll use are the Marquee tools, which includes Rectangular, Elliptical, Single Row, and Single Column tools. Some of the many uses for the Rectangular and Elliptical Marquee tools are to isolate an area for cropping, create a border around an image, or simply to use that area in the image for corrective or creative image adjustment.

1   In Photoshop, choose File > Browse or select the Go to Bridge button (🖻) in the options bar to launch Adobe Bridge. Then navigate to the ps07lessons folder and double-click on ps0701_done.psd to open the image. The completed image file that you are about to create appears. You can leave the file open for reference, or choose File > Close to close it now.

The completed selection file.

2   Return to Adobe Bridge by choosing File > Browse or selecting the Go to Bridge button in the options bar. Navigate to the ps07lessons folder and double-click on ps0701.psd to open the image. An image of a car appears.

3   Choose File > Save As. When the Save As dialog box appears, navigate to the ps07lessons folder. In the File name text field, type **ps0701_work**. Choose Photoshop PSD from the format drop-down menu and press Save. If the Photoshop format options dialog box appears, press OK.

4   Select the Rectangular Marquee tool (▭), near the top of the Tools palette.

5   Position your cursor (crosshair) in the upper left side of the guide in the car image and drag a rectangular selection down toward the lower right corner of the guide. A rectangular selection appears as you drag, and stays active when you release the mouse.

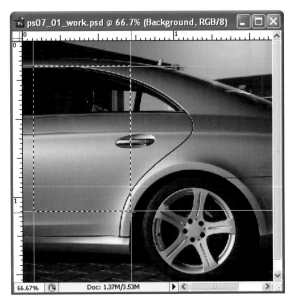

Creating a rectangular selection in the image.

You'll now apply an adjustment layer to lighten just the selected area of the image. You are lightening this region so that a text overlay can be placed over that part of the image.

6   If the Layers palette is not visible, choose Window > Layers.

7   With the Background layer selected, click on the Create a new fill or adjustment layer button (●). Select Curves from the list, and the Curves dialog box appears.

Select the Curves adjustment layer.

8   To make sure you get consistent results, first check the arrow to the left of Curve Display Options in the Curves dialog box (to show additional options) and then select Light, if that radio button is not already selected. The Light option bases the anchor points of the curve on values based upon light. You would choose Pigment for corrections that are more representative of ink on paper.

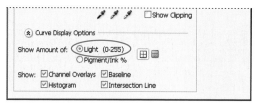

Select Light in the Curve Display Options..

Curves displays the intensity values for RGB images in a range from 0 to 255, with black (zero) at the bottom left corner. The diagonal line in the middle of the Curves pane represents the tonal values of the image. Since the image is in the Light display mode, the lower left anchor point of the diagonal line represents the shadow (or darkest) tonal values in the image, and the upper right anchor point represents the highlights (or lightest) tonal values in the image.

9 Click and drag the lower left anchor point (shadow) straight up, keeping it flush with the left side of the curve window, until the Output text field reads approximately 192, or type **192** into the Output text field. Press OK. The rectangular selection in the image is lightened.

Since you used an adjustment layer, you can double-click on the Curves thumbnail in the Layers palette to re-open the Curves palette as often as you like, to readjust the lightness in the rectangular selection.

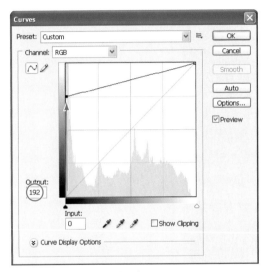

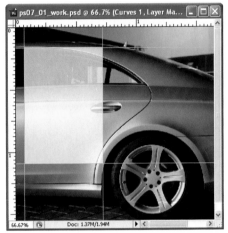

Make a curve adjustment to the selection.   *Result.*

10 Now, click the box to the left of the text layer named poster text; the eye icon (👁) appears and the layer is now visible. The text appears over the lightened area.

Creating a square selection

In this section, you learn how to create a square selection using the Rectangular Marquee tool.

1 Click on the Background thumbnail in the Layers palette to make sure it is still active.

2 Select the Rectangular Marquee tool (⬚) and position your cursor over the taillight of the car. Click and drag while holding the Shift key. Note that your selection is constrained, creating a square selection. When you have created a square (size doesn't matter), first release the mouse and then the Shift key.

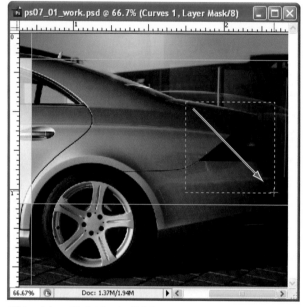

Click and drag while holding the Shift key.

3 With the square selection still active, position your cursor over the selected region of the image. Notice that an arrow with a dashed box appears (⬚). This indicates that this selection shape can be moved without moving any of the pixel information in the image.

4 Click and drag the selection to another location. Only the selection moves. Reposition the selection over the taillight.

5 Select the Move tool (⤢) and position the cursor over the selected region. Notice that an icon with an arrow and scissors appears. This indicates that if you move the selection, you will cut, or move, the pixels with the selection.

6   Click and drag the selection; the selected region of the image moves with the selection.

When the Move tool is selected, the pixels are moved with the selection.

7   Select Edit > Undo Move, or use the keyboard shortcut Ctrl+Z (Windows) or Command+Z (Mac OS) to undo your last step.

You'll now alter that section of the image. Note that when you edit a region of an image without creating a layer, you are affecting the actual pixels of the image and cannot easily undo your edits after the image has been saved, closed, and reopened.

8   With the square region of the tail light still selected, choose Image > Adjustments > Hue/Saturation. You will now adjust the Hue, or color, of this region. Click and drag the Hue slider to change the color of the selected region. You can select any color that you like. In this example, the Hue slider was moved to -163.

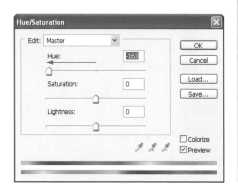

Changing the hue of the selected region.   *Result.*

With the Hue/Saturation dialog box still open, choose View > Show > Selection Edges, or use the keyboard shortcut Ctrl+H (Windows) or Command+H (Mac OS). This is a toggle feature that allows you to turn the selection marquee off and on.

9   Press OK in the Hue/Saturation window. The new hue is applied to the taillight region.

10 Choose Select > Deselect, or use the keyboard shortcut Ctrl+D (Windows) or Command+D (Mac OS) to deactivate that region of the image.

11 Choose File > Save; keep the image open for the next part of this lesson.

Creating a selection from a center point

1   Click and hold on the Rectangular Marquee tool (▣) and select the hidden Elliptical Marquee tool (○).

Limber up your fingers, because this selection techniques requires you to hold down two key modifiers as you drag.

2   You'll now draw a circle selection from the center of the image. Place your cursor in the approximate center of the tire, then hold down the Alt (Windows) or Option (Mac OS) key and the Shift key. Click and drag to pull a circular selection from the center origin point. Release the mouse (before the modifier keys) when you have created a selection that is surrounding the tire. If necessary, you can click and drag the selection while you still have the Elliptical Marquee tool selected.

Hold down Alt/Option when dragging, to create a selection from the center.

3   Whether you need to adjust your selection or not, choose Select > Transform Selection. A bounding box with anchor points appears around your selection. Use the bounding box's anchor points to adjust the size and proportions of your selection.

Transform your selection.

4   When you are finished with the transformation, press the check mark (✔) in the upper right of the options bar to confirm your transformation change, or press the ESC key in the upper left of your keyboard to cancel the selection transformation.

5   Choose File > Save. Keep this file open for the next part of this lesson.

Changing a selection into a layer

You will now move your selection up to a new layer. By moving a selection to its own independent layer, you can have more control over the selected region while leaving the original image data intact. You'll learn more about layers in Lesson 9, "Getting to Know Layers."

1   With the tire still selected, press Ctrl+J (Windows) or Command+J (Mac OS). Think of this as the "Jump my selection to a new layer" keyboard shortcut. Alternatively, to create a new layer for your selection, you can select Layer > New > Layer via Copy. The selection marquee disappears and the selected region is moved and copied to a new layer, named Layer 1.

A new layer created from the selection.

2   Now you will apply a filter to this new layer. Choose Filter > Blur > Motion Blur. The Motion Blur dialog box appears.

3   In the Motion Blur dialog box, type **0** (zero) in the Angle text field and **45** into the Distance text field, then press OK. A motion blur is applied to the tire.

Applying the Motion Blur.

Result.

4 Select the Move tool (▸+) and move the tire slightly to the right, and press **5**. By pressing 5, you have changed the opacity of this layer to 50%.

5 Congratulations! You have finished the marquee selection part of this lesson. Choose File > Save, then File > Close.

The Lasso tool

The Lasso tool is a freeform selection tool. It is great for creating an initial, rough selection. The selection that you create is as accurate as your hand on the mouse or trackpad allows it to be, which usually isn't all that accurate. The best advice for this is not to worry about being too precise; you can modify the selection, as you will see later in the section.

1 Choose File > Browse, or select the Go to Bridge button (📷) in the options bar to open Adobe Bridge. Navigate to the ps07lessons folder inside the pslessons folder you copied to your computer. Double-click on ps0702.psd to open the image. An image of a building appears.

2 Choose File > Save As. When the Save As dialog box appears, navigate to the ps07lessons folder. In the File name text field, type **ps0702_work**. Choose Photoshop PSD from the Format drop-down menu and click Save.

3 Select the Lasso tool (ℓ) in the Tools palette.

4 Position your cursor in the sky area, just outside and to the left of the top of the Capitol Building. Click and drag (don't let go until you reach your starting point!) with the Lasso tool around the outside top portion of the building. Don't worry if you do not get an accurate selection around the top of the building. The selection will be adjusted in the next few steps.

Selection made with the Lasso tool.

Adding to and subtracting from selections

Once a selection is created, there are many ways to modify it; this section focuses on just a few basic methods.

1   You will now add to your existing selection. Using the Lasso tool (⌒), position your cursor over the image and hold down the Shift key. You will see the Lasso tool displayed, with a plus sign next to it.

While holding down the Shift key, click and drag the Lasso tool to make a new path that overlaps the already active selection. Release the mouse when you have circled back to your original starting point. The new Lasso selection you made is added to the existing selection.

The original selection.   *After adding to the selection.*

2   To subtract from your selection, hold the down Alt (Windows) or Option (Mac OS) key. This time, you see the Lasso tool with a minus sign next to it.

Click and drag outside the selected area and into the active selection. Release the mouse when you have circled back to your original starting point. The new Lasso selection you made is deleted from the existing selection.

The original selection.   *After subtracting from the selection.*

Using Shift and Alt/Option, you can add to and delete from selections created with any of the selection tools.

3   Keep this image open for the next part of this lesson.

Using the Quick Selection tool

The Quick Selection tool is a new tool in Adobe Photoshop CS3 that allows you to paint your selection on an image.

1 Make sure that ps0702_work.psd is open and that there is no active selection. If you have a selection, deselect it by choosing Select > Deselect, or pressing Ctrl+D (Windows) or Command+D (Mac OS).

2 Choose View > Fit on Screen to see the entire image in your document window.

3 Choose the Quick Selection tool () in the Tools palette.

4 Position your cursor over the building. You'll see a circle with a small crosshair in the center (⊙).

The circle and crosshair will not appear if you have the Caps Lock key down.

5 Now, click and drag to paint over the building, making sure that the edge of your brush does not extend into the sky or over the trees. You can release the mouse and continue painting. The new regions are added to the existing selection. Note that when you paint over the statue at the top of the building, the selection will extend into the sky; this is due to the active brush size. You will fix this later.

Initial selection with the Quick Selection tool.

6 Now you'll delete some of the selection of the sky around the statue. If it helps, zoom into the statue. Press and hold the Alt (Windows) or Option (Mac OS) key, and paint around the statue over the sky. Note that by holding down the Alt/Option key, you are deleting from the existing selection.

7 If it helps, adjust the Quick Selection selection size by pressing the [(left bracket) repeatedly to reduce the selection size, or the] (right bracket) to increase the selection size.

8 Keep the selection active for the next section.

Understanding the new Refine Selection Edge feature

The new Refine Selection Edge feature in Adobe Photoshop CS3 allows you to alter the edge of a selection using a choice of selection previews, making it easier to view your edits. In this section, you'll experiment with the varying results of this new feature.

1 With the ps0702_work.psd image still open and the building selection still active, select the Refine Edge button on the options bar at the top of your screen. The Refine Edge dialog box appears.

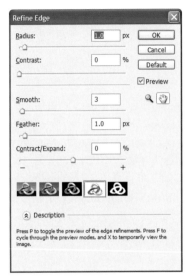

The Refine Edge dialog box.

2 The selected area of the image appears, previewed on a white background. Press the letter **F** on your keyboard to toggle through the different previews. At the bottom of the dialog box, you'll see the preview buttons highlight as you toggle through them.

Refine Edge with white background.

3   You'll now change some of your edge selection settings. Type **13** in the Feather text field, and **+50** in the Contract/Expand text field, then press OK.

Preview your selection in the Refine Edge dialog box.

4   Select the Dodge tool (✎) from the Tools palette. The Dodge tool is used to lighten or darken areas of a image. It is based on a traditional photographer's technique for regulating light exposure in specific areas of an image while creating a print. You must be careful with this tool because the more you paint over an area with the Dodge or Burn tool, the lighter or darker it becomes.

5   In the options bar, select Highlights from the Range drop-down menu. This instructs the Dodge tool to lighten only the highlight areas of the image.

6   With the Dodge tool selected, paint in the center archway to lighten it up.

7   Choose File > Save, then File > Close to close the file.

Working with the Magic Wand tool

The Magic Wand makes selections based on tonal similarities; it lets you select a consistently colored area (for example, a blue sky) without having to trace its outline. You control the range it automatically selects by adjusting the tolerance.

1   Choose File > Browse or select the Go to Bridge button (📷) in the options bar to launch Adobe Bridge. Then navigate to the ps07lessons folder and open the image ps0703.psd.

2   Choose File > Save As; the Save As dialog box appears. Navigate to the ps07lessons folder and type **ps0703_work** into the Name text field. Make sure that Photoshop is selected from the Format drop-down menu and press Save.

3   Select and hold on the Quick Selection tool (✎) to locate and select the hidden Magic Wand tool (✳).

4   Position your cursor over the top right portion of the statue's hat and click once. You will notice that similar tonal areas that are contiguous (touching) are selected. Place your cursor over different parts of the statue and click to see the different selections that are created. The selections pick up only similar tonal areas that are contiguous, which is generally not the most effective way to make selections.

5   Choose Select > Deselect, or use the keyboard shortcut Ctrl+D (Windows) or Command+D (Mac OS).

6   Click once in the lower portion of the background (the lighter portion of the sky). The entire background is selected. If the sky is not entirely selected, you can Shift+click on the areas that were missed to add them to the selection.

Image with the background selected.

To see what is included in a selection, position any selection tool over the image. If the icon appears as a hollow arrow with a dotted box next to it, it is over an active selection. If the icon of the tool or crosshair appears, then that area is not part of the active selection.

Notice that some of the sky between the arm (holding the lantern) and the body and between the legs was not selected. This is because those areas are not touching the part of the sky that you selected with the Magic Wand tool.

7   Press Ctrl+0 (zero) (Windows) or Command+0 (zero) (Mac OS) to fit the window to the screen. Then hold down the Shift key and click the area of sky that was left unselected between the legs and arm. They are added to the selection of the sky.

8   Choose Select > Inverse. Now the selection has been turned inside out, selecting the statue. Inversing a selection is a helpful technique when solid colors are part of an image, as you can make quick selections instead of focusing on the more diversely colored areas of an image.

If you have control over the environment when you capture your images, it can be helpful to take a picture of an object against a solid background. That way, you can create quick selections using tools like Quick Selection and the Magic Wand.

9   Don't worry if you accidentally deselect a region, as Photoshop remembers your last selection. With the selection of the statue still active, choose Select > Deselect and the selection is deselected, then choose Select > Reselect to reselect the statue.

10 Now you will sharpen the statue without affecting the sky. Choose Filter > Sharpen > Unsharp Mask. The Unsharp Mask dialog box appears.

11 Drag the Amount slider to the right to about 175, or type **175** into the Amount text field. If the Radius is not set at 1.0, type **1** into the Radius text field now. Slide the Threshold slider to about 10, or type **10** into the Threshold text field. Refer to Lesson 6, "Creating a Good Image," for more information on what these Unsharp Mask settings mean.

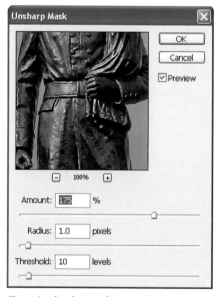

Sharpening the selection only.

12 Notice that in the preview pane of the Unsharp Mask dialog box only the statue is sharpened. Position your cursor over the statue in the preview pane and click and hold. This temporarily turns the preview off. Release the mouse to see the Unsharp Mask filter effect applied. Press OK.

13 Choose File > Save. Then choose File > Close to close this file.

See the Quick Mask feature in action!

Use the video that accompanies this lesson to gain a better understanding of how to use the Quick Mask feature. Open the file PS07.swf located in the Videos folder to view the video training file for this lesson.

Using Quick Mask

Earlier in this lesson, you learned how to add to and subtract from selections. Another method for modifying selections is to use Quick Mask. Rather than using selection tools to modify the selection, you'll use the Paint Brush tool in the Quick Mask mode and paint to modify your selection. This is a type of art therapy for those who are selection-tool-challenged. Note that when creating a mask, it is the inverse of a selection; it covers the unselected part of the image and protects it from any editing or manipulations you apply.

In this lesson, you create a mask using the Quick Mask feature, save the selection, and then copy and paste the selection into another image.

1 To see the file in its completed stage, choose File > Browse and navigate to the ps07lessons folder. Locate the file named ps0705_done.psd and double-click to open it in Photoshop. A picture with a duck and penguins appears. You can keep the file open for reference or choose File > Close now.

The completed exercise.

2 Choose File > Browse, or select the Go to Bridge button (📁) in the options bar to launch Adobe Bridge. Then navigate to the ps07lessons folder and open the image named ps0704. psd, an image of a duck appears.

3 Select the Lasso tool (𝒫) and make a quick (and rough) selection around the duck. Make sure that as you click and drag, creating a selection that encompasses the duck, the Lasso tool finishes where it started, creating a closed selection around the duck. Don't worry about the accuracy of this selection, as you are going to paint the rest of the selection using Photoshop's painting tools in the Quick Mask mode.

4 Select the Quick Mask Mode button (⊚) at the bottom of the Tools palette, or use the keyboard shortcut **Q**. Your image is now displayed with a red area (representing the mask) over areas of the image that are not part of the selection.

Now you will use the painting tools to refine this selection. Select the Brush tool (✎) in the Tools palette.

Create a rough selection using the Lasso tool.

The selection in the Quick Mask Mode.

5 Click the Default Foreground and Background Colors button at the bottom of the Tools palette, or press D on your keyboard to return to the default foreground and background colors of black and white. Painting with black adds to the mask, essentially blocking that area of the image from any changes. Painting with white subtracts from the mask, essentially making that area of the image active and ready for changes.

These tips will help you to make more accurate corrections on the mask:

Brush function	Brush keyboard shortcuts
Make brush size larger	] (right bracket)
Make brush size smaller	[(left bracket)
Make brusher harder	Shift+] (right bracket)
Make brush softer	Shift+[(left bracket)
Return to default black and white colors	D
Switch foreground and background colors	X

6   With black as your foreground color, start painting close to the duck, where there might be some green grass that you inadvertently included in the selection. Keep in mind that the areas where the red mask appears will not be part of the selection.

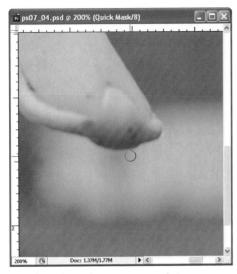

Paint the mask to make a more accurate selection.

7   If you accidentally paint into, or select some of the duck, press **X** on your keyboard to swap the foreground and background colors, putting white in the foreground. Start painting with white and you will see that this eliminates the mask, thereby making the regions that you paint with white part of the selection.

8   Continue painting until the selection is more accurate. When you are satisfied with your work, view the selection by clicking on the Quick Mask Mode button, at the bottom of the Tools palette, again or pressing **Q** on your keyboard. This exits the Quick Mask Mode and displays the selection that you have created as a marquee. You can press **Q** to re-enter the Quick Mask Mode to fine-tune the selection even further, if necessary.

9   Keep the selection active for the next section.

Saving selections

You spent quite some time editing the selection in the last part of this lesson. It would be a shame to lose that selection by closing your file or clicking somewhere else on your image. In this part of the lesson, you'll learn how to save a selection so that you can close the file, reopen it, and retrieve the selection whenever you like.

1   With your duck selection active, choose Select > Save Selection.

2   Type **duck** in the Name text field and press OK.

3 Choose Window > Channels to see that you have a saved channel (or selection) named duck. Selections that are saved with an image are known as alpha channels. Channels are not supported by all file formats. Only Photoshop, PDF, PICT, Pixar, TIFF, PSB, and Raw formats save alpha channels with the file.

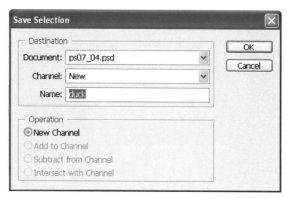

Name your saved selection.

The Channels palette.

4 Choose Select > Deselect, or press Ctrl+D (Windows) or Command+D (Mac OS) to deselect the active selection.

5 Once a selection is saved, you can easily reselect it by choosing Select > Load Selection. Select duck and press OK. The duck selection is reactivated.

You can save multiple selections in an image, but take note: your file size will increase each time you save a new selection. When multiple selections are saved, you will need to click on the Channel drop-down menu and choose which saved selection to display.

Copying and pasting a selection

There are many different methods for moving a selection from one image to another. In this lesson, you will simply cut out a selection and paste it into another image.

1 Choose Edit > Copy, or use the keyboard shortcut Ctrl+C (Windows) or Command+C (Mac OS).

2 Choose File > Browse, or press the Go to Bridge button in the options bar, and navigate to the ps07lessons folder. Double-click the file named ps0705.psd to open it in Photoshop. A photograph of penguins appears.

3 Choose File > Save As. In the Save As dialog box, navigate to the ps07lessons folder and type **ps0705_work** in the Name text field. Leave the format set to Photoshop and press Save.

4   With the image of the penguins in front, select Edit > Paste, or use the keyboard shortcut Ctrl+V (Windows) or Command+V (Mac OS). The duck selection is placed in the penguin image on its own independent layer, making it easy to reposition.

A new layer is created when the selection is pasted.

5   Select the Move Tool (✣) and reposition the duck so that it is flush with the bottom of the image.

6   Choose File > Save, then choose File > Close to close the file. Close any other open files without saving.

Using the Pen tool for selections

The Pen tool (◊) is the most accurate of all of the selection tools in Photoshop. The selection that it creates is referred to as a path. A path utilizes points and segments to define a border. Paths are not only more accurate than other selection methods, they are also more economical, as they do not increase file size, unlike saved channel selections. This is because paths don't contain image data; they are simply outlines. In this section, you will learn how to make a basic path, and then use it to make a selection that you can use for adjusting an image's tonal values.

Pen tool terminology

Bézier curve: Originally developed by Pierre Bézier in the 1970s for CAD/CAM operations, the Bézier curve became the underpinning of the entire Adobe PostScript drawing model. The depth and size of a Bézier curve is controlled by fixed points and direction lines.

Anchor points: Anchor points are used to control the shape of a path or object. They are automatically created by the shape tools. You can manually create anchor points by clicking from point to point with the Pen tool.

Direction lines: These are essentially the handles that you use on anchor points to adjust the depth and angle of curved paths.

Closed shape: When a path is created, it becomes a closed shape when the starting point joins the endpoint.

Simple path: A path consists of one or more straight or curved segments. Anchor points mark the endpoints of the path segments. In the next section, you will learn how to control the anchor points.

1   If you would like to see this next exercise in its completed form, choose File > Browse and navigate to the ps07lessons folder. Locate the file named ps0706_done.psd and double-click to open it in Photoshop. An image of a billboard appears. You can keep this file open for reference or choose File > Close to close the file.

The completed exercise.

2   Choose File > Browse or click on the Go to Bridge button (📷) in the options bar to launch Adobe Bridge. Then navigate to the ps07lessons folder and open image ps0706.psd.

3   Choose File > Save As. When the Save As dialog box appears, navigate to the ps07lessons folder. In the File name text field, type **ps0706_work**. Choose Photoshop PSD from the format drop-down menu and press Save. If the Photoshop format options dialog box appears, press OK.

4   Select the Pen tool (◊) from the Tools palette.

5   Position the cursor over the image and notice that an X appears in the lower right corner of the tool. This signifies that you are beginning a new path.

6 When the Pen tool is selected, the options bar displays three path buttons: Shape layers, Paths, and Fill pixels. Click the second icon for Paths.

7 Increase the zoom level by pressing Ctrl+plus sign (Windows) or Command+plus sign (Mac OS), so you can view the entire sign in the image window as large as possible. If you zoom too far in, zoom out by using the minus sign with the Ctrl or Command key.

8 Place the pen tip at the top left corner of the sign and click once to create the first anchor point of the path. Don't worry if it's not exactly on the corner of the sign, as you can adjust the path later.

9 Place the pen tip at the top right corner of the sign and click once. Another anchor point is created, with a line connecting the first anchor point to the second.

10 Click on the lower right corner of the sign to create another anchor point, and again the point is connected.

11 Click in the lower left corner.

12 Position your cursor over the starting point to close the path. When the cursor is on the starting point, a small circle appears next to the Pen cursor. Click once, and the path is closed.

Sign with the closed pen path.

13 To edit the position of the points on the path, you'll use the Direct Selection tool (⬡). Click and hold on the Selection tool (▶) and select the hidden Direct Selection tool.

14 Position the Direct Selection tool over the path and click once. You see the points at the corners, called anchor points, appear. Click and drag one of the corner anchor points to reposition the point. Position the corner points so that they are accurately located on each corner of the sign.

Image with the path selected.

15 Choose Window > Paths. The Paths palette appears. This is where path information is stored. You see one path in the palette, named Work Path.

16 Double-click on the name Work Path in the Paths palette. The Save Path dialog box appears. Type **Sign** in the Name text field and press OK.

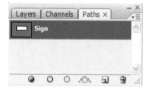

Paths palette with renamed path.

17 In the Paths palette, click below the name of the path to deselect the path. To reselect the path, simply click on the path name.

18 Now you'll apply an adjustment to this path selection. If the Layers palette is not visible, choose Window > Layers.

19 Click and hold on the Create new fill or adjustment layer button (●) at the bottom of the Layers palette and select Curves. The Curves palette appears.

20 Select the center point (the midtones) of the diagonal line that appears in the Curve control pane to add an anchor point, and then click and drag it up to lighten the sign. Simply make a visual adjustment at this time. In the example shown, the anchor point was adjusted until 174 appeared in the output text field. Once you have made your adjustment, press OK.

A new adjustment layer is created, named Curves 1. The pen path you created is visible to the right of the Curves adjustment layer thumbnail and acts as a mask, blocking the adjustment from occurring outside of the path.

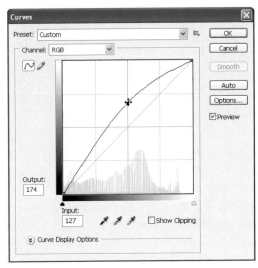

Creating a curve adjustment. *The new adjustment layer with vector mask.*

If you want to have multiple paths in the Paths palette, deselect any active path before you begin drawing a new path. If you don't deselect, the new path you create will be added to and become part of the currently active path.

21 Choose File > Save, then choose File > Close to close the file.

More pen selections

In last section, you created a basic rectangular path. Now you'll create a path with a combination of straight lines and curves.

1 Choose File > Browse or select the Go to Bridge button (🔳) in the options bar to launch Adobe Bridge. Then navigate to the ps07lessons folder and open image ps0707.psd.

2 Choose View > Fit on Screen, or use the keyboard shortcut Ctrl+0 (zero) (Windows) or Command+0 (zero) (Mac OS).

3 With the Pen tool (◊), create the first anchor point at the bottom left side of the door by clicking once.

4 Staying on the left side of the door, click again at the location that is aligned with the top of the door frame's crossbar.

Second path point.

5 Now, to set up the path for a curve segment around the arc of the door window, place the pen over the last anchor point. When you see a right slash next to the pen cursor, click and drag to pull a Bézier directional line. Drag until the directional line is even with the top horizontal bar inside the door window. The purpose of this handle is to set the direction of the curve segment that follows.

Bézier handle.

6   To form the first curve segment, place the pen cursor at the top of the arc of the door window and click, hold, and drag to the right until the curve forms around the left side of the window's arc, then release the mouse button.

Curve and its anchor point.

7   To finish off the curve, place your cursor at the right side of the door, aligned with the top of the door frame's crossbar. Click and drag straight down to form the remainder of the curve.

The completed curve's anchor point.

8   Since the next segment is going to be a straight line and not a curve, you'll need to remove the last handle. Position the cursor over the last anchor point; a left slash appears next to the Pen cursor. This indicates that you are positioned over an active anchor point. Click with the Alt/Option key depressed; the handle disappears.

9   Click on the bottom right side of the door to create a straight line segment.

10 To finish the path, continue to click straight line segments along the bottom of the door. If you need some help, look at the example.

Completed, closed path, selected with the Direct Selection tool.

11 Editing paths requires a different strategy when working with curve segments. With the Direct Selection tool (⬚), select the path in the image to activate it, and then select the anchor point at the top of the door. Two direction handles appear next to the selected anchor point. You also see handles at the bottom of each respective curve segment to the left and the right. These are used for adjusting the curve.

12 Select the end of one of the handles and drag it up and down to see how it affects the curve. Also drag the handle in toward and away from the anchor point. If you need to adjust any part of your path to make it more accurate, take the time to do so now.

13 Double-click on the name Work Path in the Paths palette, and in the Name text field, type **door**. Keep the image open for the next section.

Converting a path to a selection

Paths don't contain image data, so if you want to copy the contents of a path, you need to convert it to a selection.

1 Make sure that the file from the last exercise is still open.

2 Click on the path named Door in the Paths palette to make the path active.

3 At the bottom of the Paths palette, there are five path icons next to the palette trash can:
Fill path with foreground color fills the selected path with the current foreground color.
Stroke path with brush is better used if you first Alt/Option+click on the icon and choose the tool from the drop-down that includes the brush you want to stroke with.
Load path as a selection makes a selection from the active path.
Make work path from selection creates a path from an active selection.
Create new path is used to start a new blank path when you want to create multiple paths in an image.

4   Choose Select > Deselect, or use the keyboard shortcut Ctrl+D (Windows) or Command+D (Mac OS), to deselect the selection.

5   Choose File > Close, without saving the document.

Self study

Take some time to work with the images in this lesson to strengthen your selection skills. For instance, you used ps0702.psd with the Lasso and Quick Selection tools. Try making different selections in the image as well as using the key commands to add and subtract from the selection border. Also experiment with Quick Mask.

Review

Questions

1   Which selection tool is best used when an image has areas of similar color?

2   Which key should you hold down when adding to a selection?

3   What can you do to copy the image data inside a path?

4   Which new feature in Photoshop CS3 allows you to edit your selection using different masking options?

Answers

1   The Magic Wand is a good tool to use when you have areas of an image with like colors. The Magic Wand tool selects like colors based on the Tolerance setting in the options bar.

2   Hold down the Shift key to add to a selection. This works with any of the selection tools.

3   To select the pixel data inside of a path, you can activate the path by Ctrl+clicking (Windows) or Command+clicking (Mac OS) on the path in the Paths palette or by pressing the Load path as selection button at the bottom of the Paths palette.

4   The Refine Selection dialog box allows you to select the best masking technique and to preview edge selection changes that you are making.

What you'll learn in this lesson:

- Selecting color
- Using the Brush tool
- Applying transparency
- Using the blend modes
- Retouching images

Painting and Retouching

In addition to using Photoshop's creative painting and retouching tools to create new artwork, you can also use them to modify existing images. In this lesson, you get a quick primer in color and color models, and then you will have an opportunity to practice using all of Photoshop's painting tools, such as the paintbrush, clone, and healing tools.

Starting up

Before starting, make sure that your tools and palettes are consistent by resetting your preferences. See "Resetting Adobe Photoshop CS3 preferences" on page 4.

You will work with several files from the ps08lessons folder in this lesson. Make sure that you have loaded the pslessons folder onto your hard drive from the supplied DVD. See "Loading lesson files" on page 3.

See Lesson 8 in action!

Use the accompanying video to gain a better understanding of how to use some of the features shown in this lesson. Open the file PS08.swf located in the Videos folder to view the video training file for this lesson.

Setting up your color settings for this lesson

Before you begin selecting random colors for painting, you should have an understanding of color modes and Photoshop's color settings. Let's start with a basic introductory overview of the two main color modes that you will use in this lesson, RGB and CMYK.

Color primer

This lesson is about painting, adding colors, and changing and retouching images. It is important to understand that what you see on the screen is not necessarily what your audience will see. Bright colors tend to become duller when output to a printer, and some colors can't even be reproduced on the monitor or on paper. This is due to the fact that each device—whether it's a monitor, printer, or TV screen—has a different color gamut.

Understanding color gamut

The gamut represents the number of colors that can be represented, detected, or reproduced on a specific device. Although you may not realize it, you have experience with different gamuts already; your eyes can see many more colors than your monitor or a printing press can reproduce.

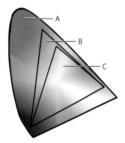

A. Colors your eye recognizes. B. Colors your monitor recognizes.
C. Colors that your printer reproduces.

In this lesson, you will learn how you can address some of the color limitations that are inherent to working with color that is displayed or output by different devices. A quick introduction to the RGB and CMYK color models will help you to get a better grasp on what you can achieve.

The RGB color model

The RGB (Red, Green, Blue) color model is an additive model in which red, green, and blue are combined in various ways to create other colors.

1 Choose File > Browse, and navigate to the ps08lessons folder. Open the file named ps08rgb. psd An image with red, green, and blue circles appears. Try to imagine the three color circles as light beams from three flashlights with red, green, and blue colored gels.

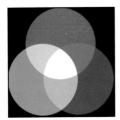

Red, green, blue.

2 Select the Move tool (✛), then check the Auto-Select check box in the options bar. By checking Auto-Select, you can automatically activate a layer by selecting pixel information on that layer. One at a time, click and drag the red, green, and blue circles around on the image.

Notice that white light is generated where the three colors intersect.

3 Now, turn off the visibility of the layers by selecting the eye icon (👁) to the left of each layer name, with the exception of the black layer. It is just like turning off a flashlight; when there is no light, there is no color.

4 Choose File > Close. Choose to not save changes.

The CMYK color model

CMYK (Cyan, Magenta, Yellow, and Black, or Key—black was once referred to as the "Key" color) is a subtractive color model, meaning that as ink is applied to a piece of paper, these colors absorb light. This color model is based on mixing the CMYK pigments to create other colors,

Ideally, by combining CMY inks together, the color black should result. In reality, the combination of those three pigments creates a dark, muddy color, so black is added to create a palette with true blacks. CMYK works through light absorption. The colors that are seen are the portion of visible light that is reflected, not absorbed, by the objects on which the light falls.

In CMYK, magenta plus yellow produces red, magenta plus cyan makes blue, and cyan plus yellow creates green.

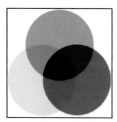

Cyan, magenta, yellow, and black.

1   Choose File > Browse, and navigate to the ps08lessons folder. Open the file named ps08cmyk. An image with cyan, magenta, and yellow circles appears. Think of the colors in this file as being created in ink printed onto paper.

2   With the Move tool (⊹) selected, and the Auto-Select check box checked, individually click and drag the cyan, magenta, and yellow circles around on the image to see the color combinations that are created with ink pigments of these three colors. Notice that black appears at the intersection of all three, but, as mentioned earlier, it would never reproduce that purely on a printing press.

3   Choose File > Close to close the ps08cmyk image. Do not save changes.

4   Uncheck the Auto-Select checkbox in the options bar.

Why you will work in the RGB mode

Unless you use an advanced color management system, you should do much of your creative work in the RGB mode. The CMYK mode is limited in its capabilities (fewer menu selections), and, if you work in the CMYK mode you have already made some decisions about your final image output that may not be accurate. Follow this mini color primer to help you achieve the results that you expect.

In this lesson, you'll use generic profiles for your monitor and output devices. If you want to create a custom monitor profile, follow the instructions in the Photoshop Help menu, under the heading "Calibrate and profile your monitor."

1   Choose File > Browse, or select the Go to Bridge icon (⬚) in the upper right of the options bar.

2 Navigate to the ps08lessons folder and open the image ps0801.psd. A very colorful image of a woman appears.

A colorful RGB image.

3 Press Ctrl+Y (Windows) or Command+Y (Mac OS); some of the colors become duller. By pressing Ctrl/Command+Y you have turned on the CMYK Preview. This is a toggle keyboard shortcut, which means you can press Ctrl/Command+Y again to turn the preview off. Note that the text in your title bar indicates whether this preview is active or not. Keep the file open for the next part of this lesson.

Essentially, the preview is visually attempting to simulate what colors would look like if you were to print this image to a printer. Understanding the color settings is important, as the settings you choose affect the colors you use and how they appear in their final destination, whether that is the Web, print, or video.

Editing Color Settings

For this lesson, you will adjust the Color Settings for Photoshop as if the final destination for this image is in print. Note that if you have any of the Creative Suite 3 Suites installed, you can adjust your color settings suite-wide, using Adobe Bridge. Applying color settings through Adobe Bridge saves you the time and trouble of making sure that all the colors are consistent throughout your production process. If you have a suite installed, follow the steps that are indicated for suite users; if you have Adobe Photoshop installed independently, follow the steps for adjusting Photoshop color settings only.

1 Choose File > Browse, or select the Go to Bridge icon (📷) in the upper right of the options bar. If you do not have the entire Creative Suite 3 installed, leave Adobe Bridge open and skip to step 3.

2 Choose Edit > Creative Suite Color Settings and select North America Prepress 2, if it is not already selected. Press the Apply button. The new color settings are applied throughout the suite applications. Note that the setting you selected is a generic setting created for a printing process that is typical in North America.

3 In Photoshop, choose Edit > Color Settings, even if you have already set them in Adobe Bridge.

4 If North America Prepress 2 is not selected in the Settings drop-down menu, choose it now. Leave the Colors Settings dialog box open.

5 While still in the Color Settings dialog box, press Ctrl+Y (Windows) or Command+Y (Mac OS) to use the toggle shortcut for the CMYK preview. You can tell if you are in the CMYK preview by looking at the titlebar of the image window.

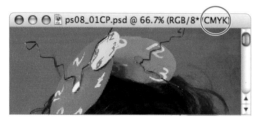

The titlebar indicates that this image is in the CMYK preview mode.

It is good to get this sneak peak into what your CMYK image will look like, but there is still the issue of having many different kinds of CMYK output devices. You might have one printer that produces excellent results and another that can hardly hold a color. In the next section, you will learn about the different CMYK settings and how they can affect your image.

6 Make sure that the CMYK preview is still on. If not, press Ctrl+Y (Windows) or Command+Y (Mac OS) again. From the CMYK drop-down menu in the Working Spaces section of the Color Settings dialog box, choose U.S. Sheetfed Uncoated v2.

Notice the color change in the image. Photoshop is now displaying the characteristics of the color space for images printed on a sheetfed press. This would be the generic setting you might choose if you were sending this image to a printing press that printed on individual sheets of paper.

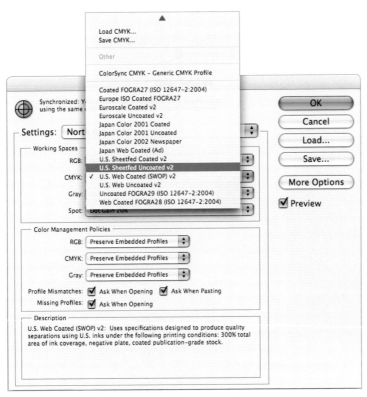

Choose various CMYK specifications from the CMYK drop-down menu.

7   From the CMYK drop-down menu, choose Japan Web Coated (Ad). Notice that color preview changes again. You might use this selection if you were sending this image overseas to be printed on a large catalog or book press. A web press is a high-volume, high-speed printing press that uses rolls of paper rather than individual sheets.

You do not want to pick a CMYK setting just because it looks good on your screen; you want to choose one based upon recommendation from a printer, or else you should use the generic settings that Adobe provides. The purpose of selecting an accurate setting is not only to keep your expectations realistic, it also helps you accurately adjust an image to produce the best and most accurate results.

8   From the Settings drop-down menu, choose the North America Prepress 2 setting again, and select OK. Keep the file open for the next part of this lesson.

Selecting colors

There are many methods that you can use to select colors to paint with in Photoshop. Most methods end up using the Color Picker dialog box. In this section, you will review how to use the Color Picker to choose accurate colors.

1   Select the Set foreground color box at the bottom of the toolbar. The Color Picker appears. It is tough to represent a 3-D color space in 2-D, but Photoshop does a pretty good job of interpreting colors in the Color Picker. Using the Color Picker, you can enter values on the right, or use the Hue slider and color field on the left to create a custom color.

2   Now, with the Color Picker open, click and drag the color slider to change the hue of your selected color. The active color is represented as a circle in the color field.

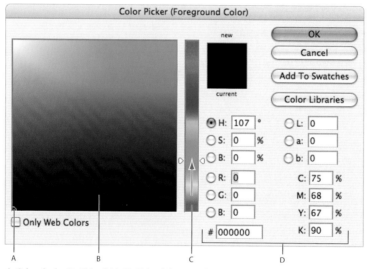

A. Selected color. *B*. Color field. *C*. Color slider. *D*. Color values.

3   Now, click in the color field, then click and drag your selected color toward the upper right corner of the color field, making it a brighter, more saturated color. To choose a lighter color, click and drag the selected color to the upper left corner of the color field. Even though you can select virtually any color using this method, you may not achieve the best results.

4   Press Ctrl+Y (Windows) or Command+Y (Mac OS) to see how the CMYK preview affects the colors in the Color Picker. Notice that your color choices look less saturated (bright). Press Ctrl/Command+Y again to turn off the CMYK preview.

Perhaps you are creating images for the Web and want to work with web-safe colors only. This is very restrictive, but you can limit your color choices by checking the Only Web Colors checkbox in the Color Picker.

5   Check and uncheck the Only Web Colors checkbox to see the difference in selectable colors in the color field.

There are also warning icons in the Color Picker to help you choose the best colors for print and the Web.

6   Click in the lower left of the color field and drag up toward the upper-right corner. Note that, at some point when you enter into the brighter colors, an Out of gamut for printing warning icon (⚠) appears. This indicates that although you may have selected a very nice color, it is never going to print, based on your present color settings. Select the Out of gamut warning icon to have Photoshop redirect you to the closest color you can achieve.

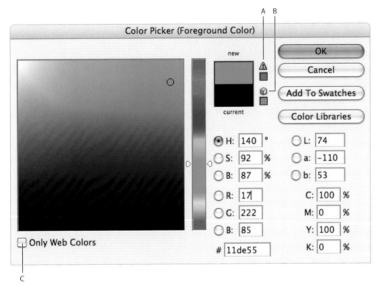

*A. Out of gamut warning. **B**. Not a web safe color warning. **C**. Only Web Colors.*

7   Click and drag your selected color in the color field until you see the Not web safe alert icon (🔘) appear. Click on the Not web safe icon to be redirected to the closest web-safe color.

8   Position the Color Picker so that you can see part of the ps0801.psd image, then position the cursor over any part of the image. Notice that the cursor turns into the Eyedropper tool (🖋). Click to select any color from the image.

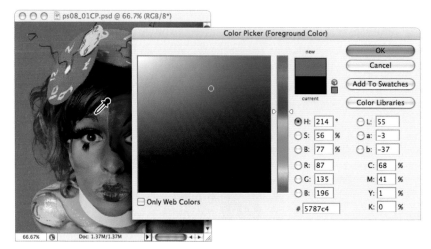

Click outside the Color Picker to sample a color from your image.

9   Press OK in the Color Picker dialog box.

10 Choose File > Close. If asked to save changes, select No.

Starting to paint

Now that you know a little more about color and finding it in Photoshop, you will start to do some painting. You will work on a new blank document to begin with, but once you have the basics of the painting tools down, you'll put your knowledge to work on actual image files.

1   Under the File menu, choose New. The New dialog box appears.

2   Type **painting** in the Name text field. From the preset drop-down menu, choose Default Photoshop Size. Leave all other settings at their defaults and press OK. A new blank document is created; keep it open for the next part of this lesson.

Using the Color palette

Another way to select color is to use the Color palette.

1   If the Color palette is not visible, choose Window > Color.

Place your cursor over the color ramp at the bottom of the palette, then click and drag across the displayed color spectrum. Notice that the RGB sliders adjust to indicate the color combinations creating the active color. If you have a specific color in mind, you can individually drag the sliders or key in numeric values.

Note that the last color you activated appears in the Set Foreground Color box, located in the Color palette as well as near the bottom of the toolbar.

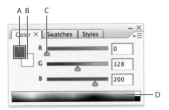

A. *Foreground color.* **B**. *Background color.*
C. *Slider.* **D**. *Color ramp.*

2   Click once on the Set foreground color box to open the Color Picker. Enter the following values in the RGB text fields on the right side of the Color Picker dialog box: R: **74** G: **150** B: **190**. Press OK.

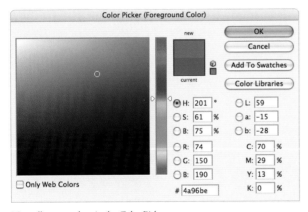

Manually enter values in the Color Picker.

Using the Brush tool

The Brush tool paints using the foreground color. You can control the brush type, size, softness, mode, and opacity with the Brush tool options.

1   Select the Brush tool (✐) on the toolbar.

2   Press the arrow next to the Brush in the options bar to open the Brush Preset picker.

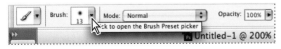

Press the arrow in the Brush options bar to pen the presets.

3   If you are not in the default palette view (Small Thumbnail), click and hold on the palette menu in the upper-right corner of the Brush Preset picker and choose Small Thumbnail View.

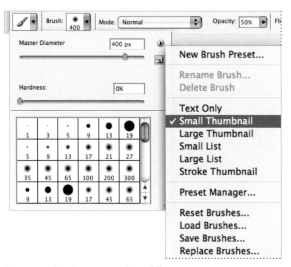

You can use the palette menu to choose different views.

4   Position your cursor over any of the brushes to see a tooltip appear. The tooltip provides a description of the brush, such as soft, airbrush, hard, or chalk, as well as its size in pixels.

5   Locate the brush with the description Soft Round 45 pixels, toward the top of the palette, and double-click on it. The brush is selected and the Brushes Preset picker is closed.

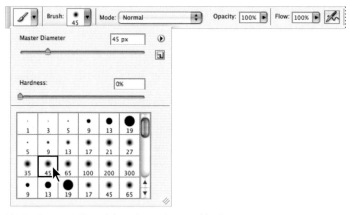

The Brush Preset picker and the Soft Round 45 pixel brush.

6   Position your cursor on the left side of the image window, then click and drag to paint a curved line similar to the example below.

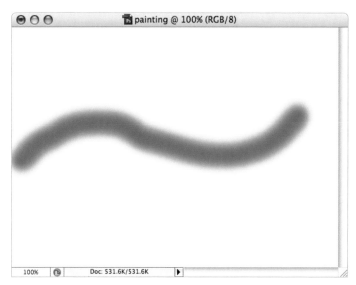

Painted brush stroke.

7   Using the Color palette, click on a different color from the color ramp (no specific color is necessary for this exercise). Then paint another brush stroke that crosses over, or intersects, with the first brush stroke.

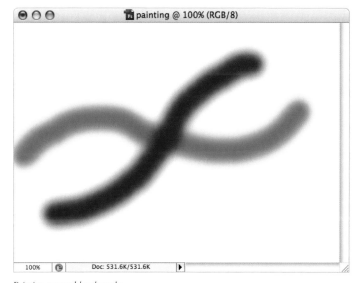

Painting a second brush stroke.

Note that when you paint, the Brush tool cursor displays the diameter of the brush that is selected. To resize the brush, you can return to the Brush Preset picker in the options bar, but it is more intuitive to resize your brush dynamically, using a keyboard shortcut.

 If you have the Caps Lock key selected, your Brush tool cursor appears as a crosshair.

8 Press the] (right bracket) to increase the brush size. Now press the [(left bracket) to decrease the size of the brush. As this blank document is for experimentation only, you can paint after resizing to see the size difference.

9 Choose File > Save to save the file. Keep the file open for the next part of this lesson.

Changing opacity

Changing the level of opacity affects how transparent your brushstrokes look over other image information. In this section, you will experiment with different percentages of opacity.

1 With the painting.psd file still open, choose Window > Swatches. The Swatches palette appears, with predetermined colors ready for you to use.

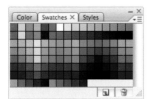

The Swatches palette.

2 Position your cursor over any swatch color and you'll see an eyedropper, along with a tooltip indicating the name of the color. Click on any one of the swatches; it becomes your current foreground color.

3 Now, to change its opacity, go to the options bar at the top and click on the right-facing arrow next to 100%. A slider appears. Drag the slider to the left to lower the opacity to about 50%, then click on the arrow to collapse the slider. Alternatively, you can type **50** into the opacity text field, if you prefer. Understand that changing the opacity of a color does not affect any of the painting that you have already completed, but it will affect future painting.

Change the opacity of the brush to 50%.

You can also change the opacity in Photoshop by holding down the Ctrl (Windows) or Command (Mac OS) key while dragging the cursor in the Opacity percentage value in the options bar. A double-arrow appears ( ), allowing you to slide the opacity down or up without even having to reveal the slider.

4 Click and drag with the Brush tool to paint over the canvas. Make sure to overlap existing colors to see how one color interacts with another. Take some time here to experiment with different colors, opacity settings, and brush sizes.

5 Choose File > Save and then File > Close to close the file.

Save time—learn the shortcuts

There are many keyboard shortcuts to help you when painting in Photoshop, most of which are integrated into the exercises in this lesson. Here is a list that will help you save time and work more efficiently:

BRUSH FUNCTION	BRUSH KEYBOARD SHORTCUTS
Open the Brush Preset picker	Right+Click (Windows) Ctrl+Click (Mac OS)
Increase Brush size	] (right bracket)
Decrease Brush Size	[(left bracket)
Make Brush Harder	Shift+] (right bracket)
Make Brush Softer	Shift [(left bracket)
Change Opacity	Type value, such as **55** for 55% or **4** for 40%
100% Opacity	Type **0** (Zero)

Applying color to an image

You can color anything realistically in Photoshop by using different opacity levels and blending modes. In this part of the lesson, you'll take a grayscale image and tint it with color. Understand that you can also paint color images to change the color of an object, like clothing for a catalog, or just to add interesting tints for mood and effect.

1 Choose File > Browse, or select the Go to Bridge button ( ) in the options bar to launch or bring forward Adobe Bridge. Then navigate to the ps08lessons folder and open image ps0802.psd.

2 Double-click on the Zoom tool ( ) in the toolbar to change the view to 100%. You may need to resize the image window to view more of the image.

3   Choose Image > Mode > RGB Color. It won't change to a color image immediately, but, in order to colorize a grayscale image, it needs to be in a color mode that supports color channels.

4   Choose File > Save As; the Save As dialog box appears. Navigate to the ps08lessons folder and type **ps0802_work** into the File name text field. Choose Photoshop from the Format drop-down menu and Press Save.

5   If you do not see the Swatches palette, choose Window > Swatches to bring it to the front.

6   Select the Brush tool from the toolbar. Right-click (Windows) or Ctrl+click (Mac OS) anywhere on the canvas to open the Brush palette, then slide the Master Diameter to 17 and the Hardness slider to 0%. Press Enter/Return to exit the Brushes palette.

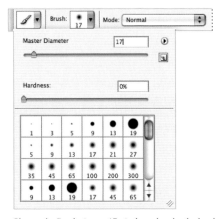

Change the Brush size to 17 pixels, and make the brush softer.

7   Using the Opacity slider in the options bar, change the opacity of the brush to 85%, or type **85** into the Opacity text field.

Settings for the first round of colorizing.

8   Position your cursor over an orange color in the Swatches palette until the tooltip indicates the color is *Pure Yellow Orange*, then click to select the color.

9   Using the Brush tool, paint over the ceramic vessels at the bottom of the image. Notice that with 85% opacity, the color is slightly transparent but still contains some of the image information underneath. You'll now experiment with blending modes to paint these vases more realistically.

Painted vases at 85% opacity.

10   Choose File > Revert to return the image to the last saved version. Leave the file open for the next part of this lesson.

Changing blending modes

Opacity is one way to alter the appearance or strength of a brush stroke. Another method is to change the blending mode of the painting tool you are using. The blending mode controls how pixels in the image are affected by painting. There are many modes to select from, and each creates a different result. This is because each blending mode is unique, but also because the blending result is based upon the color you are painting with and the color of the underlying image. In this section, you will colorize the photo by leaving the opacity at 100% and changing the blending mode.

1   Make sure that ps0802_work is still open and double-click on the Zoom tool (⊕) in the toolbar to change your view to 100%.

Make sure the Swatches palette is forward and the Brush tool (✎) is selected for this part of the lesson.

2   Right-click (Windows) or Ctrl+click (Mac OS) anywhere in the document window. This opens the contextual Brush Preset picker.

3   Click on the palette menu of the Brush Preset picker in the upper right corner and select Small List. When you release the mouse, the brushes appear as a descriptive list.

4   Select the Soft Round 17 pixels brush from the list of preset brushes.

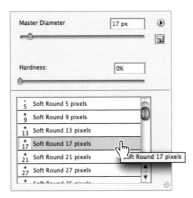

Selecting a brush in the list view.

5   Make sure that you still have the Pure Yellow Orange color selected from your Swatches palette; if not, select it now.

6   In the options bar, change the opacity to 100%, or press **0** (zero). Pressing zero is the keyboard shortcut to return to 100% opacity in any painting or retouching tool.

7   Select Color from the Mode drop-down list. This is where you select various blending modes for your painting tools. Color will be close to the bottom of this drop-down menu, so you may have to scroll to see it.

Change the blending mode to Color.

8   Using the Brush tool, paint over the ceramic vessels at the bottom of the image. Notice that the strength or opacity of the color varies according to the tonality of the painted area. This is because using the color blending mode you selected (Color) retains the grayscale information in the image. Where the image is lighter, the application of the orange color is lighter, where the image is darker, the application of the orange color is darker.

Experiment with different colors to colorize the photo, but avoid painting the stone. Also try using different modes with the same color to see how differently each mode affects the colorization. Some modes may have no effect at all. Experiment all you want with painting at this point. You can choose Ctrl+Z (Windows) or Command+Z (Mac OS) to undo a brush stroke that you do not like, or use Ctrl+Alt+Z (Windows) or Command+Option+Z (Mac OS) to undo again and again.

Ceramic vases painted in the Color Mode.

Don't like what you have done in just one area of the image? Select the Eraser tool and hold down Alt (Windows) or Option (Mac OS), then click and drag to erase to the last version saved. You can also change the brush size, opacity, and hardness of the Eraser tool, using the options bar.

9   Choose File > Save, and leave the file open for the next section.

The Eyedropper tool

The Eyedropper tool is used for sampling color from an image. This color can then be used for painting, or for use with text color. In this section, you will sample color from another image to colorize the stone building in ps0802.psd.

1   Make sure that ps0802_work.psd is still open, and choose File > Browse, or select the Go to Bridge button (🔲) in the options bar. Navigate to the ps08lessons folder and open the file named ps0803.psd.

2   Choose Window > Arrange > Tile Vertically. The images are displayed side by side.

3 Click on the titlebar for the ps0802_work.psd image to bring that image forward.

Images tiled vertically.

4 Choose the Eyedropper tool (🖋) and position it over the yellow building in the color image. Click once. The color is selected as the foreground color in the toolbar.

5 Using the options bar at the top, make sure that Color is selected from the Mode drop-down menu and that the Opacity slider is set at 100%.

6   With the Brush tool (✐) selected, paint the stone wall with the color you just sampled. You can experiment at this point and sample other colors for painting. Don't forget that you can always undo what you don't like.

Colorizing the stone wall with the Brush tool.

7   Choose File > Save, then File > Close to close both the ps0802_work.psd and the ps0803.psd files.

Retouching images

There are many techniques you can use to clean up an original image, from using any of the healing tools to that old standby, the Clone tool. In this lesson, you will retouch an image.

1   To view the final image, choose File > Browse or select the Go to Bridge button (📷) in the options bar to launch Adobe Bridge. Navigate to the ps08lessons folder and open image ps0804_done.psd.

The image after using the retouching tools.

2   You can choose File > Close after viewing this file, or leave it open for reference.

Using the Clone Stamp tool

One of the problems with old photographs is that they most likely contain a large number of defects. These defects can include watermarks, tears, fold marks, and so forth. There are many different ways to fix these defects; one of the most useful is the Clone Stamp tool. The Clone Stamp tool lets you replace pixels in one area of the image by sampling from another area. In this part of the lesson, you'll use the Clone Stamp tool, and you will also have an opportunity to explore the new Clone Source palette.

1   Choose File > Browse or select the Go to Bridge button (🔖) in the options bar to launch Adobe Bridge. Navigate to the ps08lessons folder and open image ps0804.psd.

2   Choose File Save As; the Save As dialog box appears. Navigate to the ps08lessons folder and type **ps0804_work** into the File name text field. Choose Photoshop from the Format drop-down menu and press Save.

You'll first experiment with the Clone Stamp tool (🖋) Don't worry about what you do to the image at this stage, as you will revert to saved when done.

3   Position your cursor over the nose of the girl in the image and hold down the Alt (Windows) or Option (Mac OS) key. Your cursor turns into a precision crosshair. When you see this crosshair, click with your mouse. You have just defined the source image area for the Clone Stamp tool.

4   Now position the cursor to the right of the girl's face, then click and drag to start painting with the Clone Stamp tool. The source area that you defined is recreated where you are painting. Watch carefully, as you will see a coinciding crosshair indicating the area of the source that you are copying.

The clone source and results.

5   Press the] (right bracket) key to enlarge the Clone Stamp brush. All the keyboard commands you reviewed for the Brush tool work with other painting tools as well.

6   Press **5**. By pressing a numeric value while on a painting tool, you can dynamically change the opacity. Start painting with the Clone Stamp tool again and notice that it is now cloning at a 50% opacity.

7   Press **0** (zero) to return to 100% opacity.

8 You have completed the experimental exercise using the Clone Stamp tool. Choose File > Revert to go back to the original image.

Repairing fold lines

You will now repair the fold lines in the upper right of the image.

1 Select the Zoom tool from the toolbar, and check the Resize Windows to Fit check box in the options bar. By checking this box, the window will automatically resize when you zoom.

2 Click approximately 3 times in the upper right corner of the image. There you see fold marks that you will repair using the Clone Stamp tool.

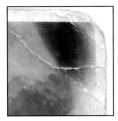

Fold marks that you will repair.

3 Select the Clone Stamp tool (⬚) from the toolbar.

4 Right-click (Windows) or Ctrl+click (Mac OS) on the image area to open the Brush Preset picker. Double-click on the Soft Round 13 pixels brush to select that brush and close the Brush Preset picker.

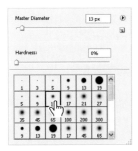

Select a soft round brush.

5 Position your cursor to the left of the fold mark, approximately in the center of the fold. Hold down Alt (Windows) or Option (Mac OS), and click to define that area as the source.

6 Position the Clone Stamp tool over the middle of the fold line itself and click and release. Depending upon what you are cloning, it is usually wise to apply a clone source in small applications, rather than painting with long brush strokes.

7   Press Shift+ [(left bracket) several times to make your brush softer. This way you can better disguise the edges of your cloning.

8   Continue painting over the fold lines in the upper left corner. As you paint, you will see crosshairs representing the sampled area. Keep an eye on the crosshairs; you don't want to introduce unwanted areas into the image.

It is not unusual to have to redefine the clone source over and over again. You may have to Alt/Option-click in the areas outside of the fold line repeatedly to find better-matched sources for cloning. You may even find that you Alt/Option click and then paint and then Alt/Option click again, and paint again; until you conceal the fold mark.

Don't forget some of the selection techniques that you learned in Lesson 7, "Making the Best Selections." You can activate the edge of the area to be retouched so that you can keep your clone stamping inside the image area and not cross into the white border.

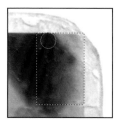

Create selections to help you clone
only the areas you want retouched.

 With the Clone Stamp tool, it is important to sample tonal areas that are similar to the tonal area you are covering. Otherwise, the retouching will look very obvious.

9   Choose File > Save. Keep this image open for the next part of this lesson.

The History palette

You can use the History palette to jump to previous states in an image. This is an important aid when retouching photos. In this section, you will explore the History palette as it relates to the previous section, and then continue to utilize it as you work forward in Photoshop.

1   Make sure that ps0804_work.psd is still open from the last section.

2   Choose Window > History. The History palette appears. Grab the lower right corner of the palette and pull it down to expand the palette and reveal all the previous states in History.

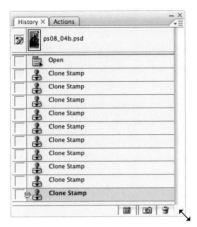

Resizing the History palette.

3   You will notice many Clone Stamp states, or a listing of any function that you performed while the image was open. As you click on each state, you reveal the image at that point in your work history. You can click back one state at a time, or you can jump to any state in the palette, including the top state, always the name of the file, which is the state of the original image when it was first opened. You can utilize this as a strategy for redoing work that does not meet with your satisfaction.

4   If you need to redo some of the cloning that you did in the previous section, click on a state in the History palette for your starting point and redo some of your work.

All states in the History palette are deleted when the file is closed.

5   Choose File > Save. Keep this file open for the next part of the lesson.

The Spot Healing brush

The Spot Healing Brush tool paints with sampled pixels from an image and matches the texture, lighting, transparency, and shading of the pixels that are sampled to the pixels being retouched, or healed. Note that unlike the Clone Stamp tool, the Spot Healing Brush automatically samples from around the retouched area.

1   With the ps0804_work.psd file still open, select View > Fit on Screen, or use the keyboard shortcut Ctrl+0 (zero) (Windows) or Command+0 (zero) (Mac OS).

2 Select the Zoom tool (Q), then click and drag the lower right section of the image to zoom into the lower right corner.

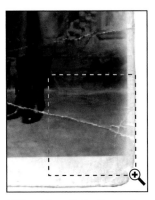

Click and drag with the Zoom tool.

Since you do not have to define a source with the Spot Healing tool, it can be easier to retouch. It is not the absolute answer to every retouching need, but it works well when retouching sections of an image that are not defined and detailed, like blemishes on skin or backgrounds.

3 Select the Spot Healing Brush tool (✐), then click and release repeatedly over the fold marks in the lower right corner of the image. The tool initially creates a dark region, indicating the area that is to be retouched, but don't panic, it will blend well when you release the mouse. Now, using the Spot Healing Brush, repair the fold lines. Use the History palette to undo steps, if necessary.

4 Choose File > Save. Keep this file open for the next part of this lesson.

The Healing brush

The Healing Brush tool also lets you correct imperfections. Like the Clone Stamp tool, you use the Healing Brush tool to paint with pixels you sample from the image, but the Healing Brush tool also matches the texture, lighting, transparency, and shading of the sampled pixels. In this section, you will remove some defects in the girl's dress.

1 Make sure that ps0804_work.psd is still open from the last section, and choose View > Fit On Screen.

2   Select the Zoom tool, then click and drag over the bottom area of the girl's dress.

Click and drag to zoom into the dress.

3   Click and hold on the Spot Healing Brush (✐) to select the hidden tool, the Healing Brush (✐).

4   Position your cursor over an area near to, but outside of, the fold line in the skirt, as you are going to define this area as your source. Hold down Alt (Windows) or Option (Mac OS) and click to define the source for your Healing Brush tool.

5   Now, paint over the fold line that is closest to the source area you defined.

6   Repeat this process; Alt/Option+click in appropriate source areas near the folds across the dress, then paint over the fold lines, using the Healing Brush tool. Don't forget to change the size using the left and right brackets, if necessary.

Define a source and then paint with the Healing Brush tool.

7   Choose File > Save, and leave this file open for the next part of this lesson.

Using the Patch tool

You may find that there are large areas of scratches or dust marks that need to be retouched. You can use the Patch tool to replace large amounts of an image with image data that you sample as your source. In this section, you will fix the large dusty area in the upper left part of the image.

1   With the ps0804_work.psd file still open, choose View Fit on Screen, or use the keyboard shortcut Ctrl+0 (zero) (Windows) or Command+0 (zero) (Mac OS).

2   Select the Zoom tool (⌕), then click and drag to zoom into the upper left area of the image.

Click and drag to zoom into the upper left corner.

3   Hold down on the Healing Brush tool (✐) and select the hidden Patch tool (◇).

4   Click and drag a selection to select an area with defects. Then, click and drag that selection over an area of the image with fewer defects, to use as a source.

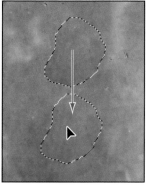

Original.   *Drag with the Patch tool.*   *Result.*

5   Continue to make selections and patch with the Patch tool to clean up most of the dust marks in the upper right corner of the image.

6   Choose File > Save. Keep the file open for the next part of this lesson.

See the new Clone Source palette in action!

Use the video that accompanies this lesson to gain a better understanding of how to take advantage of the new Clone Source palette. Open the file PS08.swf located in the Videos folder to view the video training file for this lesson.

Using the new Clone Source palette

New to Photoshop CS3 is the Clone Source palette. You can set up to five clone sources for the Clone Stamp or Healing Brush tools to use. The sources can be from the same image you are working on or from other open images. Using the Clone Source palette, you can even preview the clone source before painting, and rotate and scale the source. In this section, you will clone the upper left corner of the ps0804_work.psd image and rotate it to repair the upper right corner of the image. You will also define a second clone source to add an art deco border around the edge of the image.

1   Make sure that ps0804_work.psd is still open, and choose View > Fit on Screen.

2   Choose Window > Clone Source to open the Clone Source palette. If it helps, press Ctrl+plus sign (Windows) or Command+plus sign (Mac OS) on the upper left corner.

The Clone Source palette.

The Clone Source palette displays five icons, each representing a sampled source. You will start out using the first clone source.

3   Choose the Clone Stamp tool (🖌). Verify in the options bar that the Mode is Normal and Opacity is 100%.

4   Click on the first Clone Source icon in the Clone Source palette and position your cursor over the top-left corner of the image. Hold down the Alt (Windows) or Option (Mac OS) key and click to define this corner as the first clone source.

You will now use this corner to replace the damaged corner in the upper right.

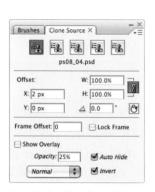

Select the first Clone Source icon.   *Alt/Option+click on the upper-left corner.*

5 If you zoomed into the upper left corner, hold down the spacebar to turn your cursor into the Hand tool (✋), then click and drag to the left. Think of the image as being a piece of paper that you are pushing to the left to see the upper right corner of the image.

6 When you are positioned over the right corner, check the Show Overlay checkbox in the Clone Source palette. A ghosted image of your clone source is displayed.

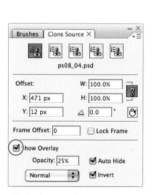
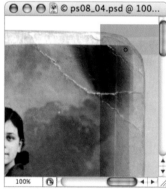

Check Show Overlay to see your clone source before cloning.

7 Now, type **90** in the Rotate text field in the Clone Source palette. The corner is rotated so that you can fit it in as a new corner in the upper right area of the image.

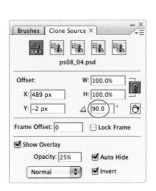
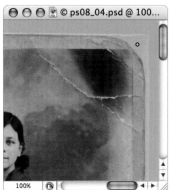

Use the Clone Source palette to Rotate your source.

8 Verify that your brush size is approximately the width of the white border. You can preview the brush size by positioning your cursor over the white border. If you do not see the brush size preview, you may have your Caps Lock key selected. If necessary, make your brush smaller, using the [(left bracket), or larger, using the] (right bracket) keys repeatedly.

9 Make sure the corner is aligned with the outside of the underlying image (original upper right corner). Don't worry about aligning with the original inside border.

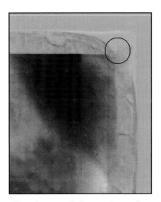
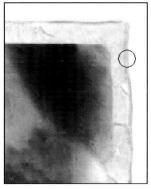

Align the corner before starting to clone.

10 Start painting only the corner with the Clone Stamp tool. Now the corner has been added to the image. Uncheck the Show Overlay checkbox to better see your results.

You can uncheck the Auto Hide checkbox in the Clone Source palette if you want the overlay to remain visible while you are painting.

11 Choose File > Save and keep this file open for the next part of this lesson.

Cloning from another source

In this section, you will open an image to clone a decoration, and then apply it to your ps0804_ work image.

1 Choose File > Browse, or select the Go to Bridge button (⬚) in the options bar. When Adobe Bridge appears, navigate to the ps08lessons folder and double-click on the image named ps0805.psd. An image with a decorative border appears.

2 If the Clone Source palette is not visible, choose Window > Clone Source. Make sure that the Show Overlay check box is unchecked.

3 Select the Clone Stamp tool (⬚) and then click on the second Clone Source icon.

4 Position your cursor over the upper left corner of the decorative border, then hold down the Alt (Windows) or Option (Mac OS) key and click to define this area of the image as your second clone source.

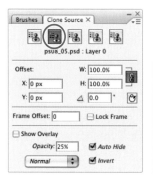

Define the upper-left corner as the second clone source.

5 Select the third Clone Source icon in the Clone Source palette.

6 Position your cursor over the upper right corner of the decorative border, then hold down the Alt (Windows) or Option (Mac OS) key and click to define this area of the image as your third clone source.

7 Choose Window > ps0804_work.psd to bring that image to the front.

8 If you cannot see your entire ps0804_work.psd image, choose View > Fit on Screen, or use the keyboard shortcut Ctrl+0 (zero) (Windows) or Command+0 (zero) (Mac OS).

9 To make the clone of the decorative border appear "antique," you will make some modifications to the Clone Stamp tool options. With the Clone Stamp tool selected, go to the options bar and select Darker Color from the Mode drop-down menu. Type **50** into the Opacity text field.

10 Select the second Clone Source icon, then check the Show Overlay checkbox in the Clone Source palette.

11 Position your cursor in the upper left of the ps0804_work.psd image and you will see the preview of the decorative border. When you have the decorative corner positioned roughly in the upper left corner, start painting. Try to follow the swirls of the design as best as you can, but don't worry about being exact. The blending mode and opacity that you set in the options bar will help blend this into the original image. If it helps to see the results, turn off the Show Overlay check box. Check it back on for the remainder of this lesson.

Paint with the clone tool.   *Result.*

Now you will clone the third source to the upper right corner of the image. This time, you can experiment with the position of the decoration on the image.

12 Navigate to the upper right side of the ps0804_work image and select the third Clone Source icon from the Clone Source palette. You will now use the Clone Source palette to reposition the upper right corner clone source.

13 Hold down Alt+Shift (Windows) or Option+Shift (Mac OS) and press the left, right, up, or down arrows on your keyboard to nudge the overlay into a better position. No specific position is required for this lesson; simply find a location that you feel works well.

14 Once you have the clone source in position, start painting. Lightly paint the decoration into the upper right corner. If you feel your brush is too hard-edged, press Shift+ [(left bracket) to make it softer.

15 Choose File > Save. Keep the ps0804_work.psd file open for the next part of this lesson. Choose Window > ps0805.psd to bring that image forward. Then choose File > Close. If asked to save changes, select No.

Self study

Return to the ps0804_work.psd image and use a variety of retouching tools, such the Clone Stamp, Spot Healing, and Healing Brush tools, to fix the rest of the damaged areas in the image. Also use the retouching tools to remove dust.

Use the Clone Source palette to repair the lower left and lower right corners of the ps0804_work.psd image.

Review

Questions

1 If you have an image in the grayscale mode and you want to colorize it, what must you do first?

2 What blending mode preserves the underlying grayscale of an image and applies a hue of the selected color? Hint: it is typically used for tinting images.

3 What is the main difference between the way the Clone Stamp and Healing Brush replace information in an image?

4 How many clone sources can be set in the Clone Source palette?

Answers

1 In order to use color, you must choose a color mode that supports color, such as RGB or CMYK. You can change the color mode by selecting the Image > Mode menu.

2 The Color blending mode is used for tinting images.

3 The Clone Stamp makes an exact copy of the sampled area, whereas the Healing Brush makes a copy of the sampled area and matches the texture, lighting, transparency, and shading of the sampled pixels.

4 You can set up to five clone sources in the Clone Source palette.

What you'll learn in this lesson:

- Understanding and using layers
- Selecting and moving layers
- Using layer masks
- Creating compositions
- Understanding clipping masks

Getting to Know Layers

Once you discover how to use layers, you can expand your capabilities to create incredible compositions, repair images like never before, and use effects that just aren't available elsewhere.

Starting up

Before starting, make sure that your tools and palettes are consistent by resetting your preferences. See "Resetting Adobe Photoshop CS3 preferences" on page 4.

You will work with several files from the ps09lessons folder in this lesson. Make sure that you have loaded the pslessons folder onto your hard drive from the supplied DVD. See "Loading lesson files" on page 3.

See Lesson 9 in action!

Use the accompanying video to gain a better understanding of how to use some of the features shown in this lesson. Open the file PS09.swf located in the Videos folder to view the video training file for this lesson.

Discovering layers

Think of layers as clear pieces of film, each containing its own image data, that can be stacked on top of each other so that you can see through transparent areas of each layer to the layers below. Each layer is independent of the others and can have its contents and opacities changed independently. You can reorder layers to create different stacking orders, and change the blending modes on the layers to create interesting overlays. Once you have mastered layers, you can create composites and repair image data like never before.

*Use the Layers palette to stack image data
in various stacking orders and opacities.*

A new image has a single layer. The number of additional layers, layer effects, and layer sets you can add to an image is limited only by your computer's memory. In this lesson, you'll find out how to take advantage of layers to create interesting composites and make non-destructive changes to your images.

The Layers palette

To help you work with layers, Photoshop provides a palette specific to layers. In addition to showing thumbnail previews of layer content, the Layers palette allows you to select specific layers, turn their visibility on and off, apply special effects, and change the order in which they are stacked.

Getting a handle on layers

In the first part of the lesson, you will work with the most fundamental concepts of using layers. Even if you have already been using layers in Photoshop, it is still a good idea to run through this section. Due to the fast pace of production, many users skip right into more advanced layer features without having the opportunity to learn basic layer features that can save them a lot of time and aggravation.

Creating a new blank file

In this lesson, you'll create a blank file and add layers to it one at a time.

1 Choose File > New. The New dialog box appears.

2 In the New dialog box, choose Default Photoshop Size from the Preset drop-down menu.

3 Choose Transparent from the Background Contents drop-down menu, and press OK.

4 You will now save the file. Choose File > Save and navigate to the ps09lessons folder. In the File name text field, type **mylayers**. Choose Photoshop from the Format drop-down menu and press Save. If the Photoshop format warning dialog box appears, press OK.

5 If the Layers palette is not visible, choose Window > Layers. Click on the Layers tab and drag it out of the docking area for this lesson so that you can more closely follow the changes you are making.

6 If the Swatches palette is not visible, choose Window > Swatches. Click and drag on the Swatches tab to take it out of the docking area as well.

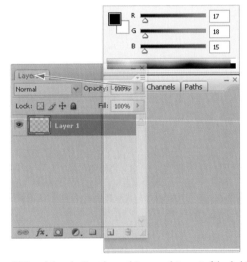

Click and drag the Swatches and Layers palettes out of the docking area.

7 Select the Rectangular Marquee tool (▭) and click and drag; to constrain the marquee selection to a square, hold down the Shift key as you drag. Release the mouse when you have created a large, square marquee. Exact size is not important for this step.

8 Select the Brush tool (✔), and then click on any red color in the Swatches palette. In this example, CMYK Red is used.

9   Choose Edit > Fill, or use the keyboard shortcut Shift+Delete, to open the Fill dialog box. Leave the settings at their default and press OK.

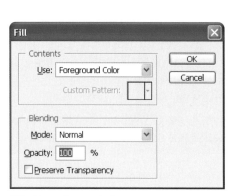

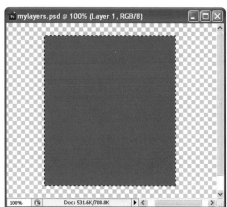

Fill with your foreground color.   *Result.*

10   Choose Select > Deselect to turn off the selection marquee, or use the keyboard shortcut Ctrl+D (Windows) or Command+D (Mac OS).

11   Choose File > Save.

Naming your layer

You will find that as you increase your use of layers, dissecting a Photoshop image can become quite complicated and confusing. Layers are limited only by the amount of memory you have in your computer, so you could find yourself working with 100-layer images. To help you stay organized, and therefore more productive, be sure to name your layers appropriately.

1   Double-click on the layer name, Layer 1. The text becomes highlighted and the insertion cursor appears. You can now type **red square** to provide this layer with a descriptive name.

2   You can also name a layer before you create it. Hold down the Alt (Windows) or Option (Mac OS) key and press the Create a new layer button (⬚) at the bottom of the Layers palette. The New Layer dialog box appears.

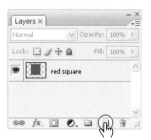

Hold down the Alt/Option key when creating a new layer.

As a default, new layers appear on top of the active layer. Use Ctrl+Alt+Shift to open the New Layer dialog box to add the new layer underneath the active layer.

3   In the Name text field, type **yellow circle**, as you are about to create a yellow circle on this layer.

Note that for organizational purposes, you can change the color of the layer in the Layers palette, which can help you locate important layers more quickly.

4   For the sake of being color-coordinated, choose Yellow from the Color drop-down menu and press OK. A new layer named "yellow circle" is created. The layer thumbnail in the Layers palette has a yellow background. This background does not affect the actual contents of your layer.

Now you will put the yellow circle on this layer.

5   Click and hold on the Rectangular Marquee tool (▯), then choose the hidden Elliptical Marquee tool (◯).

You can also cycle through the marquee selection tools by pressing Shift+M.

6   Click and drag while holding the Shift key down to create a circle selection in your image area.

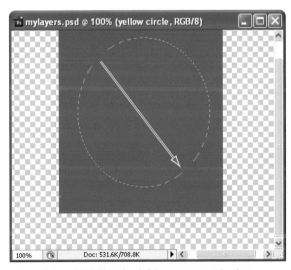

Click and drag while holding the Shift key to create a circle selection.

7   Position your cursor over the Swatches palette and click to choose any yellow color from the Swatches palette. In this example, CMYK Yellow is selected.

8 Use the keyboard shortcut Alt+Delete (Windows) or Option+Delete (Mac OS) to quickly fill the selection with yellow.

9 Choose Select > Deselect, or use the keyboard shortcut Ctrl+D (Windows) or Command+D (Mac OS).

You will now create a third layer for this file. This time, you'll use the Layers palette menu.

10 Click and hold on the Layers palette menu and choose New Layer. The New Layer dialog box appears.

11 Type **green square** in the Name text field and choose Green from the Color drop-down menu. Press OK. A new layer is created.

If you like keyboard shortcuts, you can type Ctrl+Shift+N (Windows) or Command+Shift+N (Mac OS) to create a new layer.

12 Click and hold on the Elliptical Marquee tool to select the hidden Rectangular Marquee tool. Hold down the Shift key, then click and drag a small, square selection on your document.

13 Position your cursor over the Swatches palette and click to choose any green color from the palette. In this example, CMYK Green is selected.

14 Use the keyboard shortcut Alt+Delete (Windows) or Option+Delete (Mac OS) to quickly fill the selection with green.

15 Choose Select > Deselect, or use the keyboard shortcut Ctrl+D (Windows) or Command+D (Mac OS).

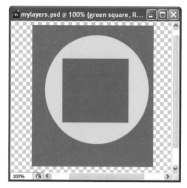

The document now has three layers.

16 Choose File > Save. Keep the mylayers.psd file open for the next part of this lesson.

Selecting layers

As basic as it may seem, selecting the appropriate layer can be difficult. Follow this exercise to see how important it is to be aware of layers by keeping track of which layer is active.

1 You should still have the mylayers.psd file open from the last exercise. If not, access the file in the ps09lessons folder and select the green square layer in the Layers palette.

2 Select the Move tool (⊹) and click and drag to reposition the green square on the green square layer. Note that only the green square moved. This is because layers that are active are the only layers that are affected.

3 With the Move tool still selected, select the yellow circle layer in the Layers palette and then click and drag the yellow circle in your image file. The yellow circle moves.

4 Now, select the red square layer in the Layers palette.

5 Choose Filter > Blur > Gaussian Blur. The Gaussian Blur dialog box appears.

6 In the Gaussian Blur dialog box, type **7** in the Radius text field, then press OK.

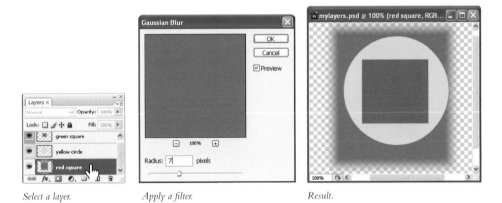

Select a layer.   *Apply a filter.*   *Result.*

7 Press Ctrl+Z (Windows) or Command+Z (Mac OS) to undo the Gaussian Blur filter.

8 Choose File > Save. Keep the file open for the next part of the lesson.

Tips for selecting layers

There are several methods you can use to make sure that you are activating certain layers and changing the properties on the specific layer you want to modify.

1 You should still have the mylayers.psd file open from the last exercise. If it is not, access the file in the ps09lessons folder and select the red square layer in the Layers palette.

2 Hold down the Ctrl (Windows) or Command (Mac OS) key and select the yellow circle in the image file. Notice that the yellow circle layer is automatically selected.

3 Now, hold down the Ctrl (Windows) or Command (Mac OS) key and select the green square in the image file. The green square layer is selected. By holding down the Ctrl or Command key, you turn on an auto-select feature that automatically selects the layer that contains the pixels you have clicked on.

You can also use contextual tools to select layers.

4 Right-click (Windows) or Ctrl+click (Mac OS) on the green square. Note that when you access the contextual tools, overlapping layers appear in a list, providing you with the opportunity to select the layer in the menu that appears. Select the green square layer.

You can select a layer using contextual tools.

5 Right-click (Windows) or Ctrl+click (Mac OS) on an area of the image file that contains only the red square pixels to see that only one layer name appears for you to choose from. Choose red square.

Moving layers

Layers appear in the same stacking order in which they appear in the Layers palette. For instance, in the file you have been working on in this lesson, the green square was created last and is at the top of the stacking order, essentially covering up the yellow circle and red square wherever it is positioned.

By moving the position of a layer, you can change the way an image looks, which allows you to experiment with different image compositions.

1 With the mylayers.psd file still open, click and drag the green square layer in the Layers palette to the bottom of the red square layer. Release the mouse button when you see a dark bar appear underneath the red square layer. The dark line indicates the location of the layer that you are dragging. Notice that the green square may not be visible at this time because it is underneath the red square, and thus hidden.

Click and drag to reorder your layers.

2 You may find it easier to use keyboard commands to move the layers' positions in the stacking order. Select the green square layer and press Ctrl+] (right bracket) (Windows) or Command+] (right bracket) (Mac OS) to move it up one level in the stacking order. Press it again to move the green square layer back to the top of the stacking order.

3 Select the yellow circle layer and press Ctrl+[(left bracket) (Windows) or Command+[(left bracket) (Mac OS) to put the yellow circle one level down in the stacking order, essentially placing it behind the red square. Press Ctrl+] (right bracket) (Windows) or Command+] (right bracket) (Mac OS) to move it back up one level in the layer stacking order.

The image layers should now be back in the same order as when the image was originally created: red square on the bottom, yellow circle in the middle, and green square on the top.

4 Choose File > Save. Keep the file open for the next part of this lesson.

See Layers in action!

Use the accompanying video to gain a better understanding of how to use layers. Open the file PS09.swf located in the Videos folder to view the video training file for this lesson.

Changing the visibility of a layer

One of the benefits of using layers is that you can hide the layers that contain pixel data on which you are not currently working. By hiding layers, you can focus on the image editing at hand, keeping distractions to a minimum.

1 With the mylayers.psd file still open, select the eye icon (👁) to the left of the red square layer. The red square disappears.

Turn the visibility of a layer off and on by selecting the eye icon.

2 Click again on the spot where the eye icon previously appeared. The red square layer is visible again.

3 This time, hold down the Alt (Windows) or Option (Mac OS) key, and click on the same eye icon. By using the Alt/Option modifier, you can hide all layers except the one you click on.

4 Alt/Option+click on the same eye icon to make all the layers visible again.

Using masks in a layer

There is one last layer fundamental to understand before you delve further into layers: the layer mask feature. Without the mask feature, making realistic composites or blending one image smoothly into another would be much more difficult.

1 With the mylayers.psd file still open, choose the red square layer in the Layers palette.

2 Select the Add layer mask button at the bottom of the Layers palette. A blank mask is added to the right of the red square layer.

Adding a layer mask.

3 To make sure your foreground and background colors are set to the default black and white, press **D** on your keyboard.

4 Select the Gradient tool (▪) from the Tools palette, and make sure that the Linear gradient option is selected in the options bar. Click and drag right across the red square in the image. Note that some of the red square becomes transparent, while some remains visible. Click and drag with the Gradient tool as many times as you like. Note that in the Layers palette, wherever black appears in the mask thumbnail, the red square is transparent, as the mask is essentially hiding the red square from view.

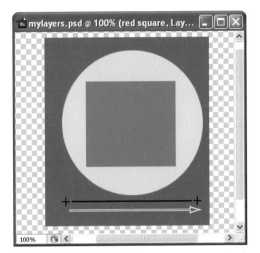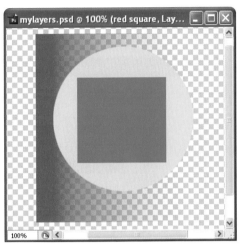

Click and drag with the Gradient tool across the image when the mask is active.

5 Choose File > Save. Keep this file open for the next part of this lesson.

Preserve transparency

The last step in this practice file will be to apply transformations to your layers. Transformations include scaling, rotating, and distorting a layer. To help illustrate how transformations work, you will first duplicate a layer and link it to the original.

1 With the mylayers.psd file still open, select the green square layer.

2 Select the Move tool (⊕) and then hold down the Alt (Windows) or Option (Mac OS) key and position the cursor over the green square in the image. You see a double-arrow cursor (⊳). While still holding down the Alt/Option key, click and drag the green square to the right. A duplicate of the layer is created; release the mouse to see that a green square copy layer has been added to the Layers palette.

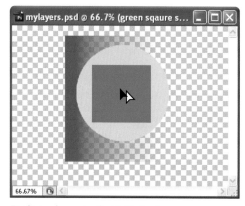

Duplicate a layer using the Alt/Option key.

3 Double-click on the green square copy layer name, when the text is highlighted, type the name **green square**.

4 Double-click on the green square layer and when the text is highlighted, type the name **green square shadow**.

5 You'll now take advantage of a feature that allows you to fill without making a selection. Choose Edit > Fill, or use the keyboard shortcut Shift+ Delete. The Fill dialog box appears.

6 In the Fill dialog box, choose Black from the Use drop-down menu. Leave Mode (in the blending section) set to Normal and Opacity set to 100%, check Preserve Transparency, and press OK.

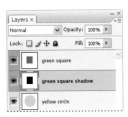

Preserve Transparency maintains the transparent sections of a layer.

Notice that since you selected to preserve the transparency, only the green pixels were changed to black and the rest of the layer (the transparent part) remains transparent. You'll use this feature later in this lesson when creating a composition from several images.

7 With the green shadow layer still active, select Filter > Blur > Gaussian Blur. The Gaussian Blur dialog box appears.

8 In the Gaussian Blur dialog box, type **8** in the Radius text field, and press OK.

9 Now, in the Layers palette, click and drag the green square shadow layer beneath the green square layer. Remember that when moving a layer from one position in the stacking order to another that you should not release the mouse until you see a dark line appear between the layers where it is being relocated.

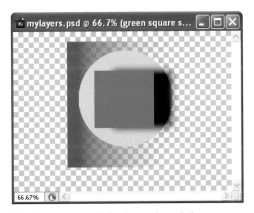

Drag the green square shadow layer underneath the green square layer.

In this section, you will link the green square layer and green square shadow layer together. This allows you to move them simultaneously and also to apply transformations to both layers at the same time.

10 Select the green square layer, then Shift+click on the green square shadow layer. Both are now selected.

11 Select the Link layers button (⊖⊖) at the bottom of the Layers palette. The link icon appears to the right of the layer names, indicating that they are linked to each other.

Keep layers together by linking them.

12 Select the Move tool and click and drag the green square to another location. Notice that the shadow moves, too. Move the squares back to the center of the image.

13 Choose Edit > Free Transform, or use the keyboard shortcut Ctrl+T (Windows) or Command+T (Mac OS). A bounding box appears around the green square and its shadow.

14 Click on the lower right corner handle and drag it to enlarge the squares. Release the mouse when you've resized them to your liking.

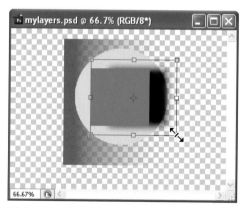

Click and drag the bounding box to scale the layer contents.

If you are not happy with the size and want to cancel the transformation, press the ESC key (on the upper left of your keyboard).

15 Now, choose Edit > Free Transform again, but this time hold down the Shift key while dragging the lower right corner of the bounding box toward the lower right corner of your image. Holding down the Shift key keeps the layer contents proportional as you scale. Release the mouse when you're done with the transformation.

16 You can also enter exact scale amounts by using the options bar. Type **150** in the W (Width) text field and then press the Maintain aspect ratio button (⚬). The layer contents are scaled to exactly 150%. Select the checkbox in the options bar to confirm this transformation.

17 Choose File > Save and then File > Close to close this practice file.

Creating a composition

Now you will have the opportunity to put your practice to work by creating a composition with images and type.

1 Choose File > Browse to open Adobe Bridge or select the Go to Bridge button (⬛) in the upper right of the options bar. Navigate to the ps09lessons folder inside the pslessons folder on your computer.

2 Double-click on the file ps0901_done.psd to see the composition that you will create. You can keep this file open for reference, or choose File > Close.

The completed lesson file.

3 Double-click on ps0901.psd to open it in Photoshop. An image of a blue sky with clouds appears.

4 Choose File > Save As. In the Save As dialog box navigate to the ps09lessons folder and type **ps0901_work** into the File name text field; leave the format as Photoshop and press Save.

Moving images in from other documents

You'll start this composition by opening another file and dragging it into this file. Be aware that when moving one document into another, an image's resolution plays an important part in how that image appears proportionally when moved into another file. For instance, if a 72-ppi image is moved into a 300-ppi image, it becomes relatively smaller, as the 72-ppi takes up much less pixel space in the 300-ppi image. On the other hand, if you move a 300-ppi image into a 72-ppi image, it takes up a larger space. If you plan to create composites of multiple images, it is best to choose Image > Image Size and adjust the pixel resolutions of the images before combining them. In this section, you will learn how to check the resolution of your images before combining them into one document.

1   With the ps0901_work.psd file open, choose Image > Image Size. The Image Size dialog box appears. Notice that this image's resolution is 300 ppi. Press OK.

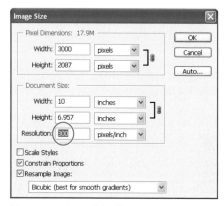

The image resolution of this file is 300 ppi

2   Choose File > Browse to open Adobe Bridge, or select the Go to Bridge button (▣) button in the upper right area of the options bar at the top of your workspace. Navigate to the ps09lessons folder inside the pslessons folder on your computer.

3   Double-click on ps0902.psd to open it in Photoshop. An image of a boy jumping appears.

For this image, you will check the resolution without opening the Image Size dialog box.

4   Make sure that the Photoshop document window is opened large enough for you to see the document size in the lower left corner of the window. If you don't see the document size in that corner, you may need to click and drag the lower right corner of the document window to make it a bit larger.

5   Hold down the Alt (Windows) or Option (Mac OS) key and click on the document size box to see a pop-up window appear that provides you with dimension and resolution information. Note that this image is also 300 ppi.

Checking the resolution right in the document window.

6   Choose Window > Arrange > Tile Horizontally to position the ps0901_work.psd and ps0902.psd documents so that you can see both of them at the same time.

7   Select the Move tool (⊹).

8   Hold down the Shift key and click and drag the jumping boy image into ps0901_work.psd. Holding the Shift key assures you that the layer is being placed in the exact center of the document into which it is being dragged. Release the mouse when a border appears around the ps01_work.psd image.

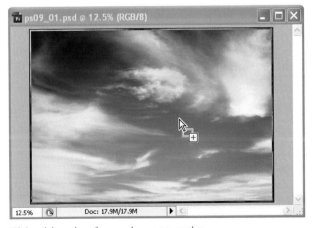

Click and drag a layer from one document to another.

9 Choose File > Save. Keep the file open for the next part of this lesson.

10 Choose Window > ps0902.psd, and then choose File > Close, or use the keyboard shortcut Ctrl+W (Windows) or Command+W (Mac OS) to close the file. If you are asked to save the file, choose No.

Creating a layer mask

You just created the first layer in this document. It is important to keep your layers organized as you work; the Layers palette can become cumbersome when additional layers are created without being properly named.

1 Double-click the word Layer 1 in the Layers palette. When the Layer 1 text becomes highlighted, type **boy**.

Now you'll select the boy and create a layer mask to cover the background sky.

2 Select the boy layer in the Layers palette to make sure it is the active layer, then select the Quick Selection tool (✎) and start brushing over the image of the boy. A selection is created as you brush. If you accidently select the area around the jumping boy, hold down the Alt (Windows) or Option (Mac OS) key and brush over that area again to delete it from the selection.

Since you will be turning your selection into a mask, you do not have to be perfectly precise. You can edit the selection later if necessary.

Create a selection using the Quick Selection tool.

3 With the selection still active, select the Add layer mask button (◻) at the bottom of the
Layers palette. A mask is created, revealing only your selection of the jumping boy.

Select the Add layer mask button.   *Result.*

Editing the layer mask

Your mask may not be perfect, but you can easily edit it using your painting tools. In the
example shown here, the hand was not correctly selected with the Quick Selection tool and
therefore created an inaccurate mask. Zoom into the image and locate a section where your
selection may not be precise; it is more than likely this will be around the boy's hands.

The mask needs to be adjusted in this section.

1   Select the layer mask thumbnail that is to the right of the boy's thumbnail in the Layers palette.

Select the Layer mask thumbnail.

2   Press **D** on your keyboard to select the default colors of black and white. Note that when working on a mask, painting with white reveals the image, while painting with black hides it.

3   Press **X** on your keyboard, and note that by pressing X you are swapping the foreground and background colors in the Tools palette. Make sure that black is the foreground color.

4   Select the Brush tool and position the cursor over an area of the image where the mask is a bit inaccurate. You see a circle representing the brush size.

If you have Caps Lock selected, you will not see the Brush size preview.

If the brush size is too big or too small for the area of the mask that needs to be retouched, adjust the size before you start painting.

5   Press the] (right bracket) key to make the brush size larger, or [(left bracket) to make the brush size smaller.

6   Start painting the areas of the mask that were not accurate; in this case perhaps where some of the sky on the boy layer still appears. Experiment even further by painting over the entire hand. The hand disappears.

7   Press **X** on your keyboard to bring white to the foreground and paint over the location where the hand was to reveal it again. You are essentially fine-tuning your mask by painting directly on it.

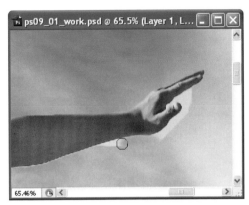

Painting the mask.

8   If you find that your brush should have a harder edge, press Shift+] (right bracket) or Shift+[(left bracket).

The benefit of working with a layer mask is that you can fine-tune and edit it as many times as you want. This gives you a lot of freedom and control, and allows you to make more accurate selections.

9   When you are finished editing your selection, press Ctrl+0 (zero) (Windows) or Command+0 (zero) (Mac OS) to return to the Fit in Screen view. Then, to deselect the layer mask thumbnail, select the boy layer thumbnail in the Layers palette.

Cloning layers

You'll now clone (or duplicate) the boy layer two times. You'll then apply filters and adjust the opacity of the new layers.

1 Select the boy layer thumbnail in the Layers palette to ensure that it is the active layer. Select the Move tool (⊹) and reposition the boy so that his feet touch the bottom of the image.

Click and drag the boy layer downwards.

2 With the Move tool still selected, click and hold the Alt (Windows) or Option (Mac OS) key while dragging the jumping boy image up toward the middle of the image. By holding down the Alt/Option key, you are cloning the layer. Don't worry about a precise location for the cloned layer as you'll adjust its position later. Release the mouse before releasing the Alt/Option key.

Clone the layer of the boy jumping.

3 Click and hold down the Alt (Windows) or Option (Mac OS) key once again and drag the newly created layer upwards to clone it. Position this new layer at the top of the image. There are now three layers with the boy jumping.

4 In the Layers palette, double-click on layer name "boy copy." When the text becomes highlighted, type **boy middle** to change the layer name.

5 Then, double-click on layer name "boy copy 2." When the text becomes highlighted, type **boy top** to change the layer name.

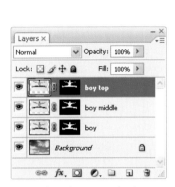

You now have three jumping boy layers.

6 Choose File > Save to save this file. Keep the file open for the next part of this lesson.

Aligning and distributing layers

The layers may not be evenly spaced or aligned with each other. This can be adjusted easily by using the Align and Distribute features in Photoshop.

1 Select the boy layer and then Ctrl+click (Windows) or Command+click (Mac OS) on the boy middle and boy top layers. All three layers become selected.

Note that when you have three or more layers selected, there are additional options in the options bar to align and distribute your layers.

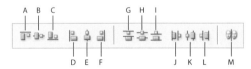

*A. Align top edges. **B**. Align vertical centers. **C**. Align bottom edges.*
*D. Align left edges. **E**. Align horizontal centers. **F**. Align right edges.*
*G. Distribute top edges. **H**. Distribute vertical centers. **I**. Distribute bottom edges.*
*J. Distribute left edges. **K**. Distribute horizontal centers. **L**. Distribute right edges.*
M. Auto-Align layers.

2 Choose the Align horizontal centers button (♣) and then the Distribute vertical centers button (♣). You may or may not see a dramatic adjustment here; it depends on how you positioned the layers when you created them.

3 Choose File > Save. Keep the file open for the next part of this lesson.

Applying filters to layers

Now you'll apply a filter to the boy and boy middle layers and then adjust their opacity.

1   Select the boy middle layer in the Layers palette.

2   Choose Filter > Blur > Motion Blur. The Motion Blur dialog box appears.

3   Type **–90** in the Angle text field, drag the distance slider to 150, then press OK. You have created a blur that makes it look like the boy is jumping up.

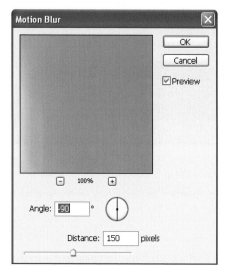

Apply the motion blur.   *Result.*

4   Choose the boy layer in the Layers palette and press Ctrl+F (Windows) or Command+F (Mac OS). This applies the last-used filter to this layer.

You will now adjust the opacity on these layers.

5   With the boy layer still selected, click on the arrow to the right of Opacity in the Layers palette. A slider appears. Click and drag the slider to the 20% mark.

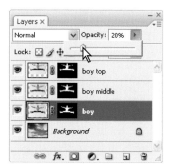

Drag the opacity slider.

6   Make sure that the Move tool (⊹) is active, and select the boy middle layer. This time, you'll change the opacity using a keyboard shortcut. Press **5**; the layer opacity is instantly changed to 50%.

The layers after the opacity has been adjusted.

*While the Move tool is active, you can type in any value to set the opacity on a selected layer. For instance, typing **23** would make the layer 23% opaque, **70** would make the layer 70% opaque. Press **0** (zero) to return to 100% opacity.*

7   Choose File > Save to save this file. Keep the file open for the next part of this lesson.

Creating a type layer

You are now going to add a text layer to this document and apply a warp as well as a layer style.

1   In the Layers palette, select the boy top layer to make it active. The new type layer will appear directly above the active layer.

2   Select the Type tool (T) and set the following options in the options bar:

From the font family drop-down menu, choose Myriad Pro. From the font style drop-down menu, choose Black. If you do not have Black, choose Bold.

Type **200** in the font size text field.

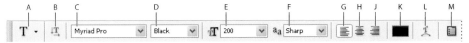

*A. Presets. **B**. Text orientation. **C**. Font family. **D**. Font style. **E**. Font size. **F**. Anti-aliasing. **G**. Left-align text.*
*H. Center text. **J**. Right-align text. **K**. Text color. **L**. Warp text. **M**. Character and Paragraph palettes.*

3   Now, click once on the Text color box in the options bar. The Color Picker dialog box appears, with a Select text color pane.

4   You can either enter a color value in this window or click on a color in the color preview pane. In this example, you will position your cursor over an area in the image that has light clouds, and click. This samples that color and applies it to the text. Press OK to close the Color Picker.

Open the Color Picker dialog box.   *Sample a color from your image.*

You are now ready to type.

5   Click once on the image near the boy's sneaker on the left side of the image. Exact position is not important, as it can be adjusted later.

6   Type **JUMP**, then hold down the Ctrl (Windows) or Command (Mac OS) key and drag the word Jump to approximately the bottom center of the image. By holding down the Ctrl/Command key, you do not have to exit the text entry mode to reposition the text.

Reposition the text using the Ctrl or Command key.

7   Select the Create warped text button (⊥) in the options bar. The Warp Text dialog box appears.

8 Select Arc Upper from the Style drop-down menu. If you like, experiment with the other style selections, but return to the Arc Upper when finished. Press OK. The text is warped.

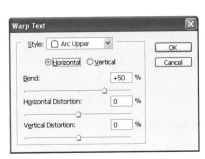

Warping the text.   *Result.*

9 Select the check mark (✔) in the options bar to confirm your text entry.

10 In the Layers palette, click and drag the Opacity slider to about 70%, or type **70** into the Opacity text field.

11 Choose File > Save and keep the file open for the next part of this lesson.

Applying a Layer Style

Layer styles allow you to apply interesting effects to layers, such as drop shadows, embossing, and outer glows, to name a few. In this section, you will add a drop shadow to your text layer.

1 Select the text layer to make sure that the layer is active.

2 Click and hold on the Add a layer style button (*fx*) at the bottom of the Layers palette. Choose Drop Shadow from the menu and the Layer Style dialog box appears.

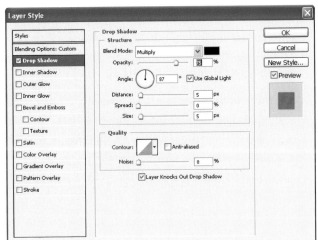

Adding a drop shadow to the text layer.

At some point you should experiment with all the layer style options listed in the column on the left, but for now you'll work with the drop shadow options.

3 With the Layer Styles dialog box open, click and drag the shadow (in the image window) to reposition it. You can manually enter values. In this example, the shadow was set to an angle of 168, the distance at 70, and the size at 30. Press OK and the drop shadow is applied.

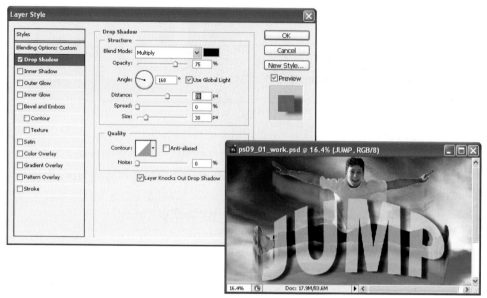

Adjusting the layer style. *Result.*

Creating a clipping mask

You will now create a clipping mask to complete this image. A clipping mask lets you use the content of one layer to mask the layers above it. In this example, you will create a shape layer and position it under the background layer. You will then clip up through several layers, masking them within that original shape layer. It might sound confusing, but it really isn't once you have seen the clipping mask feature in action.

1 First, you need to convert the background layer to a regular layer because you cannot position layers underneath the background layer.

2 Hold down the Alt (Windows) or Option (Mac OS) key and double-click on the Background layer in the Layers palette. It is automatically converted to Layer 0.

3 Double-click on the Layer 0 name, and, when the text becomes highlighted, type **sky**.

4   Click and hold on the Shape tool (□) and select the hidden Rounded Rectangle tool (□). In the options bar, make sure that Shape layers is selected, then type **1** in the Radius text field. This value is for the curved corners of the rounded rectangle you are going to create.

5   Click and drag from the boy's thumb on the left side of the image down to the bottom of the letter P in JUMP. The shape is created; don't worry about the color.

Set the shape options. Click and drag to create the shape layer.

6   In the Layers palette, click and drag the Shape 1 layer so that it is beneath the sky layer.

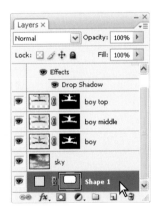

Arrange the layers so that the Shape 1 layer is at the bottom.

7   Hold down the Alt (Windows) or Option (Mac OS) key and position your cursor over the line that separates the Shape 1 layer from the sky layer. When you see the clipping mask icon (•⊙) appear, click with the mouse. The sky layer is clipped inside the shape layer.

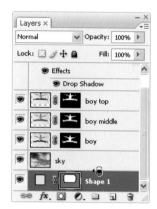 

Alt/Option click in-between the layers.   *Result.*

8   Now, position your cursor on the line separating the sky layer from the boy layer, and Alt/Option+click on the line. The clipping now extends up into the boy layer.

9   Position the cursor on the line separating the boy layer from the boy middle layer and Alt/Option+click again. The clipping mask is now extended to the boy middle layer.

10   Select the Move tool (⊹) and the Shape 1 layer. Click and drag to reposition the layer to see how the sky, boy, and boy middle layers are clipped inside the shape.

11   If you would prefer not to see the vector path creating an outline around your rounded rectangle shape, click once on the vector mask thumbnail in the Layers palette.

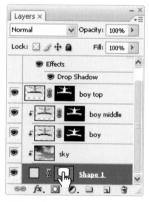

Click on the vector mask to turn off the visibility of the vector path in your image.

You will now trim the layers to eliminate areas you don't need.

12 Choose Image > Trim; the Trim dialog box appears. Leave the settings at the default and press OK. The image is trimmed down to the smallest possible size, without cropping out any image data.

13 Choose File > Save, and then File > Close. Congratulations! You have finished the lesson on getting to know layers.

Self study

Layers are fun to build and use to create professional composites. Included in the ps09lessons folder are several images (boyguitar.psd, girlguitar.psd, pianokeys.psd, and sheetmusic.psd) that you can use in any way that you want to create a composite. You can try to recreate the composition on your own, but it is meant as a reference only.

Experiment with these sample files to create new layers, layer masks, and clipping masks. Take the composition further by adding text and warping it.

Review

Questions

1 List three ways that you can create a layer in a document.

2 Why should you be concerned about resolution when compositing several images?

3 What is the difference between the Background and a regular layer?

Answers

1 You can create new layers in a document using several methods:

  a. Create a new blank layer using the Create a new layer button (⬛) in the Layers palette, or choose Layers > New > Layer, or select New Layer from the Layers palette menu.

  b. Create a new layer by clicking and dragging content from one image to another.

  c. Create a text layer; when you add text, a new text layer is automatically created.

  d. Create a shape. If the Shape tool is selected and the options bar is set to Shape tool, a new Shape layer is automatically created.

2 When combining images from several different sources, it is important for the pixel dimensions or resolutions to be similar or the images will not be proportional to each other and may not work well as a composite.

3 The Background layer is different from a regular layer in that it does not support layer features. It cannot be moved in the stacking order, repositioned, transformed, or have its blending mode or opacity changed.

What you'll learn
in this lesson:

- Making color changes with adjustment layers

- Using the new Black and White adjustment layer

- Combining layer effects

- Understanding layer fill and opacity settings

Taking Layers
to the Max

Even those who call themselves Photoshop experts can't get enough of layers. Layers provide many creative possibilities, some more evident than others. In this lesson, you will build a layered file, and then you'll take it farther than you ever thought possible, using features such as adjustment layers, layer effects, and clipping groups, among others.

Starting up

Layers, in their simplest form, offer Photoshop users an amazing amount of flexibility to create and modify images. The more advanced features of layers offer even more options, many of which you can exploit in various ways while keeping the original image information intact.

Before starting, make sure that your tools and palettes are consistent by resetting your preferences. See "Resetting Adobe Photoshop CS3 preferences" on page 4.

You will work with several files from the ps10lessons folder in this lesson. Make sure that you have loaded your pslessons folder onto your hard drive from the supplied DVD. See "Loading lesson files" on page 3.

See Lesson 10 in action!

Use the accompanying video to gain a better understanding of how to use some of the features shown in this lesson. Open the file PS10.swf located in the Videos folder to view the video training file for this lesson.

Making color changes using adjustment layers

Changing the color of an object in Adobe Photoshop is a pretty common practice, but how do you make it look realistic, and how can you recover the image if you make a mistake? What if you want to see three or four different variations? All these tasks can be completed easily and efficiently using adjustment layers. In this section, you'll change the color of a jacket on a model, and then, using the same adjustment layer, change it again, multiple times.

1   Choose File > Browse to open Adobe Bridge, or select the Go to Bridge button (⚫) in the upper right of the options bar that runs across the top of the workspace. Navigate to the ps10lessons folder, inside the pslessons folder you have created on your computer.

2   Double-click on ps1001.psd to open it in Photoshop. An image of a girl wearing a blue jacket appears.

You will take the original jacket and change the colors several times. You will also add a pattern to the jacket, using an adjustment layer.

Original image.   *Solid Color adjustment.*   *Pattern Adjustment.*

3   Choose File > Save As. In the Save As text field, type **ps1001_work**, then navigate to the ps10lessons folder. Choose Photoshop from the format drop-down menu and select Save.

The first thing that you will make is a selection with the Quick Selection tool. What's nice about using an adjustment layer is that you can paint a mask at any point in the process to modify your selection.

4   Select the Quick Selection tool (⟍), then click and drag on the jacket. If you miss some of the jacket, just paint a stroke over it to add it to the selection. If your selection went too far, hold down the Alt (Windows) or Option (Mac OS) key and click on the part of the selection that you want to deactivate.

You can also increase or decrease your Quick Selection tool size by pressing the [(left bracket) and] (right bracket).

Paint the jacket with the Quick Selection tool
to make a selection.

5   If the Layers palette is not visible, choose Window > Layers.

6   Click and hold on the Create New Fill or Adjustment Layer button (◑) at the bottom of the Layers palette.

7   Drag upwards and release on Hue/Saturation. The Hue/Saturation dialog box appears.

Hue refers to the color. By changing the hue, you can essentially change the color of an object without taking away any of the shading properties, which are normally created from the neutral gray value.

8   Check the Colorize checkbox and click and drag the Hue slider to the right to about the 70 point, or type **70** in the Hue text field.

In the next step, you will bring the saturation down a bit so the green you are creating is less bright.

9 Click and drag the Saturation slider to the right to about the 30 point, or type **30** into the Saturation text field. Press OK.

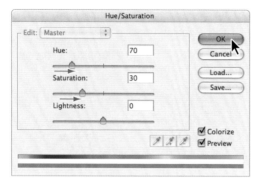

Change the color and saturation using the Hue/Saturation slider.

The jacket is now green, but your selection might not be as accurate as you would like. In the next section, you will use your painting tools to refine the mask attached to the adjustment layer.

10 Choose File > Save.

Refining the adjustment layer mask

If you take a look at the Layers palette you just created, you will see a Hue/Saturation Adjustment layer that has a mask thumbnail to the right of the layer thumbnail. You can activate this mask separately, and then use painting tools to refine it.

1 Alt+click (Windows) or Option+click (Mac OS) on the adjustment mask thumbnail, to the right of the Hue/Saturation thumbnail in the Layers palette.

The mask appears. You are not doing anything to the mask at this time, but you should take a look at what the actual mask looks like. Notice that where there is white, the hue and saturation changes take place. Where the mask is black, the changes are not occurring. Using the painting tools in Photoshop, you can edit a mask by painting black and white and even varying opacities to control the results of the adjustment layer.

Where the mask is white, the Hue/Saturation change is occurring.

2 To return to the normal layer view, click once on the word Background in the Layers palette.

You will now make changes to the adjustment mask thumbnail.

3 Click once on the adjustment mask thumbnail (to the right of the Hue/Saturation adjustment layer thumbnail).

Paint on the adjustment layer's mask to refine your selection.

4 Now, select the Brush tool (✐), and press **D** on your keyboard to set the colors to the default of black and white. Note that when in a mask, white is the foreground color and black is the background color.

5 Adjust your brush size as needed to paint the areas in the mask that might have not been selected, and thus not affected, when you created the adjustment layer.

You can make your brush size larger by pressing] (right bracket) and smaller by pressing [(left bracket). Make your brush harder by pressing Shift+] and softer by pressing Shift+[.

Paint the areas that may have been missed with your original selection.

6 Press **X** on your keyboard to swap the foreground and background colors. Black is now the foreground color.

7 Now, find a section of your image, perhaps the hand tucked in underneath the elbow, that has the Hue/Saturation change applied to it in error.

You will paint this area with the black paint brush, with the mask active, to block the change from occurring there.

 It is very easy to deselect the mask and paint on your actual image. Avoid this by clicking once on the Layer mask thumbnail, just to be sure!

8   Adjust your paint brush to the right size and softness, and paint over the hand to reveal the actual flesh color.

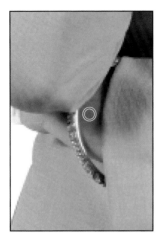

Eliminate the areas that may have been included,
in error, in the original selection.

*If you did such an accurate selection that you have no areas to repair, paint an area somewhere on your image anyway, just to see the effects of painting black on the mask. When you are done experimenting, press **X** to swap back to the white foreground color and repair the mask, as necessary.*

Adjusting the Hue/Saturation layer

Now that you have created an accurate mask, the next few steps will be rather simple. Perhaps your client has suggested that you use a more vibrant violet for the blazer. In this section, you will apply more color to the blazer and also edit the existing hue and saturation.

1   Double-click on the adjustment layer thumbnail to reopen the Hue/Saturation dialog box.

Double-click on the adjustment layer
thumbnail to change the settings.

2   Click and drag the Hue slider to the right to about the 260 point, or type **260** into the Hue text field.

3   Click and drag the Saturation slider to the right to about the 40 point, or type **40** into the Saturation text field. Press OK.

The green is now changed to a violet.

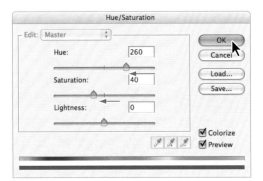

Readjusting the Hue and Saturation.

You can reopen the Hue/Saturation adjustment layer as many times as you like.

4   Choose File > Save, and keep the image open for the next section.

Adding a Pattern Fill layer

You can add a pattern and apply it to an image using a fill layer. This gives you the ability to scale the pattern, as well as adjust the opacity and blending modes. In this section, you will create a simple pattern that will be scaled and applied to the image using a new fill layer.

Defining the pattern

You can create a pattern in Photoshop out of any pixel information that you can select with the Rectangular Marquee. In this section, you will use the entire image area as the pattern, but you could also activate a smaller portion of an image and define it as a pattern.

1   Leave the ps1001_work.psd file open, and open an additional image. Choose File > Browse to open Adobe Bridge, or select the Go to Bridge button (📷) in the upper right of the options bar. Navigate to the ps10lessons folder, inside the pslessons folder you created on your computer.

2   Double-click on the file named ps1002.psd. An image of an ornate pattern appears.

Define a pattern from an entire image or just a rectangular selection.

Since you are using the entire image to create the pattern, you do not need to select anything.

3   Choose Edit > Define Pattern. The Pattern Name dialog box appears. Type **ornate** in the Name text field, and press OK.

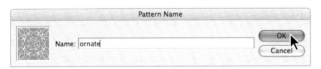

Defining a pattern for future use.

4   Choose File > Close to close the image without making any changes.

Applying the pattern

You will now apply the pattern to the jacket, using a new fill layer.

If you inadvertently close any images while working on a project, you can quickly reopen them by choosing File > Open Recent, and selecting the file from the drop-down list.

1   You spent a fair amount of time perfecting your mask, and you certainly don't want to have to do that again. Hold down the Ctrl (Windows) or Command (Mac OS) key and click on the Layer mask thumbnail of your adjustment layer. The mask is activated as a selection.

You can Ctrl or Command+click on any layer or mask to activate its contents as a selection.

2   Now that you have an active selection of the blazer, click and hold on the New Fill or Adjustment Layer button (⬤) at the bottom of the Layers palette, and choose Pattern. The Pattern Fill dialog box appears.

Your new pattern swatch should be visible. If it is not, click on the downward arrow to the right of the visible swatch to select a different pattern.

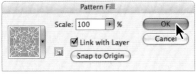

Select the Pattern Fill layer.   *The Pattern Fill dialog box appears.*

Result.

The result may be a little unexpected at first, as no scaling or blending mode has been applied to this fill pattern yet.

3   With the Pattern Fill dialog box still open, use the Scale slider to set the scale of the pattern to 25%, or type **25** into the Scale text field, and press OK.

4 With your new Fill layer still selected, click and hold on Normal in the blending mode drop-down menu on the Layers palette and choose Multiply.

Select the blending mode.　　　　*Result.*

You can experiment with other blending modes to see how it affects the final rendering of the pattern.

Want to do more with patterns? Photoshop also provides the Filter > Pattern Maker filter to create pattern presets, or you can fill a layer or selection with a custom pattern.

5 Choose File > Save and then File > Close to close this image.

Congratulations! You have finished the adjustment layer section of this lesson.

See Black & White adjustment layers in action!

Use the video that accompanies this lesson to gain a better understanding of how to take advantage of Black & White adjustment layers. Open the file PS10.swf located in the Videos folder to view the video training file for this lesson.

Using the new Black & White adjustment layer

Changing color images to grayscale is easy—you just switch the color mode using Image > Adjustments > Grayscale, right? Not if you want to achieve the best possible conversion. In this section, you will learn how to use the new Black & White adjustment layer.

1 Choose File > Browse to open Adobe Bridge, or select the Go to Bridge button (📷) in the upper right of the options bar (across the top of the workspace). Navigate to the ps10lessons folder, inside the pslessons folder you created on your computer.

2 Double-click on the file named ps1003.psd. A cityscape appears.

You will convert this cityscape image to grayscale.

3 Choose File > Save As; the Save As dialog box appears. Navigate to the ps10lessons folder. In the File name text field, type **ps1003_work** and select Photoshop from the Format drop-down menu. Press Save.

4 Click on the New Fill and Adjustment layer button (⬤) at the bottom of the Layers palette and select Black & White. The Black and White dialog box appears.

This window may appear very confusing at first. Without some assistance, it would be difficult to decipher which color adjustments are going to affect the image and where. Fortunately, Adobe has created some helpful features to make a better conversion easier for users.

5 Click and hold on the sky in the image; a pointing finger with a double arrow (👆) appears. The color that would make changes to that part of the image (the sky) is highlighted. You can see a border appear around the Blues swatch.

6 Remain holding down on the sky image, and drag to the right to notice that you automatically lightened the blues in the sky. Click and drag to the left to make the conversion darker.

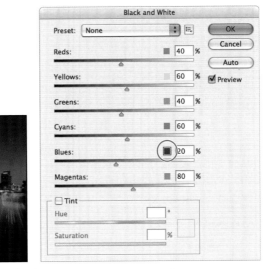

Click and drag in the sky area to automatically adjust the color.

7 Now, click on the darker streaming car lights in the image; the Reds are highlighted. Click and drag to the right to lighten them. You can just make visual adjustments for this image, but if you were concerned about dot values, you would want to have the Window > Info palette open.

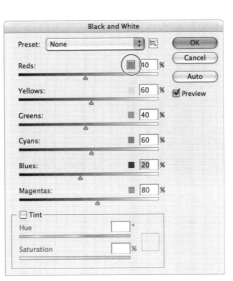

Click and drag on the car lights to lighten the conversion.

8 Press OK to close the Black & White dialog box to see the effects on your image. You can turn the visibility of this adjustment layer off and on by clicking on the visibility eye icon (👁) to the left of the Black & White 1 adjustment layer.

9 Choose File > Save. Keep the file open for the next section of this lesson.

Adding a tint

In this section, you will add a tint to your image. A tint of color can be added to an RGB image to create a nice effect.

 The Black & White adjustment layer is disabled in CMYK mode.

1 Double-click on the Black & White 1 layer thumbnail (●) icon (to the left of the Black & White 1 name and mask) in the Layer's palette. The Black and White dialog box appears with the current settings.

2 Check the Tint check box.

You can use the Hue and Saturation sliders to create custom colors, or click on the color box to the right of the sliders to assign a color from the color libraries.

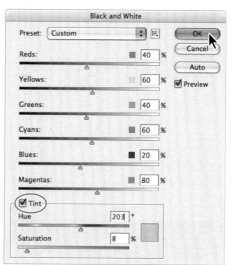

Apply a tint of color in the Black and White adjustment layer.

3 Click once on the Color box to the right of the Hue and Saturation slider in the Tint area of the Black & White dialog box. The Select Target Color dialog box appears.

4 Press the Color Libraries button; the Color Libraries dialog box appears with the present book (in the Book drop-down menu) set for Pantone® Solid Coated.

5 Type **642** quickly, with no pause between typing the numbers. There is no text field in this dialog box, so, by typing a Pantone number, you can easily locate it in the list of colors. Type too slowly and you could have an inaccurate color selection. You can try it again if PMS 642 C is not selected. Press OK to close the Color Libraries dialog box and OK again to close the Black and White dialog box. The color tint is assigned PMS 642 C.

6 Choose File > Save. Leave the file open for the next section of this lesson.

Applying a gradient to the adjustment layer

The next step is a simple one that adds an interesting blending technique for using adjustment layers. By applying a gradient to the mask, you can blend the Black & White effect into a color image.

1 Press **D** on your keyboard to make sure that you are back to the default foreground and background colors of black and white.

2 Click once on the layer mask thumbnail to select it.

3 Select the Gradient tool (▦), and press **0**. By pressing 0 you are assigning 100% opacity to the gradient.

4 Click and drag from the left side of the image to the right. A gradient is created in the same direction and angle as the line you draw.

When the Gradient tool is released, there is a blend from the black and white adjustment to the original color image. If you don't like the angle or transition, you can re-drag the gradient as many times as you want. Click and drag a short line for a shorter gradient transition, or click and drag a longer line for a more gradual transition.

If your colors are opposite of the ones in our example, your foreground and background colors could be reversed. Press **X** to reverse your colors and try again.

Click and drag with the Gradient tool to create a gradient mask on the layer mask thumbnail.

The Gradient tool can create straight-line, radial, angle, reflected, and diamond blends. Select the type of gradient from the options bar across the top of the Photoshop work area. If you want to drag a straight gradient line, hold down the Shift key while dragging to constrain the gradient to a 0°, 45°, or 90° angle.

5   Choose File > Save. Keep the file open for the next lesson.

Congratulations! You have completed the Black and White adjustment layer section of this lesson.

Layer Styles

By using Layer Styles, such as shadows, glows, and bevels, you can change the appearance of images on layers. Layer Styles are linked to the layer that is selected when the style is applied, but can also be copied and pasted to other layers. Combinations of styles can also be saved as a custom style to be applied to other layers.

Creating the text layer

In this section, you will create a text layer and apply a combination of effects to it. Then you will save the combined effects as a new style to apply to another layer. You should still have the file ps1003_work.psd open from the last lesson.

1   Select the Type tool (T) and click anywhere on the image. Type **CITY LIGHTS**.

2   Press Ctrl+A (Windows) or Command+A (Mac OS) to select all of the text. Alternatively, you can choose Select > All from the menu bar.

Get ready for a three-key command. It may seem awkward if you haven't used this combination before, but it is used in most other Creative Suite applications to resize text visually, and is a huge time-saver.

3   Hold down the Ctrl+Shift+> (Windows), or Command+Shift+> (Mac OS) and repeatedly press the > key. The text visually enlarges. You can change the combination to include the < key to visually reduce the size of the text. No particular size is needed; you can choose a size that you prefer.

If you would rather not use the key command, type **85** in the font size text field in the options bar at the top of the Photoshop workspace.

Next, you will find a typeface that you want to use. Again, no particular typeface is required for this exercise. Pick one that you like, but make sure that it is heavy enough to show bevel (edge) effects. The font in the example is Rockwell Extra Bold, but you can choose any available font from your font list.

4   Make sure the Type tool is still active and the text is selected by pressing Ctrl+A (Windows) or Command+ A (Mac OS), or choosing All from the Select menu.

5 Now, highlight the font family name in the Type tool options bar at the top of the Photoshop workspace and press the up or down arrow to scroll through your list of font families.

 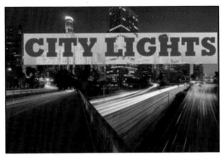

Select the text and then select the font name in the options bar.

Press the down or up arrows to change the font selection. Your font selection may differ from our example.

If you would rather not use the font shortcut, you can select the font you want from the Font family drop-down menu in the options bar.

If your Swatches palette is not visible, choose Window > Swatches to bring it forward.

6 With the text still selected, choose White from the Swatches palette. Press the Commit check mark (✔) in the far right of the options bar to commit your type changes.

 Do not leave the Type tool to select the Move tool and reposition the text. If you want to reposition your text, keep the Type tool selected and simply hold down the Ctrl (Windows) or Command (Mac OS) key while dragging.

Applying the Outer Glow layer style

Now you will apply a combination of layer effects to the text layer you just created.

1 Click on the text layer name CITY LIGHTS, which is to the right of the Text layer indicator in the Layers palette.

This selects the entire layer, not just the text.

2 Click and hold on the Add a layer style button (*fx*) at the bottom of the Layers palette, and release on Outer Glow. The Layer Style dialog box appears. The effect may be too subtle, so you will make some changes.

Select the City Lights layer.   *Select the Outer Glow style.*

There are many options available for each layer style. As a default, certain blending modes and opacities, as well as spread size and contours (edges), are already determined. In the next step, you will change the contour and the size of the outer glow.

What is a layer style contour?

When you create custom styles, you can use contours to create unique edge effects and transitions. As you can see in the samples shown below, the same style can look very different:

The Cone contour.

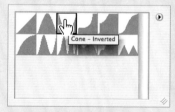

The Cone-Inverted contour.

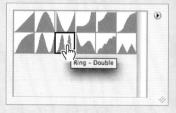

The Ring-Double contour.

3 Select the arrow to the right of the Contour thumbnail in the Quality section of the Layer Style dialog box. The Contour Presets window appears. Click on the Half Round contour. Double-click on the Half Round contour to close the window.

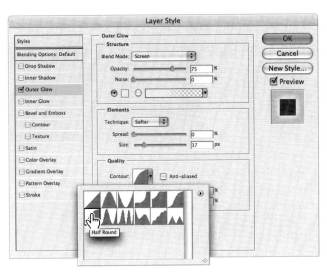

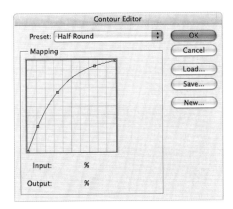

Select a preset contour for the Outer Glow style.

 You can open the Contour Editor and create your own custom contours by clicking on the Contour thumbnail instead of selecting the arrow to the right of the thumbnail.

Editing a contour.

Now you will change the size of the outer glow.

4   In the Elements section of the Layer Style dialog box, drag the Size slider to the number 60, or type **60** into the Size text field. The glow becomes more apparent.

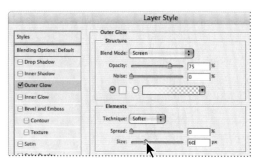

Drag the size slider to 60.   *Result.*

5   Keep the Layer Style dialog box open for the next step.

Applying the Bevel and Emboss layer style

You will now apply a second style. The Layer Style dialog box should still be open. If it is not, you can double-click on the word Effects (Layer Effects all) in the Layers palette. This reopens the Layer Styles dialog box.

1   Click on Bevel and Emboss in the Styles list on the left side of the Layer Style dialog box. The Bevel and Emboss effect is applied and the options appear on the right.

If you check a style, the options do not appear on the right. You must click on a style name for its options to appear.

2   From the Style drop-down menu in the Structure section of the Layer Style dialog box, choose Emboss.

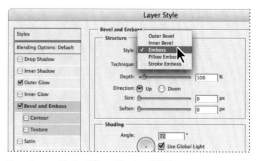

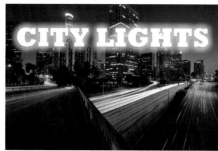

Experiment with the different Bevel and Emboss structures.   *Result.*

You can experiment with many bevel and embossing styles. You can change the Technique to be Smooth, Chisel Hard, or Chisel Soft, or even direct the embossing to go down or up, using the Direction radio buttons. Experiment with these options; no exact setting is needed for this exercise.

Changing the shading

You will now change the shading. In the Shading section of the Bevel and Emboss Layer Style dialog box, there are several choices that relate to light, including the Angle, Contour (as discussed earlier), or Highlight and Shadow colors. In this section, you will change the angle of the light and the highlight color.

1   In the Shading section to the right of Angle, there is a Direction of light source slider. You can change the current light angle by clicking and dragging the marker indicating the current light angle. Click and drag the marker to see how it affects the embossing style.

    Global light is checked as a default. This assures you that all other effects which rely on a light source use the same angle you determine for this style.

2   Click and hold to select Normal from the Highlight Mode blending drop-down menu.

3   Now, click on the white box to the right of Highlight Mode. This opens the Select highlight color picker and allows you to sample a color from your image, or create your own highlight color using the Picker. Choose any yellow-gold color; in this example, an RGB value of Red 215, Green 155, Blue 12 was used. Select OK.

4   Click on the Shadow color box, to the right of Shadow Mode, and change the color to blue. In this example, an RGB value of Red 30, Green 15, Blue 176 was used.

Select a different highlight color.

Select a different shadow color.

Result.

5   Press OK to close the Color Picker. Keep the Layer Style window open for the final step in this project.

Changing the fill opacity

In addition to setting opacity, which affects layer styles as well as the contents of the layer, you can adjust the fill opacity. The fill opacity will affect only the contents of the layer, keeping the opacity of any layer styles that have been applied at the original opacity. This is a very easy method to use to make text look like it is embossed on paper or engraved in stone, for instance.

1   Select the Blending Options: Default. This is the top-most item underneath the Styles palette.

2   Click and drag the Fill Opacity slider to the left. In the example, it was dragged to the 20% point. Keep the Layer Style dialog box open for the next part of the lesson.

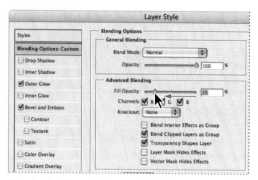

Changing the fill opacity does not affect the layer style opacity.   *Results.*

Saving the style

Now you will save the style you created.

1   With the Layer Styles dialog box still open, click on the New Style button, on the right side of the window. The New Style window appears.

2   Type **my glow** in the Name text field, and press OK.

Saving a style from combined styles.

3   Press OK in the Layer Styles dialog box. The style is now added to the Styles palette.

Accessing the style

Now you will create a new shape layer and apply the saved my glow style to it.

1 Click and hold on the Rectangle tool (□) to select the hidden Custom Shape tool (⬚).

2 Make sure that Shape layers is selected in the options bar at the top of the Photoshop workspace.

3 Click on the arrow to the right of the Custom Shape preview in the options bar and choose the Light Bulb 2 shape.

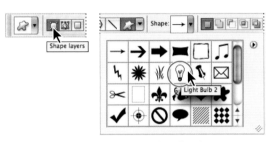

Confirm you are creating a layer shape.   *Choose the Light Bulb 2 shape.*

4 Press **D** on your keyboard to make sure you are back to the default black and white foreground and background colors.

5 Hold down the Shift key (to keep proportions correct) and click and drag in the image area to create the light bulb shape layer.

6 If any effects were automatically applied, delete them by clicking on the Effects sublayer and dragging it to the Delete button (🗑) in the lower right of the Layers palette.

7 If the Styles palette is not visible, choose Window > Styles. The Styles palette appears. It is easier to find your saved style if you view the palette as a list, rather than a thumbnail. You can change the view by selecting the palette menu and selecting Small List.

8 Scroll down if necessary, and then choose my glow.

Choose to view by Small List.   *Select your saved style, my glow.*

The same style is applied to the light bulb shape. Note that you may be viewing a path outline of the light bulb. Click once on the light bulb layer.

9 Choose File > Save.

Congratulations! You have finished the lesson on maximizing your layers.

Self study

Adjustment layers only affect the layers beneath them, leaving any layers on top of them in the layers palette unaffected.

1 To experiment with this concept, open the file named ps1005.psd.

2 Select the sky layer and create a Hue/Saturation adjustment layer for it.

3 Drag the Saturation slider all the way to the left, effectively creating an RGB grayscale image. Press OK.

4 Click and drag the adjustment layer up through the layers in the Layers palette to see how the position of the adjustment layer affects the layers beneath.

Review

Questions

1 Name three reasons why you should use an adjustment layer to change color in Photoshop.

2 What can you do to make a pattern fill layer blend in more naturally with the image underneath?

3 What does Global Lighting mean?

Answers

1 **a**. By using an adjustment layer, you keep the original image data intact.

b. Using the Color Picker and a Color adjustment layer, you can choose a specific hue, which you can then change again repeatedly until you get the color you want.

c. You can easily update or change the color by double-clicking on the adjustment layer thumbnail.

2 You can experiment with several blending modes to create a more natural blend with a pattern fill layer. In the example in this lesson, Multiply was selected, but others such as Darken and Lighten can create interesting results as well.

3 Global Lighting helps to keep the light source consistent between layer styles. This way, the light source for a shadow is the same as for the bevel and emboss, helping the image lighting effects look more realistic.

What you'll learn in this lesson:

- Opening an image as a Smart Object

- Converting a layer to a Smart Object

- Placing and editing a Smart Object

- Replacing the contents of a Smart Object layer

Using Smart Objects

Smart Objects allow you to transform pixel-based layers in new ways: you can scale, transform, and warp images without permanently destroying the original image data. In addition, Smart Objects create a link to their source files, which means that when you make changes to the source files, the Smart Objects are automatically updated with those changes.

Starting up

Smart objects will most likely change the way you work with layers. In this lesson, you will learn how to open new images as Smart Objects, in addition to how to convert existing layers into Smart Objects. Throughout this lesson, you will also have the opportunity to place and edit Smart Objects.

Before starting, make sure that your tools and palettes are consistent by resetting your preferences. See "Resetting Adobe Photoshop CS3 preferences" on page 4.

You will work with several files from the ps11lessons folder in this lesson. Make sure that you have loaded the pslessons folder onto your hard drive from the supplied DVD. See "Loading lesson files" on page 3.

See Lesson 11 in action!

Use the accompanying video to gain a better understanding of how to use some of the features shown in this lesson. Open the file PS11.swf located in the Videos folder to view the video training file for this lesson.

Creating a composition using Smart Objects

1   Choose File > Browse to open Adobe Bridge, or select the Go to Bridge (📷) button in the options bar. Navigate to the ps11lessons folder, then double-click on the image named ps1101.psd to open it in Photoshop. Alternatively, you can choose to Right-click (Windows) or Ctrl+click (Mac OS) and select Open with Photoshop CS3.

2   Choose File > Save As; the Save As dialog box appears. Navigate to the ps11lessons folder. In the File name text field, type **ps1101_work**, leave the format as Photoshop (PSD), and select Save. Keep the image open for the next section.

The ps1101.psd file.

Opening an image as a Smart Object

In this lesson, you will be bringing in multiple images of rainforest animals to create a photo illustration that could be used for a travel advertisement.

One of the defining characteristics of Smart Objects is the ability for layers to be transformed multiple times without the traditional resampling that occurs by default with Photoshop.

In this section, you will go through an exercise to help you understand the main difference between a standard Photoshop layer and a Smart Object.

1   Click on the eye icon (👁) to the left of the type layer named Visit the Rainforests of Palenque. This layer has been locked so you can't accidentally move it, and it will remain hidden for most of this lesson.

2 Select the Butterfly layer and then select the Move tool (⊕). Choose Edit > Free Transform to scale this layer. Alternatively, you can use the keyboard shortcut Ctrl+T (Windows) or Command+T (Mac OS).

3 Hold the Shift key, and then click and hold the bottom right corner of the transform box. Drag toward the center of the box to make the box smaller. Holding the Shift key ensures that the width and height are constrained proportionally.

In the options bar at the top of the screen, note that as you scale down, the percentage values begin to decrease. Scale the butterfly until the horizontal values are approximately 25%. Press the Enter/Return key to commit the transformation, or you can press the check mark (✔) on the right side of the options bar.

You can view the scale percentage in the options bar.

You have reduced the width and height of this layer by 75%. This also means that the original pixel data has been lost through the scaling process (also called downsampling). This creates problems if you decide at some point to make the image on this layer larger.

4 Choose Edit > Free Transform, or use the keyboard shortcut of Ctrl+T (Windows) or Command+T (Mac OS) to turn the transform bounding box on again. Press the Shift key, then click and drag the bottom right corner of the transform box diagonally downward and to the right to scale the image to approximately 400%. Remember to watch the percentage as it changes in the options W (Width) and H (Height) text fields. Press the Return key to commit the scale transform.

The butterfly layer after rescaling.

The image is fuzzy and pixelated because you have now enlarged the layer information, forcing Photoshop to fill in pixel information. This is called destructive editing because the original layer lost its detail through the resampling process.

You will now open the same image as a Smart Object so that you can see the benefit of non-destructive editing.

5   Click on the eye icon (👁) next to the Butterfly layer to turn the layer's visibility off. You will turn it back on shortly so you can compare the two layers.

6   Choose File > Open As a Smart Object. Navigate to the ps11lessons folder and choose the ps1102.psd file. Press Open to open the image in a new document window. In the Layers palette, note that the thumbnail for the layer is now a Smart Object thumbnail. All Smart Objects have a Smart Object icon in the lower right of the layer thumbnail to help you distinguish them from standard layers.

The image is opened as a Smart Object.

7   Reposition the image windows to see both the ps1101_work.psd and the ps1102.psd images.

8   Select the Move tool (➤+). Click and drag the butterfly image from ps1102.psd into your ps1101_work.psd image, using the Move tool to reposition the new layer at the bottom of the screen. The bottom of the butterfly wings should be touching the bottom of the image.

9   In the Layers palette, double-click directly on the layer name, ps1102. When the layer name becomes highlighted, type **Butterfly 2** and press Return to commit the change.

10   Choose Window > ps1102.psd to bring that image forward again and choose File > Close.

11   Make sure the ps1101_work file is forward and choose Edit > Free Transform or use the keyboard shortcut Ctrl+T (Windows) or Command+T (Mac OS).

12   Press the Shift key, then click and hold the top right corner of the transform box, and drag toward the center of the box. Scale the butterfly down in size until the horizontal value is approximately 25%. Press the Return key to commit the transformation.

13 Use the keyboard shortcut Ctrl+T (Windows) or Command+T (Mac OS). Press the Shift key, then click and hold then drag the top right corner of the transform box away from the center to scale the image up to 100%. Press Return to commit the change.

14 In the Layers palette, click on the eye icon (👁) to the left of the Butterfly thumbnail. Readjust the layers as needed to compare the two images. Notice that the detail has not been lost, because Smart Objects maintain their original pixel data even if they are scaled and resized.

*A. Standard layer, scaled and resized. **B**. Smart Object, scaled and resized.*

Converting a layer to a Smart Object

In the last exercise, you created a Smart Object by using the Open as Smart Object feature. However, this is not always ideal. For example, perhaps you have a document in which you have already added several layers and then you realize that you will be performing operations that require the use of Smart Objects. Rather than opening the original images again as Smart Objects, you can convert existing layers to Smart Objects.

1 Drag the Butterfly layer to the Delete button (🗑) at the bottom of the Layers palette. The Butterfly layer is deleted.

2 Select the Butterfly 2 layer in the Layers palette. Choose Edit > Free Transform. This time you will enter a scale amount into the W (width) and H (height) text fields in the options bar.

3 Type **35** into the W (width) text field and press the Maintain aspect ratio icon (⧉) in between the W and H text fields. Press Enter/Return to commit the transformation. The layer is scaled to 35%.

4 In the Layers palette, select the Toucan layer and then click on the eye icon (👁) next to the left of the Toucan layer thumbnail; the layer is now visible. You will now convert this layer to a Smart Object.

5 Choose Layer > Smart Objects > Convert to Smart Object.

Changing a layer to a Smart Object.

There is no visible change in the image, but the Smart Object icon (▣) in the Toucan layer now appears in the lower right corner indicating that it is now a Smart Object.

6 Choose Edit > Free Transform, or use the keyboard shortcut Ctrl+T (Windows) or Command+T (Mac OS) to transform the toucan image. Grab the top right corner of the bounding box, and, while holding the Shift key, click and drag a corner point to scale it to about half its current size. If necessary, reposition the image into the lower left corner. Press Enter/Return to commit the change.

Placing a Smart Object from Adobe Bridge

In addition to opening new documents as Smart Objects, and converting existing layers to Smart Objects, you can also use Adobe Bridge to place images directly as Smart Objects.

1 Choose File > Place; the Place dialog box appears. Navigate to the ps11lessons folder, and select the ps1104.psd file, and press Place. This places the parrot image into your ps1101_work.psd file.

When documents are placed, they become Smart Objects by default. Note the large "X" on the layer; this is a bounding box that allows you to transform the Smart Object before confirming the placement.

2   Click and drag the parrot image until the bottom right corner snaps against the bottom right corner of your work file. Hold the Shift key, and then click on the top left anchor point of the transform bounding box. With the Shift key still pressed, click and drag toward the center to scale the image down in size. Scale the parrot until the top is approximately even with the top of the toucan image.

Scale the parrot so that it is approximately the same size as the toucan.

3   Select the Commit button (✔) in the options bar, or press the Enter/Return key to commit the change. Remember that because this is a Smart Object by default, you can scale it back to its original size and still retain the original detail.

4   In the Layers palette, double-click the layer name ps1104. When the layer name becomes highlighted, type the name **Parrot**.

Editing a Smart Object

There are additional benefits to Smart Objects besides their ability to be resized without loss of detail. To fully understand these benefits, you should know a little bit about how Smart Objects work. When a layer is a Smart Object, Photoshop preserves the original content of the source file by embedding it into the current file. In this exercise, you will learn how to edit the contents of Smart Objects. You will also find out how multiple Smart Object layers can be modified at the same time, how to replace the source for Smart Objects, and even how to export the contents of a Smart Object.

1 Choose File > Open As Smart Object. Navigate to the ps11lessons folder, select the ps1105.psd file, and press Open to open the image in a new window. Notice that the title bar of the window reads ps1105 as Smart Object-1. This is not the original file, but rather a copy of the original file.

An image opened as a Smart Object.

2 Select the Move tool (✛), then click and drag the butterfly image into your ps1101_work.psd image. Note that the layer is named ps1105 and has the Smart Object thumbnail.

3 In the Layers palette, double-click on the layer name ps1105. When the text becomes highlighted, type **Butterfly 3**. Press Return.

4 Select the ps1105.psd image, and choose File > Close, or select the Close button in the document window. When prompted to save the file, choose Save.

5 When the Save As window appears, navigate to the ps11lessons folder, then type **Butterfly 3** in the File name text field. Choose Photoshop (PSD) from the format drop-down menu, and press Save. As noted above, this Smart Object file is separate from the original file and will always behave as a Smart Object when opened.

6 In your ps1101_work.psd file, select the Butterfly 3 layer, and use your Move tool to drag it to the center of your image window. Choose Edit > Free Transform, or use the keyboard shortcut Ctrl+T (Windows) or Command+T (Mac OS). Click and hold the Shift key while dragging any corner anchor point. Scale the butterfly to approximately 20%. Press Enter/Return to commit the change. Reposition the butterfly to the upper right corner.

7 Choose Image > Adjustments. Note that virtually all the options are grayed out. This is because image adjustments such as Levels and Curves are destructive by nature. Release the mouse without making a choice.

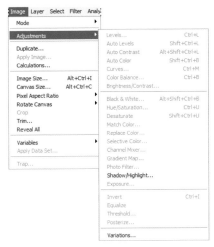

Adjustment commands are grayed out because the layer is a Smart Object.

8 Click on the Brush tool (✓). Position your cursor over the image. Don't click, but notice that the non-editable icon (⊘) appears. You cannot paint on this layer because that would be destructive.

So, what if you need to modify the layer? Perhaps you want to selectively dodge and burn parts of the image or use image adjustment commands. Photoshop must rasterize your Smart Object before you can use common editing tools. You could still apply an adjustment layer to perform non-destructive changes; it is only destructive layer changes that are forbidden.

9 Select the Blur tool (◊) from the Tools palette, or press the keyboard shortcut **R**. Click anywhere on the butterfly; a warning dialog appears, informing you that the layer will be rasterized. Press OK to rasterize the image.

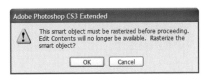

Press OK to rasterize the layer.

10 Click and drag the Blur tool several times over the edges of the butterfly to see the blur effect. You are now able to edit the image because it has been converted to pixels. However, it has also lost its Smart Object status.

All the editing tools, such as dodge, burn, clone stamp, and the eraser, are destructive and therefore not usable on a Smart Object layer.

11 Choose Edit > Free Transform, or use the keyboard shortcut Ctrl+T (Windows) or Command+T (Mac OS). While holding the Shift key, click and drag any corner anchor point to make the layer larger. Scale until you see approximately 300% in the W (width) and H (height) text fields in the options bar. Press the Return to commit the transform. The butterfly is slightly blurry now because the standard rules of resampling apply.

12 Drag the Butterfly 3 layer from the Layers palette to the Delete icon (🗑) in the Layers palette. You will be adding the layer again in the next exercise.

Editing the contents of a Smart Object

In the last exercise, you saw how you could modify a Smart Object by rasterizing the layer. The problem with this method is that rasterizing the layer removes the unique characteristics of the Smart Object layer. Using the method shown, you will edit the contents of the embedded Smart Object without changing its Smart Object status.

1 Choose File > Place, and navigate to the ps11lessons folder. Select the ps1105.psd file and click Place. The butterfly image appears in your screen.

2 Holding the Shift key, click and drag any corner anchor point towards the center until you see an amount close to 25% in the W and H text fields in the options bar. Reposition the butterfly to the upper right corner of the image. Press the Return key to commit the change.

3 In the Layers palette, double-click on the layer name ps1105 to highlight the text name. Type **Butterfly 4** and press Return.

4 Now, double-click the Butterfly 4 layer thumbnail in the Layers palette. (Do not click on the layer name or the layer itself, but specifically on the Smart Object thumbnail.) A dialog box appears, reminding you that you need to save the document after you edit the contents. Press OK. The file ps1105.psd is now open on your screen.

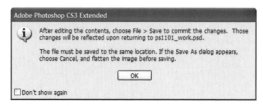

A Warning dialog box appears when you edit a Smart Object.

By double-clicking on the Smart Object layer, you open the original file as a separate document. You'll now make some adjustments to the original image. In this case, you will be adjusting the hue and saturation.

5   Click on the Create new fill or adjustment layer icon (●) at the bottom of the Layers palette, and choose Hue/Saturation from the menu.

Select the Create new fill or adjustment layer button.

The Hue/Saturation window appears. Using the adjustment layer ensures that your original pixel data remains untouched.

 For more information about adjustment layers, please review Lesson 10, "Taking Layers to the Max."

6   Drag the Hue slider to the left to approximately the –180 mark, or type **–180** in the Hue texbox. This adjusts the color of the butterfly to blue. Press OK.

7   Choose File > Save. This is the crucial step. As noted in the dialog box in step 3, you must save the current document without renaming it. Choose File > Close to close the image.

8   Select the ps1101_work.psd file, and note that the blue butterfly has been updated. This is because Butterfly 4 is a Smart Object layer connected, or linked, to the ps1105.psd file.

9   Double-click on the Butterfly 4 layer thumbnail to reopen the source file. The warning dialog box you saw previously appears. Press OK.

 This dialog box can be turned off by clicking the Don't Show Again checkbox in the lower left corner.

10 Double-click the adjustment layer icon in the Hue/Saturation layer to reopen the Hue/Saturation dialog box.

*The Hue/Saturation
adjustment layer icon.*

11 Click and drag the Saturation slider to -60, or type **-60** in the Saturation text field. This tones down the bright blue. Press OK.

12 Choose File > Save, and then File > Close to close the file.

Using this combination of adjustment layers and Smart Objects allows you to have a tremendous amount of flexibility with your layers. Adjustment layers and Smart Objects individually allow for very flexible documents; when used together, they encourage you to experiment without fear of destroying the integrity of the original image. As you will see in the next exercise, this ability to edit the contents of a Smart Object has even more power when you have multiple Smart Objects.

Modifying multiple Smart Object layers

Another benefit of Smart Object layers is that multiple layers can be modified at the same time.

1 In the main composition, ps1101_work.psd, click and drag the Butterfly 4 layer down to the Create a new layer button (⬛) in the Layers palette to duplicate it. Select the Move tool (⊹), then click and drag the copy to the far left, next to the yellow butterfly.

Duplicate the Butterfly layer.

You can also duplicate layers by choosing Layer > Smart Objects > New Smart Objects Via Copy.

2 In the Layers palette, double-click the layer name Butterfly 4 Copy. When the layer name becomes highlighted, type **Butterfly 5** to rename the layer.

3   Double-click on the Butterfly 5 layer thumbnail in the Layers palette to open the original ps1105.psd image. Press OK to dismiss the dialog box if necessary; this is the same dialog box, asking if you want to save the file. You will now add a Curves adjustment layer to increase the contrast of both butterflies.

4   Press the Create new fill or adjustment layer icon (⬤) at the bottom of the Layers palette, and choose Curves from the menu. The Curves dialog box appears.

5   Position your cursor in the middle of the curves graph, then click and drag the line upward and to the left to increase the brightness and contrast. If you would like to match our image, we used an input value of 105 and an output value of 138. Press OK when done.

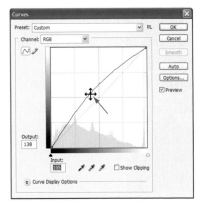

Adjust the curve.

6   Choose File > Save. Both butterflies are now brighter. Multiple Smart Object layers can be linked to the same source file. When the source file is changed in some way, all the linked files will also change.

7   Choose File > Close to close the document.

Replacing the contents of a Smart Object layer

Because multiple Smart Object layers can be controlled by the original file, you will now take it a step further and change the source file of the two Smart Object layers. To understand the usefulness of this exercise, imagine that you have created several butterflies and rotated, resized, and warped them in different ways. A replacement image is found, and instead of having to delete the existing layers and repeat the same steps, you can simply replace the existing butterfly image with a new one, and all the transformations will stay the same.

1   In your ps1101_work.psd image, click on Butterfly 5 in the Layers palette and then select Edit > Free Transform, or use the keyboard shortcut Ctrl+T (Windows) or Command+T (Mac OS), to transform the first butterfly in the left corner. Hold the Shift key, then click the top left anchor point of the transform bounding box, and drag downward and to the right, scaling the image down to approximately 15%.

2 Position your cursor slightly below and to the right of the bottom–right corner anchor point. A cursor with a rounded arrow appears. Click and drag to the left to rotate the image approximately -45 degrees. Reposition the image slightly to the right of the brown butterfly. Press Return to commit the transformation.

3 Select the Butterfly 4 layer in the Layers palette. Press Ctrl+T (Windows) or Command+T (Mac OS) to transform the layer. You will now use Photoshop's Warp feature to simulate the butterfly moving through the air.

4 Choose Edit > Transform > Warp. Feel free to create your own warping effect; however, for our effect, we clicked and dragged the top left corner down and to the right until the wing began to curl.

Clicking and dragging the warp handles to warp the image.

5 Press Return when you are satisfied with the effect.

Now you will replace the two butterflies with a new image, while maintaining the transformations you created.

6   Choose Layer > Smart Objects > Replace Contents. Locate the ps11lessons folder, select ps1106.psd, and press Place. Both the images update automatically, while retaining their transformations.

Replacing Smart Objects.

This technique can be extremely helpful, because it saves you from having to repeat similar steps.

See Smart Filters in action!

Use the video that accompanies this lesson to gain a better understanding of how to take advantage of Smart Filters. Open the file PS11.swf located in the Videos folder to view the video training file for this lesson.

Working with Smart Filters

Smart filters are one of the most exciting parts of Photoshop CS3. Now that you have a good foundation for Smart Objects, the concept of Smart Filters shouldn't be too hard to follow. A Smart Filter is simply one of the Photoshop filters applied to a Smart Object layer. Filters are usually destructive, i.e., any effect applied to a layer becomes more difficult to remove. When you use a Smart Filter, any filter you apply is not permanent. Effects can be toggled off and on, combined, or deleted. As you will see in this exercise, you can work with the built-in mask of a filter effect to customize your filter effects in ways that were previously not possible in Photoshop.

In this exercise, you will be applying a combination of two filters to create an effect of motion, then you will use the layer mask to refine the effect with the Brush tool.

1   Select the Butterfly 4 layer, and choose Filter > Sharpen > Smart Sharpen. The Smart Sharpen window appears. If necessary, change the Amount value to 100% and the Radius to 1.0, then press OK. The effect is applied; the butterfly should have a bit more detail.

2   In the Layers palette, below the Butterfly 4 layer, there is a Smart Filters line with a white thumbnail to the left. Immediately below that is the Smart Sharpen filter effect. These two lines were automatically added when you applied the filter. You will now examine how they work.

3   Click on the eye icon (👁) next to the Smart Sharpen filter effect. This turns the Smart Sharpen filter off and allows you to view the original image. Click in the now-empty space to toggle the filter back on.

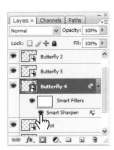

Clicking on the eye icon will toggle a filter effect on and off.

You will now add a Blur filter in addition to the Smart Sharpen filter.

4   Choose Filter > Blur > Motion Blur. You may have to click and drag down and to the left inside the filter preview window to see the image. In the Motion Blur window, type **50** in the Distance text field. This creates a blur of 50 pixels in both directions. Now you will change the angle of the blur.

5   Click on the right side of the angle dial, and click and drag counter-clockwise until the angle value is approximately –65 degrees, then press OK. Don't worry about how the effect looks; you will be editing it shortly.

6   In the line beneath the Smart Filters, the Motion Blur effect now is above the Smart Sharpen effect.

7   Click on the eye icon to the left of the Motion Blur effect. The Smart Sharpen effect is still active; it is just hidden by the blur. Click the eye icon in the Motion Blur line to bring the Motion Blur effect back.

This feature of Smart Filters is great, but what if you want only part of the filter to be applied to the layer? In this example, combining Sharpen and Blur filters doesn't make much sense. However, with a bit of masking, you can allow certain areas to remain sharp, while other areas are blurred.

8 Select the white thumbnail in the line marked Smart Filters, immediately above the two filter effects. This is the default layer mask that is created whenever you add a Smart Filter. It will allow you to mask out the areas where you don't want the filter effects to appear, while leaving the areas you do want filtered alone.

Select the Smart Filter mask.

9 Select the Brush tool (✐) and click and hold on the arrow to the right of the Brush Preset picker in the options bar. Select the 45 Pixel Soft Brush preset. Click on the options bar to make the Brush Preset picker disappear.

For more information about working with Photoshop brushes, please review Chapter 8, "Painting and Retouching."

10 Press **D** on your keyboard to revert the foreground and background colors back to the default of black and white. Press **X** on your keyboard to swap the foreground and background colors. Black is now the foreground color and white is the background color.

11 Place your brush at the top of the butterfly, and begin painting from left to right and then downward. As you paint, the filter effects are concealed by the layer mask you are adding.

For an in-depth look at layer masks, please review Chapters 9, "Getting to Know Layers."

12 Continue painting downward until the bottom half of the butterfly is blurred. Press the letter **X** on your keyboard to swap the foreground color to white. Now, paint over the top half again, and notice how the effect is revealed again. By toggling between white and black, and painting on the Smart Filter mask, you can reveal or conceal the filter effects.

13   Press **X** on your keyboard to set black as the foreground color, then paint the mask to hide virtually all the filter effect at the top part of the image. There are also areas at the bottom that you will want to hide. You want your image to look approximately the same as the example shown below. The effect is still not exactly what is desired, but, in the next section, you will fine-tune the motion blur effect.

The lesson file at this point.

Modifying a Smart Filter

Once you add a Smart Filter, you can go back and modify the effect, even if you've added a mask, as in this case.

1   In the Butterfly 4 layer, double-click on the Motion Blur effect; the Motion Blur window appears. You may have to click and drag down and to the left inside the filter preview window to see the image. Change the angle to 87 degrees by clicking and dragging the dial to the right. Press OK when you are done.

Changing the angle of the motion blur now requires you to go back with the paintbrush and modify the mask.

2   Click on the layer mask thumbnail in the Smart Filters line to select it. Then, begin to paint from the top down, leaving just a blur at the bottom of the butterfly. If you mask out too much of the effect, you can press **X** to switch to white as the foreground color to restore the effect in the desired areas.

3   Click on the eye icon (👁) next to the Smart Filter mask. This turns the mask off completely, and can help identify areas affected by a filter that you may have missed. Click to turn the mask back on and clean up any areas where you don't want the filter applied.

Change the visibility of the effect.

4   In the Layers palette, click on the eye icon to the left of the Visit the Rainforests type layer on the top. Select the Move tool, then click and drag to reposition the layers as needed.

5   Choose File > Save. Congratulations! You have finished this lesson.

The completed lesson file.

Self study

In this section, you can complete some exercises on your own. Use adjustment layers to adjust the brightness, contrast, hue, and saturation of the lesson files.

Currently, the individual butterfly and bird images do not blend as well into the background as they could. Using the techniques laid out in "Editing the contents of a Smart Object" exercise, add adjustment layers to the objects in the photo-illustration and fine-tune the appearance of the individual objects. Try to make the individual layers match each other as much as possible to create a cohesive photo illustration.

Creating multiple Smart Objects

In this lesson, you learned how to work with Smart Objects in their various forms. Create additional copies of the butterfly or bird images, and experiment with creating a collage. Apply filters to your existing Smart Objects. For different effects, try applying a black-to-white gradient on a Smart Filter mask to achieve a smooth transition that would be difficult to achieve using just the Brush tool alone.

Working with Illustrator files

If you have Adobe Illustrator, you can also place .AI files into Photoshop files as a Smart Object layer. They work in similar ways. Create an image in Illustrator, and place it into Photoshop. Create multiple copies of the Illustrator layer, and then modify the original AI file to see the changes applied to the layers in the Photoshop file.

Review

Questions

1 What are three ways that you can create a Smart Object layer?

2 Why would you convert a standard layer to a Smart Object layer? What are the advantages of doing so?

3 How do you replace the contents of a Smart Object layer? When would you do so?

4 What are Smart Filters and what are the benefits of using them?

Answers

1 You can bring an image into an existing file as a Smart Object by choosing File > Open as Smart Object and selecting the file, choosing File > Place, or, when using Adobe Bridge, selecting the file and choosing File > Place > Into Photoshop. If an image is currently inside a document and you would like to convert it to a Smart Object, select the layer in the Layers palette and choose Layer > Smart Objects > Convert to Smart Objects.

2 A Smart Object layer can be resized indefinitely without losing resolution due to resampling.

3 You can replace the contents of a Smart Object layer by choosing Layer > Smart Objects > Replace Contents. You might use this technique if you wanted to replace one image with another.

4 Any filter applied to a Smart Object is a Smart Filter. Smart filters appear in the Layers palette below the Smart Object layer to which they are applied. Because you can adjust, remove, or hide Smart Filters, they are non-destructive.

What you'll learn in this lesson:

- Working with filters.
- Fading filter effects
- Using the Filter Gallery
- Taking advantage of Smart Filters
- Using the new and improved Vanishing Point filter

Using Adobe Photoshop Filters

Filters allow you to apply artistic effects to your images. You can make images look as though they were sketched with chalk, drawn with a graphic pen, or even add perspective to them. In this lesson, you will learn how to use filters to apply interesting effects to your images.

Starting up

Before starting, make sure that your tools and palettes are consistent by resetting your preferences. See "Resetting Adobe Photoshop CS3 preferences" on page 4.

You will work with several files from the ps12lessons folder in this lesson. Make sure that you have loaded the pslessons folder onto your hard drive from the supplied DVD. See "Loading lesson files" on page 3.

See Lesson 12 in action!

Use the accompanying video to gain a better understanding of how to use some of the features shown in this lesson. Open the file PS12.swf located in the Videos folder to view the video training file for this lesson.

Filter Basics

Filters are accessed using the Filter menu. When you select certain filters, the Filter Gallery opens; other filters, when selected, open their own dedicated controls. Some, like the Clouds filter, don't even have a dialog box.

Filters are always applied to the layer you currently have selected and cannot be applied to Bitmap mode or indexed-color images. Note that some filters, such as Brush Strokes and Sketch, work only in the RGB mode and are not available when working in the CMYK mode.

Starting to use filters

Before starting, you may want to view the file that you are going to create.

1 Choose File > Browse or select the Go to Bridge button (🔖) in the options bar to open Adobe Bridge. Navigate to the ps12lessons folder and open the file ps1201_done.psd. A file of several robots and a package appears.

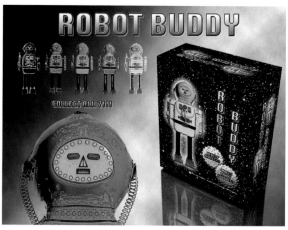

The completed lesson file.

2 You can keep this file open for reference, or choose File > Close to close it.

Using the Clouds filter

In this lesson, you will use the Clouds filter to build a smoke-like background. The Clouds filter generates a cloud pattern, using random values from the selected foreground and background colors.

1   Choose File > Browse or select the Go to Bridge button (📷) in the options bar to open Adobe Bridge. Navigate to the ps12lessons folder and open the file ps1201.psd.

2   Choose File > Save As. In the Save As dialog box, navigate to the ps12lessons folder and type **ps1201_work** in the File name text field. Choose Photoshop PSD from the format drop-down menu and click Save.

3   If the Layers palette is not visible, select Window > Layers. Click on New Background to activate this layer.

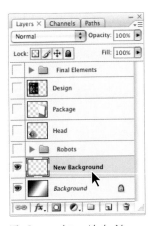

The Layers palette, with the New Background layer selected.

4   Many filters in Photoshop render differently depending on your current foreground and background colors. Press **D** on your keyboard to return to the default colors of black and white.

5   At the bottom of the Tools palette, double-click the foreground color, black. The Color Picker opens.

6 In the RGB text fields, enter these values: R: **55**, G: **71**, B: **92**. Then press OK. Your foreground color has been changed. You are now ready to apply the Clouds filter.

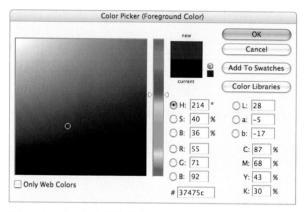

Enter custom values in the Color Picker.

7 Choose Filter > Render > Clouds.

A cloud pattern is generated, using random values of the foreground and background colors.

8 Choose File > Save. Keep this file open for the next part of this lesson.

To achieve a more high-contrast effect, press the Alt key (Windows) or the Option key (Mac OS) while selecting the Clouds filter.

Fading your filter

Now that you have made some clouds, you'll blend them into the Gradient Background layer below the New Background layer. The Fade command gives you the opportunity to change the opacity and blending mode of a filter effect immediately after you have applied it. Fade also works with the eraser, painting, and color adjustment tools.

1 Choose Edit > Fade Clouds. The Fade dialog box appears. Check the Preview option to preview the effect.

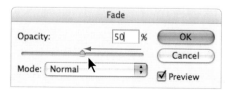

The Fade dialog box.

If Fade Clouds is not available, you did something else with the file after using the Clouds filter. Use the Window > History palette to select the Clouds state, then select Edit > Fade Clouds again.

2 Drag the slider to the left to adjust the opacity from 100% down to 50%. Leave the Mode drop-down menu set to Normal, then press OK.

The fading of the Clouds filter gives the gradient background a new, smoke-like effect.

3 In the top section of the Layers palette, click on the Set the blending mode drop-down menu and select Multiply. Keep this file open for the next part of this lesson.

Select Multiply.

Result.

Using the Filter Gallery

The Filter Gallery allows you to apply more than one filter to an image at a time, and rearrange the order in which the filters are applied.

Note that not all filters are available in the Filter Gallery, and that the Filter Gallery is not available in CMYK, Lab, or Bitmap mode.

1 With ps1201.psd open, click the eye icon (👁) next to the layer group named Robots. Three robots appear.

2 Expand the layer group by clicking on the triangle immediately to the left of the Robots layer group. This displays the Robot 1, 2, and 3 layers that are included in this group.

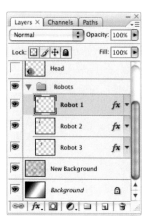

The Layers palette with the Robot 1 layer selected.

3 Select the Robot 1 layer.

4 Press **D** on your keyboard to return to the default foreground and background colors of black and white.

5   Choose Filter > Filter Gallery. The Filter Gallery dialog box appears.

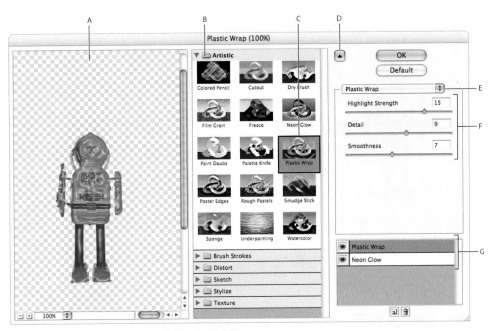

A. *The Preview pane.* *B*. *Filter categories.* *C*. *Thumbnail of filter.*
D. *Show/Hide filter thumbnails.* *E*. *Filters drop-down menu.* *F*. *Options for the selected filter.* *G*. *List of filter effects.*

Applying filters in the Gallery

You'll now apply several filters to create different versions of the robot image. When you apply
a filter from the filter categories located in the center portion of the window, a preview of
the image with the filter applied is displayed in the Preview pane. Along the right side of the
window, options for the selected filter are displayed.

1   In the filter categories section, expand the triangle next to the Stylize folder to reveal the
Glowing Edges filter.

2 Click the Glowing Edges thumbnail to add a glow to the edges of areas with color; your robot now has bright neon glowing edges. Press OK to apply the filter.

The robot with the Glowing Edges filter applied.

You'll now apply additional filters to create more versions of the robot.

3 Select the Robot 2 layer in the Layers palette.

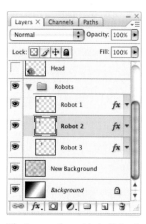

The Layers palette with the Robot 2 layer selected.

4 Choose Filter > Filter Gallery to apply a filter to this layer. Do not select the Filter Gallery menu item that appears first under the Filter menu. That is where your last-used filter appears and it does not allow you to change options. Choose the Filter Gallery menu item that appears under Extract.

5   Click on the triangle to the left of Artistic to expand and show the artistic filters, then click on the Neon Glow thumbnail. The Neon Glow filter is applied to the image in the Preview pane.

Neon Glow adds a high-tech look to the robot. This filter is useful for colorizing an image while softening its look. You can select a custom glow color from the Color Picker, which you will modify later in this section.

6   In the Filter options panel (on the right side of the dialog box), click on the color box next to Glow Color. The Color Picker opens.

7   Set the RGB values to R: **26**, G: **199**, B: **67**, then press OK.

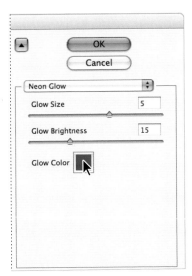

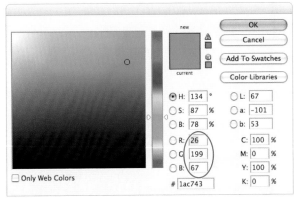

Double-click on the Glow Color.   *Enter custom values in the Color Picker.*

Now you'll apply a second filter to this layer.

8   Continuing to work in the Filter Gallery, click the New Effect Layer button (⊐) located at the bottom of filter effects area. This adds a new filter instance. There are now two instances of Neon Glow applied.

9   Click the triangle to the left of Artistic to close that filter category, and then click the triangle to the left of Texture to expand this category.

10 In the filter categories section, select Mosaic Tile. Mosaic Tiles renders the robot so that it looks like it is made of small tiles.

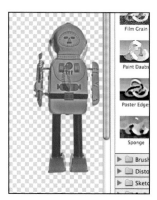

The Neon Glow and Mosaic Filters.

11 In the filter effects area of the Filter Gallery, click and drag Mosaic Tiles below Neon Glow. Notice how the overall effect changes, as Neon Glow is now the primary effect with Mosaic Tile as the secondary effect. Press OK.

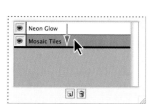

Switching the Filter Effects layer order.

12 Choose File > Save.

You can add more effect layers and drag them into different orders to produce new effects. Show and hide the visibility of each effect by clicking on the eye icon next to each effect layer.

Taking advantage of Smart Filters

The filters you applied in the last section were destructive, meaning that any changes you made using these filters affected your original image data. As you discovered in Lesson 11, "Using Smart Objects," Smart Filters are a non-destructive way to apply filters to an image. In this lesson, you will practice applying filters using the Smart Filter feature.

Applying a Smart Filter

1 Select the Robot 3 layer in the Layers palette.

2 Choose Filter > Convert for Smart Filters. A warning dialog box may appear, advising you that the layer will be made into a Smart Object. Press OK.

A Smart Object icon appears in the lower right of the Robot 3 layer. This indicates that this layer is now converted for use with Smart Filters. Next, you will apply some filters in the Filter Gallery, and then update and change the way the filters are applied to the image.

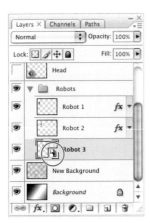

Robot 3 layer is now a Smart Object.

3 Make sure that the Robot 3 layer is selected, and then choose Filter > Filter Gallery.

Note that the last filters you used are applied to the layer by default although these can be changed.

4 Click on Mosaic Tiles (that was applied when the filter was previously used) in the filter effects area in the lower right side of the Filter Gallery dialog box.

5 In the center Filter categories section, expand the Artistic category and select Plastic Wrap. The Plastic Wrap filter replaces the Mosaic Tiles filter. Press OK to apply this new filter.

You'll now change the color of the Neon Glow so that it is different from the color on second robot, then you'll change the order in which the filters are applied. These changes will have a dramatic effect on the appearance of the image.

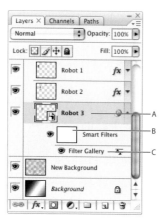

A. Smart Object.
B. The Filter Effects mask.
C. Filter.

6 In the Layers palette, Right-click (Windows) or Control+click (Mac OS) on the filter located underneath Smart Filter. By default this is named Filter Gallery; choose Edit Smart Filter from the contextual menu and the Filter Gallery dialog box opens again.

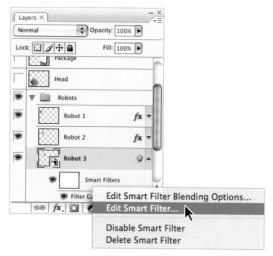

Editing a Smart Filter.

7 In the filter effects area, select Neon Glow from the list of applied filters.

8 Click once on the Glow Color box in the options panel. The Color Picker appears.

9 Enter the following values: R: **240**, G: **25**, B: **86**, and press OK.

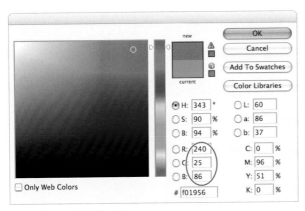

Enter values into the Color Picker.

10 In the filter effects area of the Filter Gallery, drag Plastic Wrap below Neon Glow. This changes the filter order, and creates a different effect. Press OK.

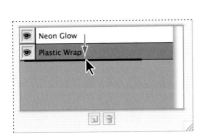

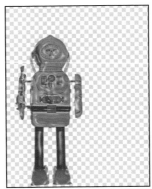

Changing the order of the filters.

11 Choose File > Save.

See Smart Filters in action!

Use the video that accompanies this lesson to gain a better understanding of how to take advantage of the Smart Filter feature. Open the file PS12.swf located in the Videos folder to view the video training file for this lesson.

Smart Filter options

Next, you will explore additional filter options. You'll start by fading the filters and by editing the Smart Filter Blending Options. You will then discover how to disable a filter and how to take advantage of the Filter effects mask thumbnail.

1   In the Layers palette, Right-click (Windows) or Ctrl+click (Mac OS) on Filter Gallery located under the Robot 3 layer Smart Filter. Select Edit Smart Filter Blending Options from the contextual menu.

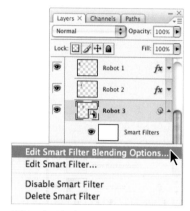

Editing the Blending options.

Like the Fade option used earlier in this lesson, the Smart Filter blending options allow you to control the intensity of a filter. However, this method is non-destructive. You can change the Fade settings multiple times and not impact the original image.

2   In the Blending Options dialog box, click and drag the opacity slider to the left, lowering the opacity to 60%. Click the Preview check box on, then off, to see the change that has been applied to the image, then press OK.

3   Choose File > Save.

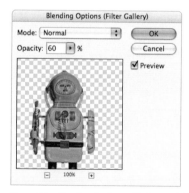

Smart Filter Blending Options with the specified opacity.

Enabling and disabling effects

Because you used a Smart Filter, you can turn the filter on or off.

1   In the Layers palette, Right-click the Filter Gallery filter under Smart Filters and choose Disable Smart Filter to hide the filter's effect.

You can also turn off the visibility of the filter by clicking the eye icon to the left of the filter name in the Layers palette; click again on the eye icon to make the filter visible. Make sure the Filter Gallery filter is visible for the Robot 3 layer.

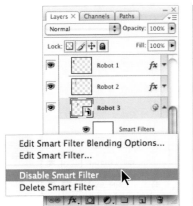

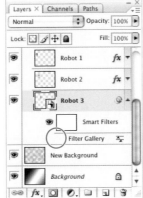

Selecting Disable Smart Filter.   *The visibility of the Smart Filter turned off.*

Using a filter effects mask

When you apply a filter to a layer that has been converted for Smart Filters, a mask, called the Filter effects mask thumbnail, is created. This provides the ability to selectively modify a filter effect. The thumbnail appears below the Smart Object layer as a white box labeled Smart Filters. You can click on the mask to activate it and then paint with shades of black or white to hide or show the filter's effect on the layer. You'll now convert a layer for Smart Filters, apply a few filters, reduce the opacity of those filter effects, and then mask the effects to appear only portions of the image.

1   To give you more room to work in the Layers palette, click the triangle next to the layer group Robots to collapse the Robot layers into the folder.

2   Click the eye icon next to the Head layer to show the Head image, and then click on the Head layer to activate it.

Select the Head layer.

3   Select Filter > Convert for Smart Filters; if a warning dialog box appears, press OK.

4   Choose Filter > Artistic > Plastic Wrap. Press OK to apply the filter.

5   Choose Filter > Artistic > Neon Glow, and press OK to also apply this filter.

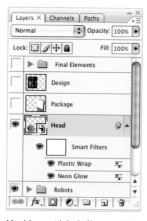

Head layer with both filters applied.

6   Right-click (Windows) or Ctrl+click (Mac OS) on the Neon Glow Smart Filter layer and choose Edit Smart Filter Blending Options. A warning dialog box appears; press OK.

7 Change the Mode to Multiply and drag the Opacity slider to the left to approximately 50%, then press OK.

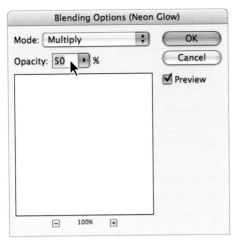

Smart Filter Blending Options with the correct settings applied.

To reveal the robot's face, you will hide a portion of the filters you have applied.

8 Click the Smart Filters mask thumbnail. You'll know it is selected when four corners appear around the edge of the white box.

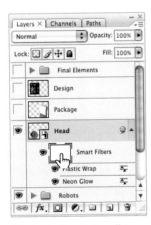

Selecting the Smart Filters effects mask thumbnail.

You will now paint inside the Smart Filters mask to expose the robot's face, essentially erasing the filters' effect in that area.

9 Select the Brush tool (✍).

10 With the Brush tool selected, Right-click anywhere in your image area to open the Brush Preset picker dialog box. Type **90** into the Diameter text field and **50** into the Hardness text field. Press Enter or Return to close the Brush Preset picker dialog box.

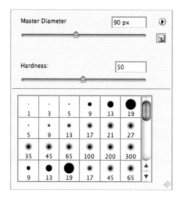

Access the Brush Preset picker contextually.

11 Press **D** on the keyboard to reset the default colors.

12 Press **X** on the keyboard to switch the foreground and background colors. Your foreground color should be black.

13 Paint with the brush inside the black oval line around the robot's face. As you paint, you are revealing a portion of the layer that will not have this filter applied to it.

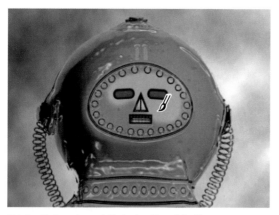

Painting black on the mask blocks the effects of the filter.

14 Continue to paint until you have completely revealed the unfiltered version of the robot's face.

15 Choose File > Save. Keep this file open for the next part of this lesson.

Using the Vanishing Point filter

The Vanishing Point filter simplifies the task of editing images that are in perspective, such as the sides of a box. With the Vanishing Point filter, you can easily add additional elements to any type of artwork that is comprised of flat planes. With this filter, you first define the planes in an image, then apply edits by painting, cloning, copying, pasting, and transforming your image. The planes you define control the perspective of the edits you make, giving your image a realistic perspective effect.

In this exercise, you'll map a pre-made design to a box so that three sides of the box are showing.

1   Turn on the eye icons (👁) next to the Design and Package layers to make them visible. Using the Layers palette, turn off the visibility of both the Robots layer group and the Head layer.

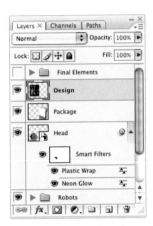

Showing the Design and Box layers in the Layers palette.

You will now cut the image on the Design layer so that it can be pasted into the Vanishing Point window.

2 Hold down the Ctrl (Windows) or the Command (Mac OS) key and click on the Design layer thumbnail in the Layers palette. A selection is now visible around the package design.

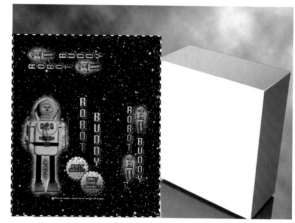

Ctrl/Command+click on the Design layer thumbnail.

The Design layer contents are selected.

3 Click on the Design layer to make sure it is the active layer, then choose Edit > Cut. The package design is now on your clipboard.

4 Choose Filter > Vanishing Point. The Vanishing Point window appears. In the first part of this exercise, the perspective planes are made for you. In the next section, you'll build your own.

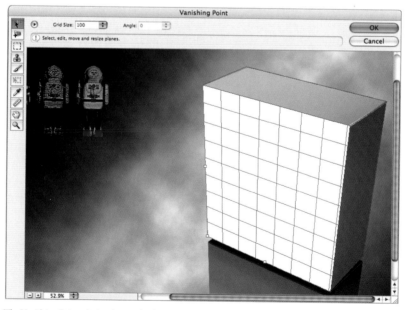

The Vanishing Point window has pre-built perspective planes.

5 With the Vanishing Point window open, Press Ctrl+V (Windows), or Command+V (Mac OS) to paste the package design you cut in step 3. When you paste, the tool changes to the Marquee selection tool.

6 Click and drag the pasted design over the perspective plane. The design artwork maps to the perspective plane. Keep the Vanishing Point window open for the next part of this lesson.

You can map artwork to perspective planes using the Vanishing Point filter.

Building perspective planes

A grid defines the four corner points of a perspective plane. When building a perspective plane, it helps to have objects in your image that can define your plane. In this example, the package itself offers a good source from which you can create your perspective plane.

Now that you know the capabilities of the Vanishing Point filter, you'll delete the existing plane and create your own.

1 Press and hold down the Alt (Windows) or the Option (Mac OS) key. This turns the Cancel button into a Reset button. Click Reset.

2 Select the Edit Plane tool (⬚), then click on the existing planes and press Backspace (Windows) or Delete (Mac OS). The perspective planes are deleted.

3   Select the Create Plane tool (⊞). You'll now create a new plane by defining each corner of the plane.

The Create Plane tool.

4   Click on the top left of the front of the box, then on the top right, then on the bottom right, and once more in the bottom left. Note that a blue grid indicates a valid plane. If your plane is red or yellow, it is invalid; use your Edit Plane tool to readjust your corners until the grid is blue.

For a plane to be valid, two sides of the plane should be parallel, while the two other sides show the perspective.

Building an attached plane

In Photoshop CS3, you can control the angle of a plane; it is no longer restricted to 90-degree angles as it was in previous versions of Photoshop.

1   Press and hold down the Ctrl (Windows) or the Command (Mac OS) key and drag the top middle edge node toward the back edge of the box top. This creates a perpendicular plane that will be used for the top side of the box..

Ctrl/Command+click.

Drag out a new perpendicular plane.

2   Press and hold the Alt (Windows) or the Option (Mac OS) key and position your cursor over the top middle edge node; a double-headed curved cursor appears. Click and drag either to the left or right to adjust the angle of the plane. You may need to zoom in to get this just right. Press **X** on the keyboard to zoom in for a better view.

You are adjusting the plane so that it follows the top side of the box. As you adjust the plane you may find that you need to release the Alt/Option key and adjust the middle edge node so that it is not extending beyond the top back edge of the box.

Alt/Option click and drag to change the angle of a plane.

3   Click inside the area of the first plane to select it. You'll now make the third plane by holding down the Ctrl (Windows) or the Command (Mac OS) key and dragging a plane from the center-right edge node in the first plane you drew.

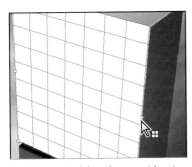   

Ctrl/Command+click on the center-right point.   *Click and drag another plane from the first.*

4   Hold the Alt (Windows) or the Option (Mac OS) key and drag from the right edge node of this plane to control the angle of the plane. The goal here is to have the new perpendicular plane align with the side of the box. Again, when you are finished adjusting the angle, you may need to release the Alt/Option key and adjust the edge node so that the plane is not extending beyond the side of the box.

5   Choose Edit > Paste to paste the package design in the Vnaishing Point window, or use the keyboard shortcut Ctrl+V (Windows) or Command+V (Mac OS).

6   Click and drag with the design over the box. As it appears over the grid, the sides of the design conform to the sides of the grid. Notice how the image automatically adjusts itself to the contours of the perspective planes.

7   Make sure the image is exactly where you want it positioned on the plane, then press OK.

8   Make the Robots layer group visible by clicking to the left of the Robots folder in the Layers palette. The visibility eye icon appears, and you see the contents of the group. Then click to the left of the Head layer and the Final Elements layer group to reveal the entire design.

9   Choose File > Save. Congratulations! You have finished this lesson.

Self study

Here are some projects that you can create on your own:

Stylize the last two robots and create the reflection of the box using the Vanishing Point filter. You can see the final outcome by opening ps1201_done.psd.

1   To experiment with this concept, open the file named ps1202.psd.

2   Select the Robot 4 layer, select Convert for Smart Filters, then apply whatever filters you like. You may also want to use the Smart Filter Blending Options.

3   Choose the Robot 5 layer, select Convert for Smart Filters, and choose some different filters.

4   Turn on the Reflection Design layer, flip it horizontally and vertically, and cut it. Open up Vanishing Point and paste it into the bottom plane. Delete the pre-made plane, make your own, and then paste. Try lowering the opacity and choosing a blend mode of Multiply for the layer, once you've closed Vanishing Point.

Review

Questions

1   When is the Fade option available for a filter that you have applied?

2   If you want to apply a filter in a non-destructive way, what is your best option?

3   How do you add a new perpendicular plane to an existing perspective plane and then control the angle of a new plane in the Vanishing Point window?

Answers

1   Unless you are using the Smart Filter feature you must apply the Fade feature as the next step after applying a filter. If you are using a Smart Filter, you can Right-click (Windows) or Ctrl+click (Mac OS) on the applied Smart Filter (listed in the Layers palette) and select Edit Smart Filter Blending Options to access the same same fade options.

2   Convert the layer for Smart Filters, then apply the filter.

3   To create a perpendicular plane from an existing perspective plane, click and hold down the Ctrl (Windows) or Command (Mac OS) key on an edge node (not a corner node) and drag out a new plane. You can control the angle of the plane by holding the Alt key (Windows) or Option key (Mac OS) and dragging an edge node (not an corner node) until the new plane is at the correct angle.

What you'll learn in this lesson:

- Creating web and video presets

- Saving a still image for use on the Web

- Saving a still image with transparency for video

- Building animation for web and video

Creating for Web and Video

Photoshop's flexibility and range of features have allowed it to gain acceptance in nearly every sector of the computer graphics industry. A very common use for Photoshop is creating imagery for web and video production.

Starting up

In this lesson, you'll create a group of projects for both web and video production. You'll work with still and animated graphics for each medium.

Before starting, make sure that your tools and palettes are consistent by resetting your preferences. See "Resetting Adobe Photoshop CS3 preferences" on page 4.

You will work with several files from the ps13lessons folder in this lesson. Make sure that you have loaded the pslessons folder onto your hard drive from the supplied DVD. See "Loading lesson files" on page 3.

In order to work with video in Photoshop, you must have the QuickTime player plug-in installed on your computer. While pre-installed with the Mac OS operating system, for Windows users, the QuickTime player is available as a free download from the Apple web site (apple.com/quicktime).

See Lesson 13 in action!

Use the accompanying video to gain a better understanding of how to use some of the features shown in this lesson. Open the file PS13.swf located in the Videos folder to view the video training file for this lesson.

Viewing the completed file

Before starting this lesson, you'll use your browser to view the completed navigational banner that you will create in this part of the lesson.

1   Open your web browser—you can use any browser for this lesson (Firefox, Safari, Opera, or Internet Explorer, to name a few).

2   Choose File > Open, or Open File. The exact menu selection may vary, depending upon the type and version of your browser, but the menu item for opening a page in your browser should be under the File menu.

3   In the Open dialog box, navigate to the ps13lessons folder on your hard drive and open the file named ps1301_done.html. An image created to help viewers navigate a web site appears.

The completed navigational banner.

4   Click on the About Us, Projects, and Sign Up text links to see that you are directed to generic pages with related titles.

You will create this navigational banner from start to finish, including adding the links and creating the web page.

5   You can keep the finished banner open in the browser for reference, or choose File > Close.

6   Return to Photoshop CS3.

Creating a preset for the Web

To start this project, you will use a new document preset. Photoshop ships with a wide variety of presets for creating print, web, and video documents. In this lesson, you will use the web and video presets. Both presets create a document with a resolution of 72 ppi, in RGB color mode. The main difference between the web and video presets is in the setting for Pixel Aspect Ratio; while web and video graphics are similar in many ways, this is the most notable and most important difference. Web graphics use pixels that are square, while video graphics use pixels that are rectangular. You will now create a preset that can be used when creating web banners.

1   Choose File > New to create a new Photoshop document. Select Web from the Preset drop-down menu. This automatically sets all of the parameters for the creation of web graphics.

If you have not reset your preferences, the size will default to the last web size used.

2   From the Size drop-down menu, choose Leaderboard, 728 x 90, as you are going to create a banner in this lesson.

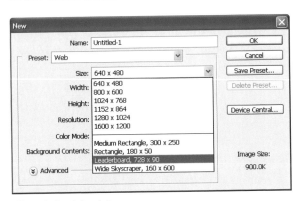

Choose the Leaderboard size.

3   Click the Save Preset button and type **webbanner** in the Name text field. Leave all the checkboxes checked in the Include In Saved Settings area.

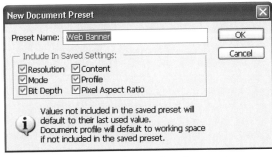

Save time when creating future documents by saving a preset.

By saving a preset, you can store presets such as resolutions, modes, and bit depths so that you can quickly create additional documents without having to input this information again. Press OK to create your new document.

4   Choose File > Save As. The Save As dialog box appears. In the Save As dialog box, navigate to the ps13lessons folder and type **ps1301_work**. From the Format drop-down menu, select Photoshop and press Save. Keep this file open.

Determining image size for the Web

This figure represents a typical monitor that is set at a screen resolution of 800 x 600. Many viewers will use a higher resolution, but this is the typical resolution that most web designers build images to fit.

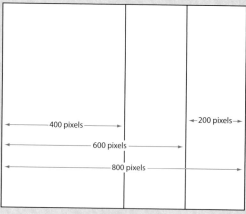

A typical screen display broken into quarters.

To determine how wide a web image should be, break down the total number of screen pixels into sections. Instead of thinking about how many pixels wide an image should be, think about what percentage of the screen you want the image to occupy. In other words, if you want the image to occupy half of the screen (typically estimated at 800 pixels for browser windows), type **400** into the Width text field in the Pixel Dimension section of the Image Size dialog box. For one quarter of the screen, type **200**, and so on. It is a different way of thinking, especially for those from the print design environment. It should also be noted that a pixel is a pixel, no matter what the ppi resolution of your image is. So, 200 pixels in a 300 ppi image takes up the same amount of disk space as 200 pixels in a 72 ppi image.

Changing your units of measurement

To verify that your measurements are set in the pixel unit, you will make a change to your Photoshop Preferences.

1   Choose Edit > Preferences > Units & Rulers (Windows) or Photoshop > Preferences > Units & Rulers (Mac OS). The Preferences dialog box appears, with Units & Rulers already selected.

2   From the Units section of the Preferences dialog box, choose pixels from the Rulers drop-down menu. Press OK.

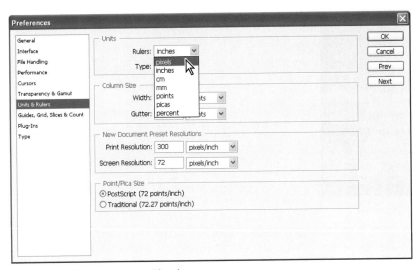

Changing the unit of measurement in Photoshop.

Creating the navigational banner

In this next part of the lesson, you will import an image from another document into your ps1301_work.psd document to create the navigation bar for a web page.

Using the Crop tool to start the banner

1   Choose File > Browse, or select the Go to Bridge button (📷) in the options bar. When Adobe Bridge appears, navigate to the ps13lessons folder and double-click to open the file named ps1301.psd. An image of a lake appears.

The ps1301.psd image.

It is apparent that this image is not going to fit well in our much smaller banner document. You will crop this image down to the same size using the Crop tool (🔲) and the options bar.

2   Select the Crop tool. The options in the options bar now reflect settings for the Crop tool.

3   In the options bar, type **728** in the Width text field and **90** in the Height text field. By typing values into the options bar, you fix the Crop tool to stay within the proportions of your final crop size.

You do not want to use the Crop tool to resize images to a size larger than they are in their present form. If you are not sure what the size is, choose Image > Image Size to open the Image Size dialog box.

4   With the Crop tool selected, click and drag from the left side of the image to the lower right. No exact location to create the crop is required at this point, but notice that your crop is restricted to the proportions of the values you entered.

5   With the Crop tool still selected, click in the center of the crop area marquee and drag to the center of the document. Then, using the corner handles, click and drag so that the cropped area is flush with the left and right sides.

Click and drag to reposition the crop area.

6   To confirm the crop, click on the Commit crop check mark (✔) in the upper right side of the options bar, or press the Return key.

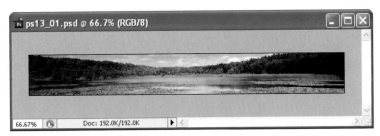

The cropped image.

7   Select the Move tool (✛), then hold down the Shift key and drag the ps1301.psd image over to the ps1301_work.psd image. When the border appears, release the mouse. By holding down the Shift key, the image is centered in the work image.

8   Return to the ps1301.psd image and choose File > Close. Choose No when asked if you want to save the changes. Keep the ps1301_work.psd file open.

Adding a logo

You will now add a logo created in Illustrator, to this banner.

1   Choose File > Place. The Place dialog box appears. Navigate to the ps13lessons folder and double-click on the image named sunny_logo.ai. The Place PDF dialog box appears. Leave the defaults as they are and press OK.

The image is placed on the document, but appears with a bounding box, waiting for you to confirm any transformations, such as scaling.

2   Do not resize the logo at this point, just press the Return key, or the Commit Transform (✔) check mark in the upper right side of the options bar.

3   Using the Move tool (✛), click and drag the logo to the far left side of the ps1301_work.psd image.

Click and drag the logo over to the left using the Move tool.

4   Choose File > Save to save this file.

Adding additional text buttons

In this section, you will add three different text layers. These text references will later be changed to hyperlinks to connect to URLs.

1   Select the Type tool (T) and click on the image document. No specific location is necessary. The cursor is blinking, waiting for you to enter text.

Before entering text, make changes to the font, style, size, and color to ensure that the text fits easily on to your image file.

2   In the options bar, select Myriad Pro from the font family drop-down menu, select Bold from the Font style drop-down menu, select 30 from the font size drop-down menu, and choose the Left align text button.

*A. Font family. **B**. Font style. **C**. Font size. **D**. Font alignment. **E**. Font color.*

3   If the Swatches palette is not visible, choose Window > Swatches and then click on the color White.

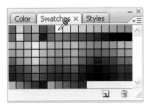

Select the color White.

4   Type **About Us**. The text appears, with the font attributes that you selected.

5   Using the Move tool (✛), reposition the About Us text layer so that it is to the right of the Sunny Lake Spa logo.

Reposition the text layer.

6   Choose File > Save to save this document. Keep the file open for the next part of this exercise.

Cloning your text layer

You will now clone this text layer in order to save time creating additional text layers.

1   With the ps1301_work.psd file still open, choose the Move tool (✛).

2   Hold down Alt+Shift (Windows) or Option+Shift (Mac OS). You will see a double-headed cursor appear. Using the Move tool, click and drag to the right. Release the mouse when a cloned copy of the About Us text is off to the right, and not overlapping the existing text layer. Make sure that you release the mouse before the key modifiers, as they allow you to clone and constrain the movement to a straight line.

3   Repeat the process of holding down the Alt+Shift (Windows) or Option+Shift (Mac OS) keys and dragging the second text layer to the right until you have a total of three text layers.

The file with three text layers.

4   Select the Type tool (T) and hover over the center About Us text. When the I-bar (⌶) appears, click and drag from the left of the text to the right to select it.

Use the Type tool to select the About Us text.

5   With the text selected, type **Packages**. The About Us text is replaced with the word Packages. Press the Commit check mark (✔) in the upper right of the options bar. The layer's name is automatically updated to be named Packages.

Type Packages.   *Text layer name is updated.*

6   With the Type tool still selected, cross over the third About Us text. When the I-bar appears, click and drag from the left to the right side of the text.

7   Type **Sign Up**. The About Us text is replaced with the words Sign Up. Press the Commit check mark in the upper right of the options bar. The layer's name is automatically updated to Sign Up.

8   Choose File > Save. Keep the file open for the next part of this lesson.

Distributing the layers evenly

You will now align and distribute the text layers so that they are more evenly spaced.

1   Make sure that you still have the ps1301_work.psd file open and select the Move tool (✛).

2   Select the About Us layer in the Layers palette, then hold down the Shift key and select the Sign Up layer. The About Us, Packages, and Sign Up layers are all selected.

Note that when you select three or more layers, the Align and Distribute options become visible in the options bar. (Align becomes visible with two layers selected.)

3 Choose Distribute horizontal centers from the options bar. The text layers are distributed evenly.

Select the three text layers.   *Distribute the text layers horizontally.*

Creating slices

A slice is a part of an image that is cut from a larger image. Think of a slice as a piece of a puzzle that, when placed alongside other related pieces, creates an entire image. What holds the pieces together is usually an html table. You will find out how to create an html table in this lesson, and then you will test it in a browser.

An example of a sliced image.

Slices can be beneficial when images are large in size, as downloading smaller packets of information on the Web is faster than downloading one large packet, and also better when you need to save parts of an image in different formats.

1 If your rulers are not already displayed, choose View > Rulers to show the rulers on the top and left side of your document window.

Using the rulers, you will create guides on your document that will later define where you want to slice your image.

2 Click directly on the top (horizontal) ruler and then click and drag to pull a guide from the ruler. Continue dragging the guide until it is just above the text layers.

Click and drag a ruler from the top ruler.

3 Now, click on the ruler to the left (vertical) and drag a guide to the right of the Sunny Lake Spa logo.

4 Click on the left ruler again and drag out a guide to the area between the About Us and Packages text.

5 Click on the left ruler and drag a guide to the space between the text Packages and Sign Up, and drag out another guide to the right of Sign Up.

 If you have the Move tool selected, you can click and drag existing guides to reposition them.

The image with the guides added.

6 Choose the Slice tool (⟋). Note that the options change in the options bar.

7 Click on the Slices From Guides button in the options bar. Your image is automatically sliced into several smaller images, based upon the location of your guides. The image is not actually sliced in Photoshop, but will be when you save the file in the Save for Web & Devices section of this lesson.

The guides converted to slices.

Selecting and combining slices

In this section, you will select several slices and combine them into one slice. You can combine and divide slices easily using contextual tools in Photoshop. You will first remove the guides since you do not need them anymore.

1 Choose View > Clear Guides. The guides are cleared, but the slices remain.

2 Click and hold on the Slice tool (⟋) to choose the Slice Select tool (⟋). Using this tool, you can click to activate and adjust your slices.

3 Using the Slice Select tool, click on the slice at the bottom of the Sunny Lake Spa logo, then hold down the Shift key and click on the top slice. Two slices that include the top and bottom of the Sunny Lake Spa logo are selected.

4 Right-click (Windows) or Ctrl+Click (Mac OS) and select Combine slices from the contextual menu. The slices are combined into one slice.

Select both slices.   *Combine into one.*

5 Now, select the slice above About Us and Shift+click on the slice to the right and the slice following. The three slices above the text are now selected.

6 Right-click (Windows) or Ctrl+click (Mac OS) and select Combine slices from the contextual menu. The slices are combined into one slice.

7 Using the Slice Select tool, select the slice in the upper right of the image and Shift+click the slice immediately beneath it. This selects the slices to the right of the Sign Up text.

8 Right-click (Windows) or Ctrl+click (Mac OS) and select Combine slices from the contextual menu. The slices are combined into one slice.

The combined slices when completed.

9 Choose File > Save to save this file. Keep the image open for the next part of this lesson.

Applying attributes to your slices

Now that you have defined your slices, you will apply some attributes to them. The attributes that you will apply in this lesson are URL and Alt Tags. By defining a URL, a link is made from that slice to a location or file on the Web. By defining an Alt Tag, you allow viewers to read a text description of an image. This is helpful if a viewer is visually impaired or has turned off the option for viewing graphics. An Alt Tag also helps search engines find more relevant content on your page.

1 With the ps1301_work.psd file still open, choose the Slice Select tool (✣) and select the slice containing the logo.

2 Click on the Set options for the current slice button (▣) in the options bar. The Slice Options dialog box appears.

You will be supplied with a link to a text page to test your links.

3 Type **http://www.agitraining.com/sunny** into the URL text field.

4 Type **Sunny Lake Spa main page** into the Alt Tag text field and press OK.

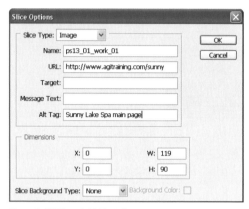

Enter the URL and Alt Tag information.

5 Now, select the slice containing the text About Us, and choose the Set options for the current slice button in the options bar. The Slice Options dialog box appears.

6 Type **http://www.agitraining.com/sunny/about.html** into the URL text field and **About Us** in the Alt Tag text field. Press OK.

7 Select the slice containing the text Packages, and choose the Set options for the current slice button in the options bar. The Slice Options dialog box appears.

8 Type **http://www.agitraining.com/sunny/packages.html** into the URL text field and **Packages** in the Alt Tag text field. Press OK.

9 Select the slice containing the text Sign Up, and choose the Set options for the current slice button in the options bar. The Slice Options dialog box appears.

10 Type **http://www.agitraining.com/sunny/signup.html** into the URL text field and **Sign Up** in the Alt Tag text field. Press OK.

11 Select the large slice spanning across the top of the text and hold down the Shift key to also select the slice on the far right. Click on the Set options for the current slice button in the options bar. The Slice Options dialog box appears.

You will not enter a URL for these slices, as they are not to be used to navigate, but you will enter an Alt Tag for them.

12 Type **lake image** into the Alt Tag text field and click OK.

13 Choose File > Save. Keep the ps1301_work.psd document open for the next part of the lesson.

Using Save For Web & Devices

The process of making an image look as good as possible at the smallest file size is called optimizing. This is important for all images that are to be used on the Web, as most viewers don't want to wait long for information to appear.

In this part of the lesson, you'll use the Save For Web & Devices feature to optimize your navigational banner.

1   With the ps1301_work.psd file still open, choose File > Save For Web & Devices. The Save For Web & Devices dialog box appears.

2   Select the 2-up tab to view your original image on the top and your optimized image on the bottom. Note that the window may display the original on the left side and the optimized image on the right.

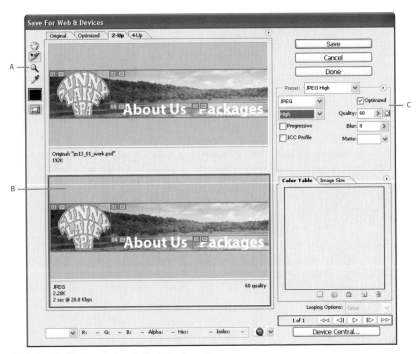

*A. Toolbox. **B**. Preview window. **C**. Optimization settings.*

The Save For Web & Devices window is broken into three main areas:

Toolbox: The Toolbox provides you with tools for panning and zooming in your image, selecting slices, and sampling color.

Preview window: In addition to having the ability to view both the original and optimized images individually, you can also preview the original and optimized images side-by-side in 2-up view or with up to three variations in the 4-up view.

Optimize menu: The Optimize menu allows you to specify the format and settings of your optimized file.

How to choose web image formats

When you want to optimize an image for the Web, what format should you choose? Based upon the image you have in front of you, choose the format best suited for that type of image.

 GIF: An acronym for Graphic Interchange File, the GIF format is usually used on the Web to display simple colored logos, motifs, and other limited-tone imagery. The GIF format supports a maximum of 256 colors as well as transparency. GIF is the only one of the four formats here that supports built-in animation.

 JPEG: An acronym for Joint Photographic Experts Group, the JPEG file format has found wide acceptance on the Web as the main format for displaying photographs and other continuous-tone imagery. The JPEG format supports a range of millions of colors, allowing for the accurate display of a wide range of artwork.

 PNG: An acronym for Portable Network Graphics. PNG was intended to blend the best of both the GIF and JPEG formats. PNG files come in two different varieties: like GIF, PNG-8 can support up to 256 colors, while the PNG-24 variety can support millions of colors, similar to the JPEG format. Both PNG varieties support transparency and, as an improvement on GIF's all-or-nothing transparency function, a PNG file supports varying amounts of transparency so that you can actually see through an image to your Web page contents. Note that not all browsers support the PNG format.

 WBMP-define: A standard format for optimizing images for mobile devices, WBMP files are 1-bit, meaning they contain only black and white pixels.

3 Choose the Slice Select tool (⋗) from the toolbar on the left and click on the slice that contains the Sunny Lake Spa logo.

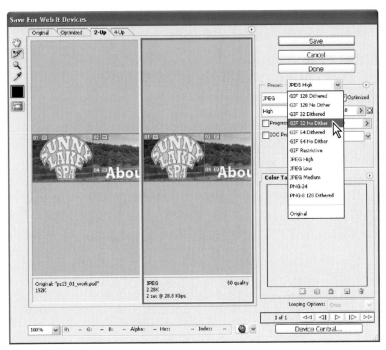

Selecting the GIF 32 No Dither format for the first slice.

Select the first slice and choose the GIF 32 No Dither from the Preset drop-down menu. This is why you selected this preset:

- The GIF format was selected because the logo contains solid colors. GIF compresses images with solid colors to the smallest possible file size.

- 32 represents the number of colors that are retained when the file is saved in GIF format. GIF files utilize a color table model that allows up to 256 colors in an image. The fewer the number of colors, the smaller the file size. You can see the color table in the Color Table palette on the right side of the Save for Web & Devices dialog box.

- No Dither indicates that you do not want Photoshop to use dithering, or pixelation, to create colors that are not included in the 32-color palette you have specified.

4 Using the Slice Select tool, select the large slice that spans above the text and choose JPEG High from the Preset drop-down menu. Note that you can increase or decrease the quality of your JPEG using the Quality slider in the optimized settings section under the Presets. You will now adjust the quality while observing the file size.

Note that the file size of the optimized image, based upon your current settings, is displayed at the bottom of the optimized image preview.

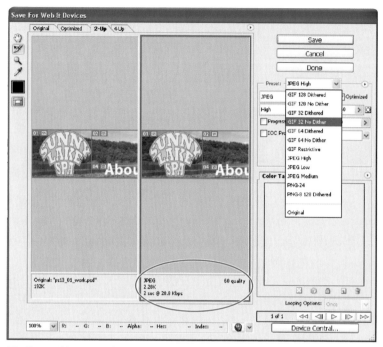

The file size of the optimized image.

5 Click on the arrow to the right of Quality and a slider appears. Click and drag the slider toward the left to about the 40 mark, or type **40** into the Quality text field. By using the Quality slider, you are able to select a quality level between the JPEG High and JPEG Medium presets. Note the size of the optimized file is reduced.

6 Using the Slice Select tool, select the About Us slice and then Shift+click on the Packages slice and the Sign Up slice. All three slices are selected.

7 Select GIF 32 No Dither from the Presets drop-down menu. All three slices are now set to GIF format.

8 Select the last slice, off to the right, and select JPEG Medium from the Preset drop-down menu.

You can test your file in a web browser directly from the Save For Web & Devices dialog box.

9   Select the Preview in default browser button at the bottom of the Save For Web & Devices dialog box. If you have a default browser installed, your image is opened on a browser page. Notice that the slices are not apparent and that the code is visible in your preview.

The Preview in Default Browser button.

10 Click on the slices that you designated as having URLs. You should be connected to the assigned URLs. Use the Back button in your browser to return to your sliced image. Close the browser window when you are finished testing the image. The Save For Web & Devices Dialog box is still open.

11 Choose Save, and the Save Optimized As dialog box appears. Browse to the ps13lessons folder and choose HTML and Images from the Format drop-down menu. Click Save. An HTML page, along with the sliced images, is saved in your ps13lessons folder. You can now open the file in Dreamweaver and continue building the page, or copy and paste the table to another page.

12 Choose File > Save to save your original image. Choose File > Close to close the file.

Saving files for video

If you are saving into Adobe applications such as After Effects, Premiere, or Flash, you do not need to take extra steps to maintain transparency. In fact, you can simply browse, search, and organize native .psd images directly in Adobe Bridge from the other Adobe Creative Suite applications.

When importing into a non-Adobe video application, you have to be concerned about transparency. Each video application has its own set of importable formats. For this lesson, you will open a pre-built file and save it as a TIFF with an alpha channel. Video editing applications recognize alpha channels when defining transparent areas on an image.

1   Open the file ps1305.psd. The image that appears is intended to overlay a video file.

An image with transparency applied to it.

2   If the Layers palette is not visible, choose Window > Layers to open the Layers palette.

3   Hold down the Ctrl (Windows) or Command (Mac OS) key and click on the layer thumbnail for the lake layer. This selects everything on that layer that is not transparent.

4   Click and hold the Ctrl+Shift (Windows) or Command+Shift (Mac OS) keys, and click on the layer thumbnail for the balloon layer. This adds the balloon layer to the selection.

5   Choose Window > Channels to open the Channels palette.

6   Click the Save Selection as channel button (⊡) at the bottom of the Channels palette. This creates an alpha channel from the active selection.

Create an alpha channel from the selection.

In your alpha channel, the areas that are black are fully transparent, the areas that are white are fully opaque, and any areas that are gray will be varying degrees of transparency. This is the standard way that video editing applications treat alpha channels.

7   Choose File > Save As. When the Save As dialog box appears, navigate to the ps13lessons folder and type **ps1305_work** into the File name text field. Select TIFF from the Format drop-down menu.

8   In the Save Options field, make sure that Layers is not checked and Alpha Channels is checked. A warning stating that this image needs to be saved as a copy appears, which means that your original file will keep layers intact. Press Save. The TIFF Options dialog box appears.

9   In the TIFF Options dialog box, make sure that None is selected in the Image Compression section and leave other settings at their default settings. Select OK in the TIFF Options window. You have saved a TIFF file with an area that will appear transparent in your video editing application.

10   Close the original Photoshop document by choosing File > Close. If asked if you would like to save the changes, choose Don't Save.

Creating animation

In this lesson, you will create an animation using the default animation palette. If you have Photoshop CS3 Extended, you can take the lesson further and use the Advanced timeline in the video lesson that follows.

Working in Frame mode

Working in the Frame mode of the animation palette is much like creating an animation using a flip book. When played, each frame is converted into a final animation. Using the Frame animation palette, you can also build individual frames and then have Photoshop automatically create transitions between the frames for you. This process is called tweening. For this part of the lesson, you will add a floating hot air balloon to the image of the lake.

1   Choose File > Browse and navigate to the ps13lessons folder. Select the images named ps1302.psd and ps1303.psd, then Right-click (Windows) or Ctrl+click (Mac OS) and select Open from the contextual menu. An image of a lake and an image of a red hot air balloon open.

2   Choose Window > Arrange > Tile Vertically to view both images at the same time.

3   Select the Move tool (⊕) and click and drag the balloon image over to the image of the lake. Release the mouse when you see the border appear around the document window of the ps1302.psd image.

4   Click on the ps1303.psd image to bring it forward, and choose File > Close.

5   Choose Window > Animation to open the Photoshop Animation palette. As a default, the Animation palette displays as a frame animation palette. If you see the Advanced timeline, choose Convert to Frame Animation from the palette menu.

Using the Frame Animation palette, you will create two different key frames and have Photoshop automatically build the additional frames for you.

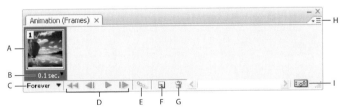

A. Key frame. *B*. Selects frame delay time. *C*. Selects looping options. *D*. Player controls. *E*. Tween.
F. Duplicates selected frames. *G*. Delete selected frames. *H*. Palette menu. *I*. Convert to timeline.

6 If the Layers palette is not visible, choose Window > Layers. Select the balloon layer to make sure that it is the active layer, then, using the Move tool, click and drag the balloon so that it is in the lower left corner of the lake image.

Position the balloon to be in the lower left corner.

7 Type **15** to change the layer to a 15% opacity.

8 At the bottom of the Animation palette, click on the Duplicate selected frames button (⊡). A second frame is added to the right of the original.

9 Verify that you still have the balloon layer selected, then, using the Move tool (▶+), click and drag the balloon to the upper right corner of the lake image. Then type **0** (zero) to set the layer opacity at 100%.

10 Click and hold on the Add a layer style button (*fx*) at the bottom of the Layers palette, and choose Outer Glow from the list of styles. The Layer Style dialog box appears with Outer Glow selected.

11 In the Elements section of the Layer Styles dialog box, click and drag the Size slider to the right until you reach approximately 70, or type **70** into the Size text field. Press OK. A glow has been applied to the balloon layer.

12 From the Animation palette menu, select Tween or click on the Tween button (⬮⬮⬮) at the bottom of the Animation palette.

13 On the Tween menu, press OK to add five frames to your animation. Your former frame 2 now becomes the seventh and last frame in your animation.

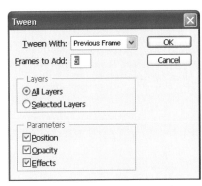

Choose to insert five frames in between the frames.

In addition to the number of frames to add to the animation, the Tween menu gives you the ability to choose which layers to include in your frames and which parameters to animate. As the default, all layers and parameters are included.

14 Select all the frames of your animation by clicking on the first frame, holding down the Shift key, and clicking on the last frame.

15 With all your frames selected, click on the value for Selects frame delay at the bottom of any frame and select 0.5. Because all the frames are highlighted, the delay time of all your frames is adjusted. Press the Play button at the bottom of the Animation palette to preview your animation. When you are finished viewing your animation, press the Stop animation button (same location as the Play button) to stop the animation.

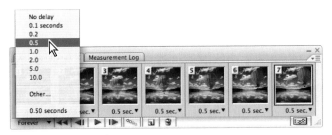

Select 0.5 as the frame delay time.

As a default, your animation is set to replay over and over again. If you prefer to set the number of times your animation plays, click and hold on the text, "Forever," that appears in the lower left corner of the animation palette and select Once, or choose Other to input a custom value.

16 Choose File > Save As. The Save As dialog box appears. Navigate to the ps13lessons folder and then type **animation_done** in the File name text field. Choose Photoshop (PSD) from the Format drop-down menu and press Save. Keep the file open for the next part of this lesson.

Saving an animated GIF

Now you will save the animation in a format that will recognize the frames and can be posted to the Web.

1 Choose File > Save For Web & Devices. The Save For Web & Devices dialog box appears.

2 Choose 2-up from the display tabs at the top of the dialog box. This allows you to see the original image next to a preview of the optimized image.

3 Choose GIF 128 Dithered from the Preset drop-down menu. This is a good preset to use for an animation with multiple colors. It creates a good balance between file size and image quality.

4 Press the Save button to save your file as a GIF animation. Navigate to the ps13lesson folder and type **animation_done.gif** in the File name text field.

5 In the Format drop-down menu, choose Images Only and press Save.

6 Choose File > Close to close your Photoshop document.

Creating animation for video

For this part of the lesson, you will create a type of on-screen graphic called a lower third. Usually seen on television and in documentary-style films, a lower third is the text and graphics that usually appear on screen to introduce a speaker. They take their name from the fact that they take up the lower third of the frame. To create the lower third, you'll bring a graphic into a blank document and animate its opacity parameter so that it fades in. Then you'll render the video file so that it can be imported into a video editing application.

Photoshop CS3 Extended is required for the following part of this lesson.

Working in Timeline mode

The Timeline mode of the Animation palette functions differently from the Frame mode. In the Timeline mode, each layer has parameters for position, opacity, and effects that can each have key frames assigned to them individually.

1 Choose File > New and choose Film & Video from the Preset drop-down menu. Leave the size at the default, NTSC DV. Choose Transparent from the Background Contents drop-down menu. Press OK.

A warning dialog box appears, telling you that the pixel aspect ratio is for previewing purposes only. Press OK.

2   Choose View > New Guide. While the presets include guidelines to define the Action and Title safe areas of the video frame, there is nothing to indicate where your lower third should end.

3   In the New Guide dialog box, select the Horizontal radio button and type **66%** in the Position text field, and press OK. This creates a new guideline 66% from the top of your document and marks the lower third of the video frame.

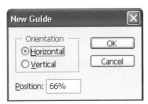

Create a guide indicating the lower third.

4   Choose File > Open and open ps1306.psd from the ps13lessons folder. When the pixel aspect ratio warning box appears, press OK.

5   Using the Move tool (⊹), drag and drop the contents of ps1306.psd into your empty document.

6   Position the graphic so that it is below the lower third guide.

Position the graphic so that it is in the lower third.

7   If the Layers palette is not open, choose Window > Layers. Layer 1 was created automatically when you created your document and you don't need it, so delete it by highlighting it in the Layers palette and dragging it to the Trash Can icon (🗑) at the bottom of the palette.

8   If the Animation palette is not open, choose Window > Animation. If it is not already in Timeline mode, select Convert to Timeline from the Animation palette menu. Note that the timeline appears only in Photoshop CS3 Extended.

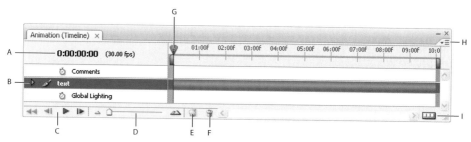

A. Current Time. B. Layers. C. Player controls. D. Zoom Slider. E. Toggle Onion Skins. F. Delete Keyframes.
G. Current Time Indicator. H. Palette menu. I. Convert to Frame Animation.

9   In the Animation palette, click the triangle to the left of the layer name to reveal its animatible parameters.

What are animatible properties?

When you edit a layer's properties over time, the computer builds an animation by interpreting the change. In Adobe Photoshop, animation information is stored in keyframes. Keyframes represent extremes of animatible properties. For example, if you wanted to have a circle move from left to right, you would need to create two keyframes, one with the circle on the left and the other with it on the right. You would then have the computer analyze the change and build the rest of the animation for you.

10 Click the stopwatch (🕑) next to the Opacity parameter to enable animation. A keyframe is created at the beginning of your timeline.

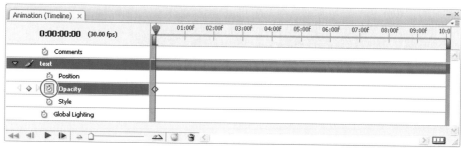

Select the stopwatch.

The stopwatch enables animation when it is clicked on. If clicked off, it disables animation. A by-product of disabling the animation of a property is that all the keyframes for that property are deleted.

11 In the Layers palette, type **0** in the Opacity text field and press the Enter or Return key.

Adjust the opacity so the text layer is not visible.

12 Double-click on the Current Time field (top left of Animation palette). The Set Current Time dialog box appears. Type **3:00** and press OK. This moves your Current Time Indicator to the three-second mark on your timeline. The Current Time Indicator (the blue wedge at the top of your timeline) indicates your animation's current time.

13 In the Layers palette, type **100** in the Opacity text field, and press Enter/Return. This creates a new keyframe where your Current Time Indicator is located.

This is the nature of timeline-based animation in Photoshop. If animation is enabled for a parameter, any change made to that parameter will create a new keyframe at the location of the Current Time Indicator.

14 Return the Current Time Indicator back to the starting point by clicking on the 0.0 at the beginning of the timeline.

15 Press the Play button (▶) at the bottom of the Animation palette to preview the animation. The text fades in over three seconds.

16 Choose File > Save As. The Save As dialog box appears. Navigate to the ps13lessons folder and type **ps1307_animation.psd** into the File name text field. Select Photoshop from the Format drop-down menu and press Save. Keep the file open for the next part of this lesson.

Rendering a video file

1   Select File > Export > Render Video. This opens the Render Video window.

Note that the Render Video Window is divided into four areas: Location, File Options, Range, and Render Options.

Location: Allows you to specify a name for the file that you are going to export and a location to save that file.

File Options: Controls the type of file you want to create from your animation. QuickTime export will create video files in a wide variety of common formats for mobile, video, and web distributions, while the Image Sequence option renders video as a series of sequential still images. This area also allows you to specify the exported files' dimensions.

Range: Controls the amount of the animation to export. By default, it will export the entire animation timeline, but you can limit the export range to lesser parts of the timeline.

Render Options: Controls whether an alpha channel is included in the output file along with the file's frame rate. Some exportable formats will not allow you to include an alpha channel.

2   In the Location section, type **ps1307** into the Name text field, click the Select Folder button, and navigate to the ps13lessons folder.

3   In the File Options field, make sure that QuickTime Export is selected and QuickTime Movie is selected from the drop-down menu on the right. The Size drop-down menu at the bottom of the File Options field should be set to Document Size. The default setting used here produces a QuickTime movie optimized for playback on a computer as well as a variety of mobile devices.

The settings button to the right of the drop-down menu can be used to format a QuickTime movie for other media such as TV and video.

4   In the Range field, make sure that the radio button next to All Frames is clicked on.

5   In the Render Options section, select "Premultiplied with White" from the Alpha Channel drop-down menu and also make sure that the Frame Rate drop-down menu is set to Document Frame Rate.

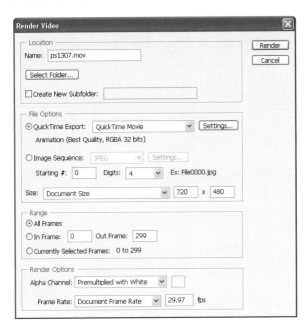

6   Press the Render button to create your video file. The rendering time will vary, depending on your computer hardware.

7   Choose File > Close. You can return to the native Photoshop file to make edits at a later point, if necessary.

The default settings rendering video are designed to produce a high-quality video file with an alpha channel that can be imported into a video editing or motion graphics program. Areas of your animation that are transparent will be transparent when you import them into these applications; however, they will not appear transparent when you view them in the QuickTime player.

Self study

1 Using the Standard Frame Animation palette, create a text layer and experiment with animating its position so that it moves around your document.

2 Using the Advanced Timeline Animation palette, experiment with animating the effects on a layer. Animate a drop shadow so that it moves over time.

Review

Questions

1 What is more important to note in an image size to be used on a web page, pixel dimensions or resolution?

2 When would you need to save a video file with an alpha channel?

3 Name four web image formats and provide an example of when to use each one.

Answers

1 It is more important to have the pixel dimensions of an image accurate, rather than the resolution. As a web and video creator, you would only use the top section of the Image Size dialog box.

2 While other Adobe applications can read native PSD files with transparent areas, non-Adobe applications cannot. The alpha channel is the only way for these applications to understand which parts of your graphic are transparent and which are opaque.

3 **a.** The JPEG format is used for saving photographs and other continuous-tone imagery.

b. The GIF format is used for saving limited-tone imagery (images with lots of solid color) such as logos and other graphics. GIF supports transparency and animation.

c. The PNG format is used for saving either photographic imagery or images with a lot of solid color. It can also support transparency in varying amounts.

d. The WMBP format is used for saving images for mobile content devices like cell phones.

Index

Where innovation, creativity, and technology converge.

There's a revolution in how the world engages ideas and information. As our culture becomes more visual and information-rich, anyone can create and share effective, interactive, and extraordinary visual and aural communications. Through our books, videos, Web sites and newsletters, O'Reilly spreads the knowledge of the creative innovators at the heart of this revolution, helping you to put their knowledge and ideas to work in your projects.

To find out more, visit us at digitalmedia.oreilly.com

O'REILLY®

Don't just get a book.

Introducing O'Reilly Dynamic Learning—a comprehensive, self-paced training system that includes books, video tutorials, online resources, and instructor guides. Written by product experts and trainers who have produced many of Adobe's training titles, the books are organized into practical, easy-to-follow lessons that cover everything you need to know about the applications in CS3.

Look for the complete Dynamic Learning series at your favorite bookseller, or online at www.oreilly.com/store

  oreilly.com/store/series/dynamiclearning

Try the online edition
free for 45 days

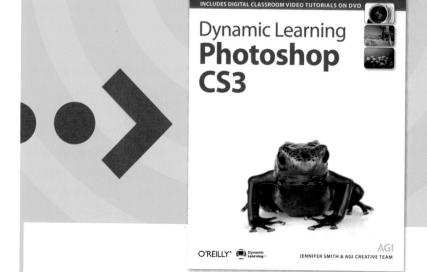

Get the information you need, when you need it, with Safari Books Online. Safari Books Online contains the complete version of the print book in your hands, as well as all of the other Missing Manuals.

Safari is designed for people who are in a hurry for information, so you can learn just what you need and put it to work right away. And with new content added as soon as it's published, you can be sure the information in Safari is the most current and relevant to the job at hand.

**To try out Safari and the online edition of the above title FREE for 45 days,
go to www.oreilly.com/go/safarienabled and enter the coupon code OCCHGCB.**

To see the complete Safari Library visit:
safari.oreilly.com

70359